ADVANCE PRAISE

"With the Strategic Analysis Cycle books, Erik Elgersma has produced
an impressive and thought-provoking volume on intelligence to be
used by firms in a highly competitive environment. He substantiates
his claim to the concept of xenocentric intelligence as a field in its own
right amid other concepts such as business intelligence or competitive
intelligence. He addresses all the stages of the so-called intelligence
cycle, such as setting requirements and direction, collection, analysis
and dissemination, showing similarities with other types of intelligence,
which make his books useful to students of strategic intelligence as well."
Professor Bob de Graaff, Professor of Intelligence and
Security Studies, University of Utrecht & Netherlands
Defense Academy, and Author of *Villa Maarheeze*

"Elgersma has produced a masterful study of how to collect data and
develop a robust capability to generate strategic analysis. Proper attention
is paid to identifying your principal, establishing what the principal
wants and tailoring training to the work environment. The books provide
a compelling road map for analyzing the capabilities and potential
challenges posed by competitors. Elgersma has identified a solid set of
analytic tools to support business success, recognizing both the strengths
and weaknesses of scenarios analysis and the underappreciated utility
of pre-mortem analysis. Throughout the books, he makes a persuasive
case for engaging decision-makers in the analytic process.
Elgersma's comprehensive and well-documented books belong
on everyone's bookshelf."
Randolph H. Pherson, CEO, Globalytica, LLC,
and co-author of *Critical Thinking for Strategic Intelligence*

Published by
LID Publishing Limited
The Record Hall, Studio 204,
16-16a Baldwins Gardens,
London EC1N 7RJ, United Kingdom

31 West 34th Street, 8th Floor, Suite 8004,
New York, NY 10001, U.S.

info@lidpublishing.com
www.lidpublishing.com

A member of:

BPR
Business Publishers Roundtable

www.businesspublishersroundtable.com

This book contains examples which originate from a business context. These have usually been constructed by taking bits and pieces of real-life examples. Subsequently my imagination has added many twists and turns to highlight the point the example aims to make. As a result, every resemblance with single real-life examples that the reader may believe to recognize, constitutes an example of the illusory bias. If the resemblance is strong, it is co-incidental.

Printed in Great Britain by TJ International
ISBN: 978-1-911498-37-7

Cover and page design: Caroline Li

ERIK ELGERSMA

THE STRATEGIC ANALYSIS CYCLE

HOW ADVANCED DATA COLLECTION AND ANALYSIS UNDERPINS WINNING STRATEGIES

TOOL BOOK

LONDON   MONTERREY
MADRID   SHANGHAI
MEXICO CITY BOGOTA
NEW YORK   BUENOS AIRES
BARCELONA   SAN FRANCISCO

THE STRATEGIC ANALYSIS CYCLE

HANDBOOK

HOW ADVANCED DATA COLLECTION AND ANALYSIS UNDERPINS WINNING STRATEGIES

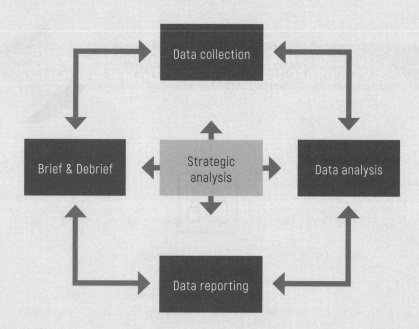

To Louise

CONTENTS

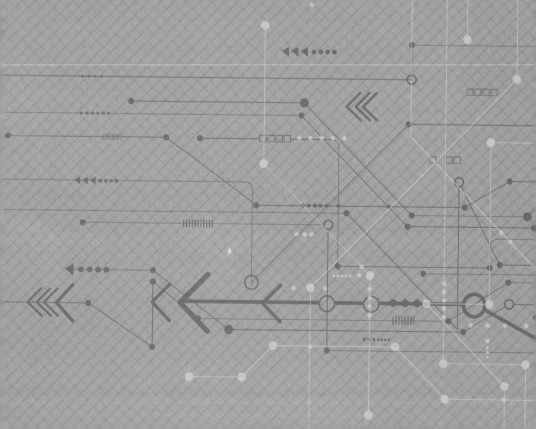

CHAPTER 1
TOOLS AS INSTRUMENTS OF PROBLEM-SOLVING

1.1 INTRODUCTION

This book is almost all about tools, but that doesn't mean that tools are always present in strategic analysis. Strategic analysis and the tools used in strategic analysis are only a means to an end. An important means, but no more than a means. Analysis is only justified when it supports and improves management decision-making in a company. Good management decisions lead to strong cash flows and higher profits. Tools may, or rather tools should, assist in substantiating such good management decisions.

Strategic analysis as a discipline first and foremost should be decision-support-focused rather than tool-focused. The more defined the decision that needs to be taken, the clearer the substantiation that needs to be developed. When the substantiation is clear, the right tools may be defined and ultimately the right data to feed the tools may be collected.

Stressing the importance of decision-support by no means understates the relevance of good tools. Without tools, no house can be built and no strategy can be defined. As a practitioner of strategic analysis I have, over the past two decades, greatly benefited from having had a few dozen tools in my toolbox. These tools helped me tackle a myriad of strategic analysis challenges. I enjoyed working with some of the tools so much that it made me write this concise book. This book covers some of the tools that worked best for me.

In this book, I will discuss 19 different commonly applicable analytic tools. The list of tools is not exhaustive. There is a good reason for this. The best tools are almost by definition tailor-made by the analyst for the particular decision to be substantiated. Equally the best quantitative metrics and units to make sense of whatever business phenomenon are also tailor-made. Even when self-made tools outperform generic tools – such as discussed in the following chapters – some generic tools may either serve as building blocks to create a self-made tool or may inspire when designing an original tool. Even when self-made tools are the best, generic tools are worth knowing and mastering. Therefore, reading this book may make some sense after all.

Tools are a means to solve problems. In the remainder of this intro-ductory chapter, a generic problem-solving methodology will be introduced that is also useful in solving strategic analysis problems. This methodology is called 'The Fermi Solution'. The Fermi Solution is an approach aiming to break down complex questions into a set of manageable sub-questions. The Fermi Solution constitutes a form of generic problem-solving methodology. For more details on generic problem-solving methodologies, I refer you to Polya's work that is both elegant and generically applicable (Polya, 1957).[1]

>>>> 1.2   THE FERMI SOLUTION

The Fermi Solution refers to the Italian scientist and Nobel Prize laureate (1938, Physics) Enrico Fermi. The essence of the Fermi Solution is that it allows and supports the solving of problems with a characteristic profile (Von Baeyer, 1993, quoted in Clark, 2007c):

> *Upon first hearing it, one doesn't have even the remotest notion of what the answer might be, and one feels certain that too little information has been provided to find a solution. Yet when the problem is broken down into sub-problems, each one answerable without the help of experts or reference books, an estimate can be made, either mentally or on the back of an envelope, that comes remarkably close to the exact solution.*

Fermi, as a physics professor, taught his students a classic example of what others now call a Fermi Solution. The question is: "How many piano tuners are there in Chicago?" (Von Baeyer, 1993):

> *There is no standard solution (that's exactly the point), but anyone can make assumptions that quickly lead to an approximate answer. Here is one way: If the population of metropolitan Chicago is three million, an average family consists of four people, and one third of all families own pianos, there are 250,000 pianos in the city. If every piano is tuned once every five years, 50,000 pianos must be tuned each year. If a tuner can service four pianos a day, 250 days a year, for a total of 1,000 tunings a year, there must be about 50 piano tuners in the city. The answer is not exact; it could be as low as 25 or as high as 100. But, as the yellow pages of the telephone directory attest (this was a pre-internet source.), it is definitely in the ballpark.*

The Fermi Solution approach is frequently applicable in strategic analysis among others in market sizing. The beauty of the Fermi Solution is that none of the estimates required in the problem-solving process may be exactly correct, but that the inaccuracies cancel out, as some estimates are too high, whereas others are too low. The cancelling out results in a remarkably accurate outcome. For strategic analysis, it means that prior to starting an analysis, when applicable, a Fermi Solution approach plan may be drafted. The Fermi Solution will identify the key information pieces to collect, which may assist in getting to the right sources thereof.

For applying the Fermi Solution in strategic analysis, some sound advice is given below (Von Baeyer, 1993):

Prudent physicists – those who want to avoid false leads and dead ends – operate according to a long-standing principle: Never start a lengthy calculation until you know the range of values within which the answer is likely to fall (and, equally important, the range within which the answer is unlikely to fall). They attack every problem as a Fermi problem, estimating the order of magnitude of the result before engaging in an investigation.

The essential 'knowing the range' competency only develops with experience. Strategic analysis is partly a science, but it is also partly an art. To the art-part the old, perhaps frustrating, paradigm applies that indeed experience is the best teacher. With experience come the right order of magnitude estimates that are so useful in Fermi Solution approaches, as the example below will hopefully show.

The example below is a real-life one. It illustrates how to apply the Fermi Solution in strategic analysis and/or market intelligence. In doing so, I hope to prove that the Fermi Solution is easy applicable and not abstract.

The question to be answered was: "What is the volume of coffee a particular factory stores in its plant in X-city, Y-country?" One hint was given: the volume matched three days of production of the owner company, Z.

The approach was:

- The player has a 60+% market share in Y-country.
- Y-country is an island. Z has a modest presence in coffee outside Y-country; they serve Y-country from their single factory, so assume the factory focuses exclusively on the Y-country market.
- Y-country has 17 million consumers, of which an estimated 12 million consume coffee daily.

- A Y-country coffee consumer takes four cups of 150ml coffee a day.
- A 200g pack of instant coffee serves about 25 cups; so per-cup dosing is about 8g.

Calculation:
- 12 million cups x 4/day x 3 days = 144 million cups in 3 days.
- 144 million cups x 8g = 1,152 million grams (1,152 tons) of coffee consumed per three days.
- 60% market share of Z: so 60% of 1,152 tons = 691 tons +/- 150 tons.

This figure matched our implicit estimate. A number of big, 20+ meter high storage silos belonging to the plant are visible from the nearby main road. These could easily contain a 1,000 metric tons, but not 10,000 metric tons. They would also be too bulky for containing only 100 metric tons. A source in the know later revealed that the actual volume was 700 tons.

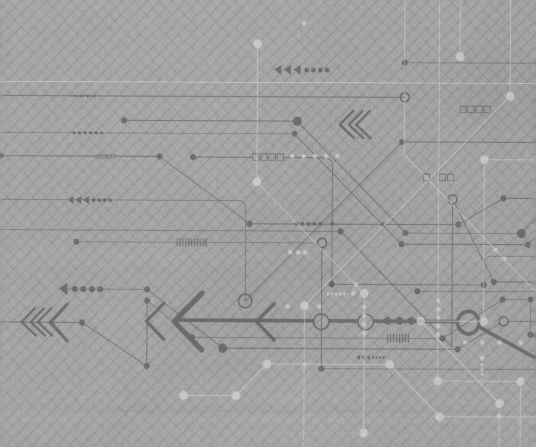

CHAPTER 2

COMPETITOR CAPABILITY PROFILING

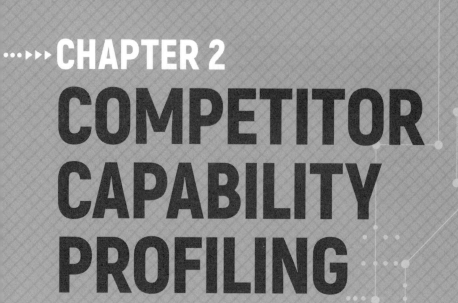

 # 2.1 INTRODUCTION

A competitor profile is a common tool in strategy. It is likely to be one of a strategy or market intelligence department's most common deliverables. Competitor profiles inform strategy design, strategy execution and even strategy progress monitoring. A well-prepared competitor profile informs management in an insightful format of the competitor's capabilities, intent and competitiveness in those functional or market areas where the competitor may affect the firm's current and future performance. In-depth company analysis may also be carried out by, for example, security analysts who review a company as a potential target for investing the assets that have been entrusted to them by their principles (Porter, 2004b).

Although the focus of this chapter is on competitors, the text below may, with limited imagination, equally be applied to profiling customers, suppliers or other corporate entities that affect a firm's current and/or future success in value creation.

ANATOMY OF A COMPETITOR PROFILE

COMPETITOR PROFILES MAY BE PERIODIC UPDATES OR ONE-OFF AND DEMAND-DRIVEN

Prior to discussing what a competitor profile exactly is, it is relevant to note that a competitor profile may both be supply-driven and demand-driven.

In the **supply-driven** case, a strategy department agrees with its customer (i.e., senior management) that every six months, for example, senior management will receive an update on key developments at one or more particular competitors. Such updates may focus on qualitative details. Topics may include mergers and acquisitions (M&A) transactions and investments announced or completed, management or policy changes, new products launched and/or marketing campaigns started. Also the most recent financial results of the competitor may be reported on, but the focus is on the total picture rather than on the competitor's financial performance or market share developments. In what is recommended to be a separate periodic update, the focus may be on quantitative details.

In a supply-driven case, competitor profiles may simply be made 'for the record' – to empower whomever in the firm wishes to understand the competitor better with a structured format of actual (basic) facts. An online intranet-based database run by the strategy department may be the channel to disseminate such standard profiles to the firm's broader organization.

Demand-driven competitor profiles tend to be requested by management in support of one-off decisions to be made. A competitor profile may, for example, be requested to underpin an initiative to fill the funnel of the M&A transaction target pipeline or to prepare an executive for meeting a competitor. When a marketing executive requests a competitor profile, the focus of the profile may be on brands and branding execution. In other words, in demand-driven profiling, the competitor profiles are tailor-made for the occasion and so are the topics that these profiles should cover.

A COMPETITOR PROFILE SHOULD COVER BOTH THE COMPETITOR'S CAPABILITIES AND INTENT

In a supply-driven, standardized format of an overall competitor profile, coverage of both key competitor capabilities (in the broadest sense) and competitor intent is essential.

Diagram 2.1 gives an overview of the dimensions of a generic competitor profile. Capabilities include the quality and structure of the competitor's organization; their business positions as starting points for further moves; their marketing, research and development skills; their fixed assets and distribution base; and their financial firepower. The intent consists of two elements: a communicated strategy and the strategy that the strategy department perceives to be executed. The two will usually overlap, but may not be entirely equal. A perceived strategy may, for example, be 'corrected' for propaganda. When a company says it wants to become a world market leader in a product range that may work well for their staff's morale for which strategy communication may well be intended. It may, however, be far from the strategy that will actually be pursued given the capabilities a company really has. Capabilities add up to what a company can do; intent summarizes what a company wants to do. Together, this results in what a company is xenocentrically expected by the strategy analyst to really do next. When, over time, it becomes clear what a company has really done, a feedback loop emerges that allows for an ever-refined understanding of the competitor (Courtney, 2009).

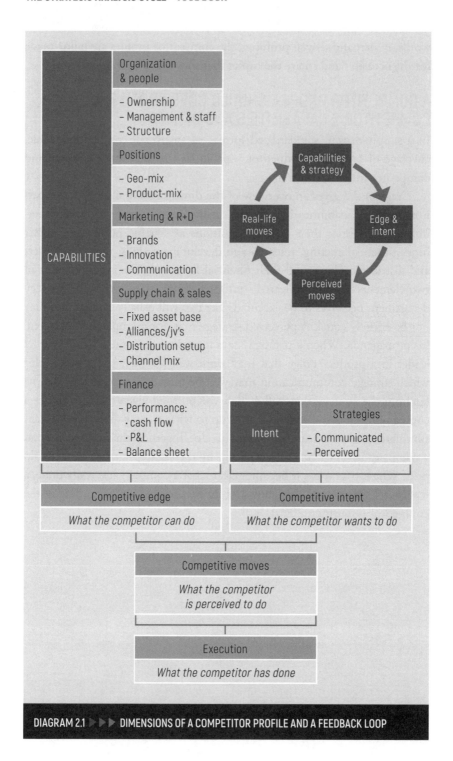

Organization & people
- Ownership
- Management & staff
- Structure

Positions
- Geo-mix
- Product-mix

Marketing & R+D
- Brands
- Innovation
- Communication

Supply chain & sales
- Fixed asset base
- Alliances/jv's
- Distribution setup
- Channel mix

Finance
- Performance:
  · cash flow
  · P&L
- Balance sheet

CAPABILITIES

Capabilities & strategy

Real-life moves

Edge & intent

Perceived moves

Intent

Strategies
- Communicated
- Perceived

Competitive edge

What the competitor can do

Competitive intent

What the competitor wants to do

Competitive moves

What the competitor is perceived to do

Execution

What the competitor has done

DIAGRAM 2.1 ▶ ▶ ▶ DIMENSIONS OF A COMPETITOR PROFILE AND A FEEDBACK LOOP

Authors sometimes recommend setting up dedicated, multidisciplinary teams per competitor to build and continuously improve competitor profiles. Each team should be dedicated to a competitor (Rothberg, 1997). This may work, but only when two strict conditions are met. The first condition is that the team includes at least one seasoned strategic analysis specialist. The second condition is that the team should get a clear briefing to produce a deliverable that is more than 'just an overview'. The deliverable should be guided by a concrete and clear set of management decisions. It is useless for a team to write an encyclopedic review of a competitor if they have not been set up in advance to support a certain view. For those that still want to prepare a competitor profile 'by the book' regardless of its end-user specific needs, Michael Porter's Four Corners model may be a good way to start. This model is discussed in the intermezzo.

INTERMEZZO: FOUR CORNERS MODEL AS GUIDE TO PROFILING COMPETITORS

In his seminal work Competitive Strategy, *first published in 1980, Michael Porter dedicated a chapter to defining a framework for competitor analysis (Porter, 2004a).*

The Four Corners model is designed to profile a competitor, depicted in Diagram 2.2. *The left hand of the diagram considers the competitor's drivers. In this book, we refer to this as the competitor's intent. Intent makes up the second term in the threat analysis equation: threat = competences + intent + surprise. Within intent, the competitor's future goals and the assumptions on the industry it is operating in are distinguished. The right-hand side of the diagram consists of the competitor's competences: its strengths and weaknesses. These become evident from analysing what assets the competitor competes with and how.*

The purpose of this model is to facilitate the prediction of the competitor's future strategy shifts and moves. It provides a useful checklist for a quick scan of a competitor's competences and intent, as it allows users to segment different data elements under different headers. The latter always assists in turning information overload into a competitive advantage. When using this model, it is recommended to use a xenocentric view on the competitor goals and assumptions, to avoid an ethnocentric bias from flawing the analysis.

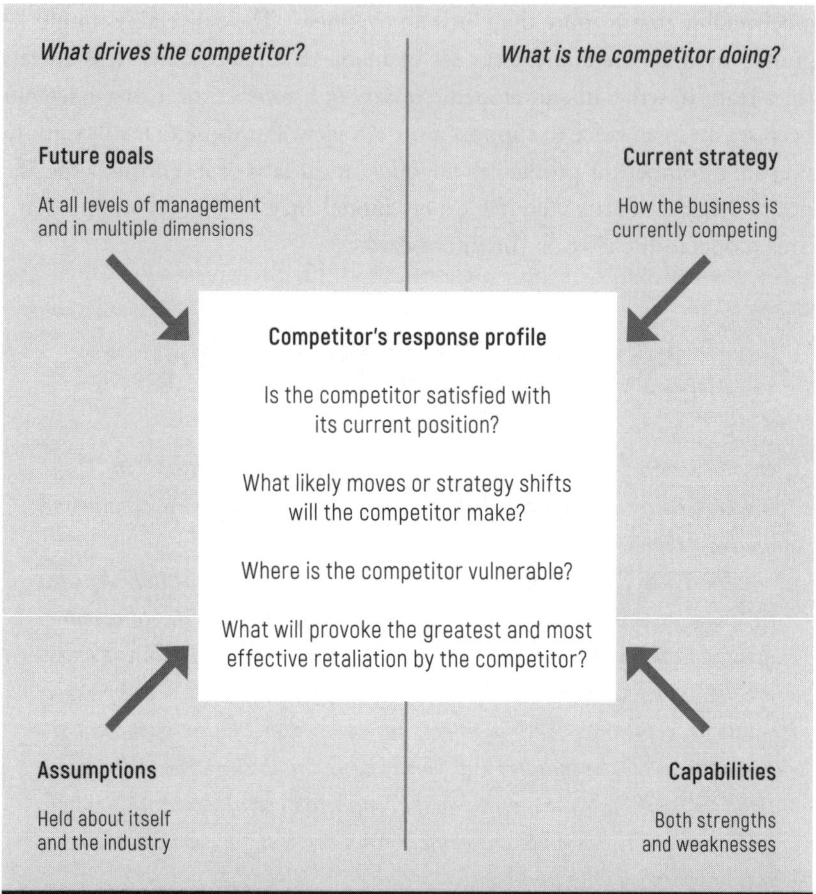

What drives the competitor? | *What is the competitor doing?*

Future goals

At all levels of management
and in multiple dimensions

Current strategy

How the business is
currently competing

Competitor's response profile

Is the competitor satisfied with
its current position?

What likely moves or strategy shifts
will the competitor make?

Where is the competitor vulnerable?

What will provoke the greatest and most
effective retaliation by the competitor?

Assumptions

Held about itself
and the industry

Capabilities

Both strengths
and weaknesses

DIAGRAM 2.2 ▶ ▶ ▶ FOUR CORNERS MODEL FOR COMPETITOR PROFILING

2.3 COMPILING A COMPETITOR PROFILE: THE USE OF SOURCES AND CHECKLISTS

Compiling competitor profiles is not only an analytical, but also a creative activity. A competitor profile that really reflects the other party's business requires us to xenocentrically think through all the aspects of a competitor's business. These aspects may both organizationally and otherwise be fundamentally different than the firm's own business, even when the firm and the competitor operate in the same industry.

Emirates and Ryanair are both airlines, but the back-office systems at both airlines may differ profoundly. Working at either one will not automatically enable you to *imagine* how to summarize the other's business in a competitor profile in the way the other party sees and operates it. Rather than starting, often implicitly, with taking their own business as the template to fill in for the competitor, it may be better to instead start with neutral, generic questions. The Appendix offers checklist questions by functional discipline. As the questions are neutral, they may assist in preventing ethnocentric biases creeping unintentionally into the profile and/or the subsequent competitor analysis.

Aiming to create a competitor profile is great, but no profile is better than the sources upon which it's based. As a result, a great profile requires access to great sources. There are multiple sources and, in the case of competitors, using information in the public domain for many aspects of competitor profiling is the best start. However, xenocentrically understanding the mind and thus the intent of the competitor by only using public domain sources is rarely enough. Applying human sources that personally know the competitor is almost inevitable.

Unlocking competitor-related insights that as tacit knowledge have never been properly captured, let alone shared, may require organizing competitor-profiling workshops. The format for such workshops is simple. The strategy or market intelligence department first uses public sources and possibly some competitor back-engineering to compile a draft competitor profile. This profile should of course remain within the scope of the overall strategy-analysis assignment. There is no point in covering topics that are irrelevant to the problem at hand. The draft has two functions. The first and foremost function is to act as a stimulus. The second is to assess and gather facts to prevent costly collection of existing knowledge later in the process.

In the working process, the stimulus is the input to a meeting of the strategic analyst who prepared the draft profile with a group of staff in a business unit. The meeting is preferably live. A WEBEX meeting may be used but is not recommended, as so much non-verbal communication gets lost in a WEBEX. Moreover, WEBEX is less engaging. The staff invited preferably report to the management team. A typical group size is 10–15 for this type of session. The group of staff should preferably consist of multiple functional disciplines, such as supply chain, finance, marketing, sales, research & development (R&D), etc. – so typically each discipline is represented by two or three staff members. The management team, however, is explicitly not welcome in the meeting, so as to avoid implicit or explicit 'yesmanship' from the team. The strategic analyst wants to hear the story as it is, not as managers believe their bosses want to hear it to be.

The session starts with the analyst presenting the draft competitor profile to the group of managers. Every slide of the presentation should be used as a stimulus by the analyst to trigger a conversation in the group: "Do you recognize this fact?" "What does this mean?" "Why do they do that?" "What objectives do they seem to have in mind?" "What incentives do they give these salespeople?" "Why do they only use these type of trucks?"

A good analyst is insatiably curious. This is the moment that behavioural competence is needed. Make the team of managers talk – they generally love it. The tacit knowledge they offer is matched by that of their peers, turning the session into a learning experience for all. When the analyst has done their homework well, they will also be able to share some facts no one in the room knew before, adding to the group's trust in and commitment to working with the analyst. The analyst meanwhile, as efficiently as possible, takes notes of all that is shared, in doing so enriching their competitor profile. When a business has three to five key competitors, talking through all five may require a full day. In the evening, the analyst may need to polish up the draft profiles a bit, as they'll need them again the next day.

The next day, the analyst runs the same session. This time, however, they use the upgraded competitor profiles. The audience now is the management team of the same business. Almost inevitably, that session will have a different character: Egos are likely to be bigger, experiences will probably be different, politics may be around the corner. The analyst simply starts by using the same stimulus. This time the stimulus is positioned as what the public-domain sources, complemented by insights from your team reports, tell us about this competitor.

"Now, what do you say about this?" "What have we missed?" "What have we misunderstood?" "What can we learn from this?" Inevitably, a management team may try to colour the picture of the competitor a bit more in their favour than a (corporate) analyst would do. If that happens, it generally takes the form of downplaying capabilities or assets mentioned as strong by their direct reports. When the analyst has used a morning with the management team to discuss the competitor profiles, they may reconvene with the management team at say 4pm for a final session.

For all competitors, *as well as the firm's own business,* they have now compiled a draft list of capabilities; an implicit or even explicit extract of the various competitor profiles. For each capability, for example, 'talent management', the firm is ranked against the competitors. The firm either excels, plays on par or plays below par versus the competitor or competitors that make up the key competition. The output of this exercise is again used as a stimulus with the management team. This time, the stimulus guides a management team in deciding which capabilities in their competitive environment they are up against now and possibly in the future. Based on the capability comparison picture, capability development by functional discipline can be prioritized by the management team. This prioritization, for example, may result in the choice to become on par, where today the firm plays below par, or in the choice to further invest in a capability in which the firm already excels. In doing so, a competitor profiling exercise serves multiple purposes. It starts with unlocking tacit staff knowledge and applying it for mutual learning. It then usually confronts a management team with competitor insights they had never heard from their staff in regular sessions. Finally, the capability mapping exercise offers the management team a tool to assist them in prioritizing what capabilities to build for today and tomorrow.

MAKE OR BUY A COMPETITOR PROFILE

Once a standard profile for mapping a number of competitors has been agreed upon, the question for the strategy or market intelligence department is whether or not to outsource the production of these profiles to a trusted third party. Outsourcing comes at an out-of-pocket cost. This price would normally be charged to the principle that assigned this task to the strategy department, subject to the principle's approval, so should not be too much of an issue. The major benefit of outsourcing is that the strategy department does not have its hands tied in the tedious work that preparing multiple standard profiles may be.

When the only purpose of the profiles is to inform management on the key data of the competitors, to allow an initial selection of the companies to be put on an M&A long-list, for example, the strategy department is probably happy for the work to be outsourced.

Parties to whom competitor profiling may be outsourced include generic parties, such as Euromonitor in FMCG markets. Specialist consultancies that can provide an expert focus on a firm's market may also be considered. Especially in the latter case, revealing what companies need to be profiled is in itself information. Next to quality considerations, the full trust of the discretion of the consultancy may well be the guiding factor on whether or not to assign a third party to this type of work. For a strategy department that does not feel comfortable with either the discretion or the quality (or worse, both) of potential suppliers, the default option remains to think twice and do the work internally. *Table 2.1* summarizes competitor profiling as a tool.

DIMENSIONS	DESCRIPTION
What use does this tool have?	Competitor profiles are broadly used, for example, as a briefing document for a senior executive meeting their counterpart at the competitor company, or as a brief description prior to a management team compiling an M&A target list. Competitor profiles should at all times be tailored to the purpose they serve.
When to apply this tool?	There are multiple occasions when competitor profiles are useful. The two applications mentioned above are just a selection. Competitor profiles may serve as input to multiple management decision documents (see Chapter 11).
Who to involve when applying this tool?	Prior to preparing a competitor profile, the ultimate decision maker needs to have provided their input on what they really want to know about the competitor. Preparing competitor profiles offers a great opportunity to waste time when data and information that is irrelevant to the decision-making at hand is being painstakingly collected, analysed and reported. In preparing a competitor tool, unlocking tacit knowledge from multiple human sources may require involving staff from inside and outside the perimeter of a company.

TABLE 2.1 ▶ ▶ ▶ **BRIEF DESCRIPTION OF COMPETITOR PROFILING AS A TOOL**

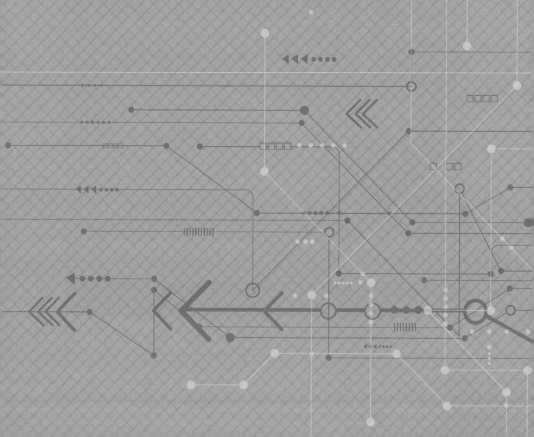

CHAPTER 3

COMPETITOR CAPABILITY ANALYSIS

3.1 INTRODUCTION

Strategic analysis inevitably features competitors. This chapter discusses four ways to study competitors. There are, of course, more than four ways to do so, but we have selected the lenses below both because they are widely applicable in support of management decisions and because they are relatively easy to apply.

In this chapter, we first look at competitor benchmarking – mapping how we perform against best-in-class companies and competitors. Subsequently, we discuss how to understand a competitor's cash position, as cash so often matters more than profits. To complete this chapter, we cover mapping a competitor's product and patent portfolio.

 3.2

COMPETITOR BENCHMARKING

Benchmarking has been adequately defined by former Xerox CEO David Kearns as (Bosomworth, 1993):

> *...the continuous process of measuring products, services and practices against the toughest competitors or those companies recognized as industry leaders.*

Benchmarking is thus an elegant term for comparing a company quantitatively but also qualitatively, along one or more chosen measurement dimensions with other companies. The definition should imply that benchmarking is not a goal in itself but an instrument to guide management decisions, followed by management implementation actions. It is the nature of management decisions that leads to the choice of *why* and *how* to apply benchmarking.

BENCHMARKING: QUALITATIVE/QUANTITATIVE, FUNCTIONAL/ COMPETITIVE, SYNDICATE/MARKET INTELLIGENCE

Table 3.1 segments benchmarking into four commonly practiced forms (quantitative/qualitative; functional/competitive). The table also includes potential sources (syndicate/market intelligence).

	Qualitative dimension(s)	Quantitative dimension(s)	Syndicate as source	Market intelligence as source
FUNCTIONAL		Process or performance comparison against a 'best-in-class' company	✓✓✓	✓
COMPETITIVE		Process or performance comparison against direct competitors (that are not per se 'best-in-class')	✓	✓✓✓

TABLE 3.1 ▶ ▶ ▶ FOUR COMMONLY PRACTICED FORMS OF BENCHMARKING

An anecdote may help to elucidate the difference between functional and competitive benchmarking. Two students visit South Africa's Kruger National Park. They violate park regulations by setting up their tent outside a designated, protected tourist area. The following morning, they hear a hungry lioness roar outside their tent. This does not sound like good news. One of the two students keeps calm and puts on his sneakers. The other student laughs at him. "What is the point of putting on your sneakers?" he asks. "Do you think you can outrun the lioness?" The other simply replies: "No, I don't believe I can outrun the lioness, but I can outrun you!" This metaphor is timeless.[1]

When a company wishes to outrun the lioness, it needs to do a functional benchmark. The outcome may be that the company decides to become a cheetah. To ensure the company survives the next downturn in its industry, it only needs to outrun its direct competitor. In that case, it needs to do a competitive benchmark. The timely putting on of their corporate sneakers may suffice in meeting that target.

In benchmarking, two sourcing strategies exist. For a functional benchmark it is common – but not critical – to run a 'syndicate project'. For a competitive benchmark, it is common that market intelligence does the collection work. Syndicate projects in competitive benchmarking do exist, but are rare.

This is due both to legal compliance sensitivities related to anti-trust/cartel law and obviously due to most companies having a sheer lack of interest in sharing non-public performance data – even when disguised – with competitors in a comparison project.

SYNDICATED PROJECTS MAY BE UNSOLICITED OR ORDERED

Syndicate projects come in two forms: the unsolicited and the ordered benchmark. An unsolicited benchmark is normally offered by an external consultant to an industry sector. The consultant believes a benchmark along some managerial dimension (e.g., supply chain order-to-cash efficiency) in a sector may be of enough interest to sector customers to justify running a project. The consultant pitches their idea (both the sourcing side and the promise of a slick report at a modest cost) to a number of industry sector players. When enough participants sign up, the project is executed. Participating companies provide requested (confidential) data and, after some time, receive a report in which a mutual comparison along the promised managerial dimension is presented. Data sourcing is all done by the consultant.

The second form of a syndicated project is the ordered benchmark. In this case, an industry sector participant *requests* a consultancy to run a benchmark project. This participant usually pays all the cost. Now, the only thing the consultancy needs to do is to persuade other sector participants to join in the project by providing data and afterwards, free of charge, receiving a summary of the outcomes (but usually not the whole report).

REPORTS MAY BE FULLY TRANSPARENT OR MAY DISGUISE THE PARTICIPATING COMPANIES

In syndicate reports, either ordered or unsolicited, two approaches to reporting exist. Most common is the disguised report; less common is the fully transparent report. A disguised report lists all participating companies only by letter, e.g., A–H. Only the consultant knows who is who. This approach is sometimes referred to as a 'black box'. The disguise is aimed to be so well executed that none of the participating companies will be able to identify which of the other participating companies is which. One way to achieve this is to constantly use A–H for different companies when comparing the results of different benchmarking dimensions. The major advantage of a disguised report is that legal compliance is easier and participating companies feel that their corporate secrets are less exposed. The obvious disadvantage is that disguised reports are less informative for competitive analysis. The latter, however, is usually less of a driver for syndicate-based benchmarking, as the latter type of benchmarking usually focuses on functional benchmarking.

In competitive benchmarking, disguised reporting is useless. There is a role here for syndicates when compiling a report on, for example, *how* a set of competitors organizes their supply chain or distribution organization, but less on comparing *quantitative data* that are not already in the public domain. Most participants, after all, will shy away from distributing confidential data, even when knowing that these data will only be used and reported in a disguised, black box type of approach.

Diagram 3.1 provides a flow sheet of a typical benchmarking process. In this diagram, the various choices are summarized. It also shows where the strategic analysis department is responsible and respectively may be involved in the process or even may only be observing the process.

Diagram 3.1 shows that a number of choices need to be made in the benchmarking process. The first choice is what the benchmark study should focus on: Will it be competitive or functional? In general, functional benchmarks are syndicated, and competitive are market intelligence based. Generally, the narrower the focus of a benchmark study, the more useful the outcome.

The next choice to make is to define the metrics in a benchmark. In qualitative benchmarks, these metrics may be less sharply defined when it comes to, for example, comparing different companies' organization charts. Still, a factor as simple as headcount in a particular functional discipline may be as quantitative as it gets. To ensure a useful comparison is made, comparability of different companies' data, including differences in accounting methods, need to be taken into account. Management needs to approve the metrics. Given the need for focus, having more than ten different metrics of comparison is not advisable.

For competitive benchmarking, tools like cash flow and profit analysis, as well as profit pool analysis, may overlap. When the decision to be taken and/or to be substantiated is clear, defining the metrics is less of a problem. When profitability is an issue, metrics for direct and indirect cost are best benchmarked. When growth is too slow, a geo- or channel-mix analysis of access to and success in growth market (channels) may define the metrics.

A good topic for a functional benchmark could be the 'order generation to order delivery process' of an e-based business model in different companies. Well-known e-business powerhouses like Amazon, Alibaba, eBay, etc., could be benchmarked as best-in-class as input to a company setting up or reorganizing their e-business organization. When choosing functional best-in-class benchmark companies, factors like their reputation (including ethics), profitability and professionalism matter. Often, one call to a friendly management consultant is enough to get inspiring names for a functional benchmark. Choosing competitors is often easy enough: it is those companies against whom orders are won (or lost).

Whereas a strategic analysis-based sourcing methodology focuses on publicly available data, possibly enriched with information obtained from human sources, a syndicate-based methodology may include collection instruments like interviews and questionnaires.

In *Diagram 3.1* the role of an in-company strategic analysis department is added, showing what is and what is not to be expected from a strategic analysis function in ordering a benchmark.

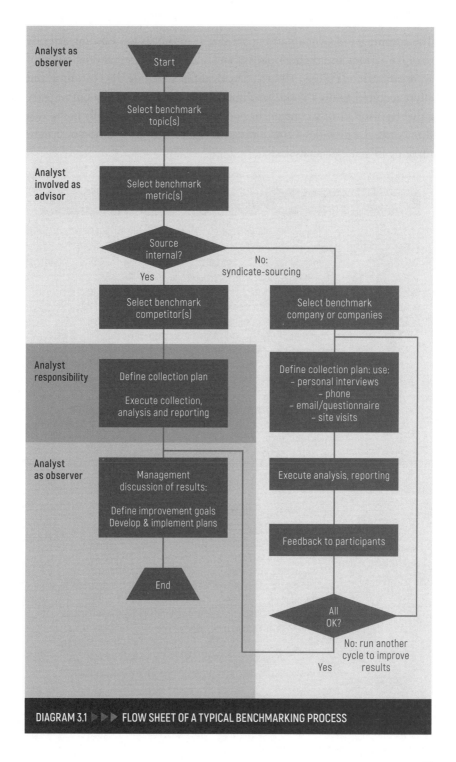

DIAGRAM 3.1 ▶ ▶ ▶ FLOW SHEET OF A TYPICAL BENCHMARKING PROCESS

The advantages of benchmarking are that it improves the learning attitude of organizations and their employees and adds to the external orientation of an organization (Philips, 1999b). Disadvantages include the cost, time and effort required to do a good benchmark, and the risk that the output may either be insufficiently concrete or poorly comparable to be really useful to a firm. *Table 3.2* provides a concluding overview of the application of benchmarking in strategic analysis.

DIMENSIONS	DESCRIPTION
What use does this tool have?	Benchmarking allows a company's management to compare its own managerial choices and performance along chosen dimensions against that of other companies. This facilitates defining what dimension a company performs above par, on par or below par versus its business environment. When benchmarked external companies include competitors, it allows to identify the basic dimensions that provide a company its competitive edge. Knowing and subsequently building a competitive edge is critical input to any future allocation of the company's resources. Thus, benchmarking is a vital input to strategy, as resource allocation is and remains the heart of what corporate strategy is about.
When to apply this tool?	Benchmarking may be applied in a one-off exercise when, for example, a part of an organization needs to be redefined. It may also be applied periodically to monitor a company's performance on a chosen dimension versus its peers. As always, it is only useful to apply it when the outcomes are directly linked to management actions that are to be based on the outcomes.
Who to involve when applying this tool?	As benchmarking is useless when it is not followed up by management action, prior to investing time in benchmarking analysis, senior management's commitment to such action is critical. Timing is everything. To secure such a commitment, the strategy department needs to define benchmarking in such a way that the data that are delivered by the exercise are critical to decision-making. Depending on the choice of the benchmarking data sourcing, involvement of in-company or external knowledgeable sources may be essential. The involvement of outside consultants may be imperative for selecting best-in-class companies in a functional benchmark and/or for running a syndicate (black box) benchmark.

TABLE 3.2 ▶ ▶ ▶ APPLICATION OF BENCHMARKING AS A TOOL

 3.3 COMPETITOR
CASH FLOW ANALYSIS

This section should start with a word of warning. Financial analysis is a craft, similar to psychology being a craft, that is needed to map the executives in a competitor's top team. In the few lines below I don't even dream of covering all the subtle details of competitor financial analysis. For the sake of brevity, let's just pick out a single piece of financial analysis that is – or rather should be – commonly used. It's simple to grasp for strategists with less of a financial background and is too often overlooked. This is a cash flow analysis. For more detailed financial analyses (of which there are many), a strategist is either advised to make a deep-dive into obscure professions like accountancy and control or should in-source such knowledge from specialists. As with any analysis, the analysis should lead to better decision-making. The decision to be substantiated commercially or strategically thus determines what competitor financial analysis should be made. This golden rule is best not violated when as a strategist your effectiveness in decision-making support is your key driver.

CASH MAY MATTER MORE THAN PROFIT

A competitor – or any other company for that matter – does not file for bankruptcy because the company makes losses. At the end of the day, filing for bankruptcy is caused by only one thing. It happens when a company runs out of *cash* to pay invoices, interest or the principal of its loans at payback day. The relevance of the cash position of a company is often underestimated when assessing a company's potential next steps or the (lack of) options a company may have. A company may objectively face some fantastic opportunities, but when it doesn't have cash funds to harvest these opportunities, they will not materialize. Cash equals undifferentiated buying power: it is the ultimate competence of a company. Therefore, some of the best-run companies emphasize their free cash flow and show off with high dividend payments when expressed as percentage of net profit. The latter may also be a sign of the lack of ideas a company has for value accretive investments, but that is not the point here.

In assessing competitors in support of strategy design, also in strategy monitoring and business tactics, considering a competitor's cash position may offer the missing critical data point that suddenly illuminates why companies do what they do, rather than do what they say. Companies rarely admit that cash constraints determine business choices. As a result, a strategy analyst will have to do some deep diving in the company's financial statements to reconstruct why companies did what they did rather than did what said they would do.

What is true for a cash flow and a cash position is to a lesser extent also true for a profit and loss account (P&L). A single company's P&L reveals in detail the various cost items (raw materials, other direct costs, indirect costs, etc.), allowing a direct comparison with another company's comparable cost-line items.

Profitability is of course a critical indicator of a company's health. Still, when having to assess companies, never forget the tested wisdom that 'profit is an opinion, but cash a reality'. This one-liner cynically hints at the fact that accounting rules permit all kinds of options to change the profitability of a company, provided these are properly documented. Today's accounting rules are stricter than they used to be, but profit polishing is still feasible. Profit may thus be seen as a management opinion rather than as an undisputable fact. For cash, no such options exist. Cash is tangible and artificially changing it is not possible. The intermezzo at the end of this section provides illustrative examples of some common ways used by companies to legally manipulate the profits reported by a daughter company or even at the holding level.

COMPETITOR CASH FLOW ANALYSIS MAY BE PERFORMED IN REAL-TIME

In one case, the cash flow of a financially weak competitor was on a month-by-month, realtime basis modeled in some analysis I was involved in. The objective was to predict the competitor's upcoming pricing strategy and the choices they would make in upcoming tender businesses. To model a cash position, start with the cash position at the balance sheet date, e.g.,

31 December. On a monthly basis, estimate all cash outputs (cost) and cash inputs (returns from sales, etc.). At the end of the month, the calculation will result in the cash position on 31 January, etc.

Company owners rarely want their companies to be net cash consumers. In other words, they loathe being obliged to every month send fresh cash to their company to keep it afloat. In investment banking parlance this is colloquially known as 'burning cash'. The owners of a cash burner usually push management to urgently effect change. When cash is the key parameter on a weak company's dashboard, be sure the market intelligence or strategy department has built a model to predict that cash position every month again.

COMPETITOR CASH FLOW ANALYSIS IS A TYPICALLY A STRATEGY DEPARTMENT RESPONSIBILITY

The steps to create a competitor cash flow analysis are all within the responsibility of the strategy department. The information collection includes liaising with people in the know within the company. Modelling a cash flow may require input from the finance department. Involving the finance department may also add to the credibility of the output of the analysis, as most managers only believe financial analysis when the finance department has been involved in the preparation thereof. Still, the responsibility from the definition of the analysis to the delivery of the output remains typically with the strategy department. Do not underestimate what is at stake here. A decent P&L or cash flow model for a competitor that is so well thought through to be used in decision-making requires massive efforts (Long, 2007). Prior to putting in the time, the balance between efforts and returns in terms of better decision-making needs to be considered. What is the value of knowing in so much detail what a competitor's cash or profitability situation is? How does knowing this improve a firm's own competitiveness? What decisions would we change if we get different answers out of our analysis? How do we ensure that those who have to act on the outcome of the analysis to harvest the benefits for our firm are so engaged that they commit to acting upon the outcome?

In *Table 3.3* the focus will be on cash flow analysis, as the drivers for a P&L analysis have already been discussed in the above text.

DIMENSIONS	DESCRIPTION
What use does this tool have?	Cash flow analysis, among others, has value in assessing the limits a company (competitor) may face to take certain business decisions. Such decisions may relate to short-term product pricing, but also being able or unable to fund an acquisition, for example. In the latter case, not just cash but other balance sheet items also matter. Typically, ratios like leverage (net debt/EBITDA), interest coverage and solvability are the criteria banks use to provide or withhold loans to customers. What the minimum figure in these ratios equates to varies from company to company. Some companies report the bank covenants' criteria. Based on company balance sheets, monitoring over the shoulders of the banks may have a merit to a strategy analyst to predict what 'room to play' another company may have.
When to apply this tool?	Cash flow analysis is especially relevant for judging whether and if so how financially weak companies can sustain their day-to-day operations. Financially weak companies may include start-ups that are building a company in a net-cash-consuming way – but from their owners only have got a limited amount of cash to start with.
Who to involve when applying this tool?	Cash flow analysis requires creating a financial model for the company under study. The strategy department is well advised to involve at least one specialist in financial control and, together with the financial controller, involve internal specialists per business discipline to assess the cost items the company under study likely has to work with. An internal manager from the sales department may, for example, be qualified to estimate the sales cost of a competitor; similarly a supply chain expert may do so for the supply chain cost, etc. In the section on industry cost curves, later in this book, a similar approach will be discussed.

TABLE 3.3 ▶▶▶ **APPLICATION OF (COMPETITOR) CASH FLOW ANALYSIS AS A TOOL**

INTERMEZZO: LEGAL WAYS TO MANIPULATE COMPANY PROFIT REPORTING

Three classic options to manipulate profits – there are many others, but covering more options is outside the scope of this book – that strategy analysts have to look out for when analysing a company's financial statements are:

- *activating cost'*
- *marking assets to market*
- *intra-company transfer price systems*

Activating cost: pretending costs are investments that keep their value

When a company starts to activate cost, raise the alarm! Activating cost means that a company is pretending that what most other companies would perceive to be costs are actually investments. Research and development expenditures in most companies are taken as cost. Costs are subtracted from profits in the year that the costs are incurred. Some companies, however, reason that today's research expenditures will tomorrow deliver license or other incomes on the intellectual property generated by the R&D department's cost spent today. As a consequence, such R&D costs should be seen as investments. Investments normally maintain their value and therefore only have to be taken partly or even not at all as costs in the same year that these costs are incurred. This is a way to avoid costs that in reality have been made to push down profits in a particular book year, by postponing the costs in gradual investment write-offs to later book years. Fokker Aircraft, the Dutch aeroplane manufacturer, in the early 1990s suddenly activated its R&D expenses. Bankruptcy followed in 1993.

Marking assets to market: valuing or revaluing assets to create profits

'Marking assets to market' is another common option to alter profitability figures in a direction that the management would like to show to their owners/investors. The direction is usually up, although tax reasons may result in management wishing to artificially lower profits at times.

A simple example will be given to explain 'mark to market'. In the book year 2013, company X lost €100,000 in its day-to-day business on sales of €10 million. Reluctant to show an ugly 1% negative return on sales to its investors, the company's management looked for ways to increase their profit. The financial director reminds management that the company owns a large piece of land. Land prices have lately been on the up. So, an official real estate broker is invited to assess the current value of the land. This value is €500,000 higher than the current book value. Thus, management decides to take an exceptional one-off profit of €500,000 in the book year, using the broker's valuation as evidence to convince the accountant that the value increase is real. The accountant has limited legal means to dispute this approach. Possibly the accountant may ask for a second opinion of the broker's valuation. When the second opinion confirms the increased valuation, the new amount is a true representation of the value of the land. The increase in value may as a result indeed be perceived as an exceptional profit for the year. After accounting for this exceptional profit, the company now suddenly reports a profit of €400,000; or 4% return on sales. Easy as that.

Do not think this only happens as an example in a book on strategy tools. This is a disguised and simplified real-life example of a company listed on the New York Stock Exchange that aimed to protect itself against a hostile takeover in 2014, by pumping up their 2013 profits through asset revaluations. In doing so, they made the takeover more expensive, as takeover bids are usually calculated as multiples of recent profits. A smart buyer will see through this accountancy change, but would you count on the smartness of all investors at all times, especially those who in their view see a company they own stock in being sold at a perceived undervalued price? As an aside, the company mentioned in this example was acquired in 2017 and taken off the stock exchange, so – as in the example of Fokker – there is limited safety in accountant magic.

Transfer prices: why some companies flourish without making visible profits

Another all-time favourite to change company profit levels at will is for an owner of a company to create multiple different legal entities, preferably having their statutory seats in different countries. It is not unusual for tax planning to motivate large, international companies to smartly choose legal structures across different countries. Profit changes are feasible because within the holding different 100%-owned legal entities start trading with each other. Once trading starts, these different entities have to internally charge prices for products to each other. Such prices are called transfer prices. Tax authorities will demand a consistent logic to be applied in transfer pricing schemes in international companies, to avoid through fictive costs allocation that all corporate profits are made in a small legal entity based in a tax haven, such as the Cayman Islands. Within the rules of tax authorities there is, however, still a remarkably wide range of options to move profits across legal entities. Two common forms are license fees and leasing fees. There are many others – often related to interest payments – but they fall outside the range of discussion here.

License fees may dilute profits of local entities in favour of international holdings

When a large international holding is, for example, based in Switzerland, all global brands they own are the property of a Swiss legal entity. Any entity that reports a P&L in a local country other than Switzerland will, somewhere in the cost lines, have to account for the license fee this local entity must pay to the Swiss holding to use the brand names owned by them in their local geo-market. This will dilute the local entity's profit and increase the Swiss entity's profit. More favourable tax rulings in Switzerland than in the country of the local entity may, as a net result of this licensing model, increase the net profit of the holding. When judging the profitability and relevance of local entities of international holdings, never underestimate the fact that, as an analyst, what you see is far from the complete picture. Absence of evidence of profits or losses is not the same as evidence of absence!

Leasing fees may almost invisibly shift profits across different legal entities

In family-owned companies that operate within a single country, a veritable Christmas tree of legal entities may have been set up. Again, the driver for doing so is often either estate planning or tax reasons. The operational entity of a dairy processor for many years in a row delivered virtually no profits. Without understanding the role of the different entities in their legal structure, the operational company at face value was hardly worth pursuing for the family owner. A meeting with the owner clarified the *company's choices and made them meaningful. The operational company is trading in highly volatile markets. The whole entity may suddenly face a perfect storm of a fast upswing in raw material cost, while as a company having a portfolio of fixed longer-period product price contracts with the company's key customers. The contracts would disenable the company to pass on any increases in raw material cost. The company, however, is still legally bound to deliver loss-making goods. The company's customers do not, as a rule, accept short-term pricing contracts and the company does not have the negotiation power toward its customers to change that. If this is the business environment an operational company has to trade in, legal structures may offer at least partial protection. In this case, the company was legally split in two parts. One mother company held all fixed assets (land, buildings). This company leased its land and buildings to the operational company that had almost no fixed assets on its balance sheet. The leasing fee pulled profits out of the operational company through some smart formulas that formed the heart of the lease agreement. Should the perfect storm hit the operational company and heavy losses be incurred, the only assets lost in a bankruptcy proceeding would be those in an almost empty shell. No wonder the operational company was hardly profitable: it wasn't designed to be. Only a truly xenocentric view on this company may have resulted in an unprompted discovery of the logic behind these choices. An analysis tool like pre-mortem analysis may have revealed this discovery, reasoning back from a perfect storm driven bankruptcy. In this case, the owner was so helpful to reveal the choices. The lesson here is that companies make choices that affect the profitability of various legal entities they own. In the absence of a complete overview, avoid being too judgmental as an analyst: cash, at the end of the day, does matter more than profits.*

What is the role of the accountant in all this?

Accountancy firms that check a company's books will validate the compliance of a company's financial statements with the chosen accounting standards. Within the compliance, accountants may not accept all tricks that management proposes but some, provided properly documented, may pass their scrutiny. The fact that the fall-out of fraudulent energy giant Enron's bankruptcy brought down one of the world's largest accounting firms has made accountants less understanding toward management. The Enron disaster has also resulted in stricter rules. Still, even today, reading a P&L without knowing the valuation principles behind the P&L remains tricky. A deep-dive into a company's financial statements – especially note 26 to the profit & loss account, presented in a small font on page 479 – may be required to reconstruct what a company did and how they did it. The footnote may uncover what this company's annual profit figures may have looked like had they not done it. Assuming there is no fraudulence at play, the financial statements will provide the details needed for such a reconstruction, provided the search is intensive and persuasive enough. A good strategy or market intelligence department should either have their analysts trained in reading financial statements or should liaise closely with an internal or external expert to find the need-to-know details for the analysis at hand.

3.4 COMPETITOR PRODUCT PORTFOLIO ANALYSIS

Competitor product portfolio analysis has a role both in strategy design and in strategy execution. Analysing a product portfolio may either consist of understanding products that are for sale in a particular market or that are offered by a specific competitor. In strategy design, the analysis may generate input to an R&D plan, a market entry plan and/or a marketing plan. In strategy execution, making an assessment of the innovation capabilities of a potentially to-be-acquired company and of its portfolio of products and brands is input to an M&A feed-the-funnel exercise and/or possibly to a target approach. In the latter case, the *value* of the innovation capabilities and the products/brands must also be assessed.

Competitor product portfolio analysis enables us to:

- Assess the value or strength of a particular company's innovation capabilities and brands portfolio, either as input to a M&A decision or as input to a broader assessment of a supplier, a customer or a competitor.
- Assess the competitive entry barriers of a market or a category or a technology: What barriers would our firm encounter when trying to enter a geo/product market?

Technology intelligence and patent analysis of other companies are discussed elsewhere in this book. In this section, the focus is on how to analyse an individual company's portfolio of trademark registrations and products/brands and its portfolio of (new) product (launches). In addition, a so-called 'white space analysis' will be discussed to identify innovation opportunities that may exist in markets based on new product launch analysis.

TRADEMARKS AND BRANDS

In a competitive entry barrier assessment, trademarks and competitor brands must feature. Trademark registrations will inform the strategy analyst which portfolio of brands are registered in a country, by which companies, in which (strictly defined) product categories and with which typical colour schemes and or characteristic images.

Assessing the value of brands is a specialist's work (Salinas, 2009). In this section, a few parameters are mentioned as first, tentative indicators to be collected by strategic analysts:

- Brand sales   (by country, by channel, by product range)
- Brand awareness   (by consumer target group – aided and spontaneous, top-of-mind percentage, by country, by product range)
- Brand equity/image   (by country, by consumer target group)
- Perceived brand promise   (by country, by consumer target group)
- Brand identity   (by country, by consumer target group)
- Brand distribution   (by country, by channel, weighted/numeric)

In carrying out this analysis on the brand portfolio of a competitor, finding answers to the above questions is virtually impossible without committing substantial resources and involving specialist research agencies. It is relevant to be realistic about what a strategy department, with its range of collection instruments and capabilities, can do itself and what it can thus promise to deliver to the principal of the project within a particular (out-of-pocket) budget and timeframe.

Brands, especially those being sold in different countries, may have very different identities in different countries. Generalizing based on too few data points and/or on ethnocentric thinking may lead to serious mishaps in the analysis. Two examples are shared to illustrate the importance of never jumping to conclusions when it comes to what international brands mean to consumers in different countries:

- The Heineken beer brand in the US and in many other countries represents a premium positioned lager. This is absolutely not the case in the Netherlands (Heineken's country of origin) where Heineken is a mainstream priced product and positioned as an everyday brand.
- When I was talking to the advertising agency that ran the car manufacturer Fiat's account in Brazil in 2012, the topic of Fiat's tie-up with Chrysler surfaced. In Europe, this deal led to mixed feelings among car lovers. The Fiat Group decided to modify the Lancia brand after the tie-up, pulling it close

to what Chrysler used to stand for – at least for Lancia's premium car segment offerings. In Europe, Lancia used to be an exclusive brand. Lancias were driven by architects and artists: perhaps not offering the best value for money, but uniquely styled and indicating a truly Italian lifestyle. The Brazilian advertising man was shocked. In Brazil, Chrysler was US-based and thus, almost by default, aspirational and the values of the Lancia brand were, as a consequence, lifted after the Chrysler deal.

This type of strategic analysis may also be applied to new product launches, regardless of whether the objective is to assess a market entry barrier, a competitor's innovativeness or a (company's or brand's) value.

NEW PRODUCT LAUNCH ANALYSIS

A new product launch analysis maps and analyses historical product launches, meticulously researches the most recent launches and, based on a thorough understanding of current and future relevant technologies and trends, predicts future directions of product launches. New product launch analysis normally either focuses on a market (geo/product) or a company (competitor/supplier/customer). In the latter case, the term 'shadow innovation roadmap' is sometimes used. The intermezzo at the end of this section covers how to source new product launch data (in FMCGs).

The new product launch analysis may either focus on the functional benefits of newly launched products or focus on the emotional benefits of newly launched products to its customers/consumers. The latter is best carried out by analysing communication materials like TV commercials. Analysing both the functional and the emotional benefits of newly launched products and the simultaneous connection or interaction between the two is possible as well.

Communication analysis is a specialist subject. It may be beneficial for a strategy department to involve an advertising agency or a (neutral) in-house expert. New product launches and the related communications may, gradually and over time, aim to change a brand's identity, as was made clear in the Lancia/Chrysler example. Such slow changes may strategically be highly relevant for the competitive dynamics in a market, but does not involve overnight visible changes: the weak signals of change and the direction that is apparently aimed for by the other brand/company may be difficult to notice by a strategy department without expert guidance.

The ultimate objective of new product analysis at large remains to predict – with a reasonable accuracy and probability – the future of in-market competition. To do so, a strategy department needs to uncover patterns in the behaviour of other market players. The patterns should unravel the script the other market players use (the thinking of the Fiat Group on where to take the Lancia brand in terms of positioning) – leading to an assessment of the other players' innovation roadmaps. The standard underlying model for a (shadow) innovation roadmap is:

Past: Historical launches following particular now-known technologi-
             cal developments (applied patented knowledge and technologies).
Present: Current launches possibly linked to known patents/technolo-
             gies/licenses.
Future: Expected launches based on current (published/patented)
             technological developments that have not yet been brought
             to market.

The above model highlights the technology dimension. The same model is valid once it is clear what identity a brand owner gradually wants to move its brand to. Below, follow some questions that may assist in unraveling other players' innovation agenda:

- What connections are visible between technologies/patents, launches, brands?
- How much time typically elapses between a technology mastered and a new product launched?
- What repeatable sequence of new product launches is visible?
- What, if any, market is used as a test market (trying to stay under the RADAR)?
- What, if any, is the market where an international innovation is always launched first (market can mean a specific channel or a geo-market or a customer group)?
- How much time elapses between roll-out in the launch country and in other countries – or markets/channel/customer groups?
- What channel is the first that is chosen for the launch? Why? What pattern is visible?
- What pricing strategy is seen in new product launches (if any)?
- What (consumer) occasion is (first) targeted when launching an innovation (this may not be relevant for all products, but it is relevant in consumer food)?
- What emotional benefit/identity direction is a brand apparently heading?
- What evidence is available to substantiate this view? What (consumer) trends does this movement apparently tap into and why? How defendable

is the new emotional territory for the brand? How many other players try to occupy a similar or almost similar consumer mind space? Which brand is the consumer image leader in this territory and why?

- What, if any, claims are made as functional 'reasons to believe' for the new product?
- What, if any, legal framework (think Codex Alimentarius, think Federal Drug Agency) is applicable that may regulate these claims? What compliance issues could emerge?
- What do the answers to the above questions tell us about what to expect next in terms of competitive pressure by market – be it a country, a channel, a customer group, etc.?

WHITE SPACE ANALYSIS

An R&D and/or a marketing/brand plan may also wish to identify which channels/occasions/product areas in the market are heavily crowded with multiple, overlapping and probably competing competitor propositions and which are not. The latter are white spaces or blue oceans, the former red oceans (Chan Kim, 2005).

Table 3.4 gives a simple example of the output of a white space innovation analysis. In the columns, different typical consumer health benefit platforms are listed that may be delivered through tailored food concepts on the basis of yogurt. The rows show different countries. The numbers indicate, for example, the number of new products launched in the past year by category and by country in the retail channel.

	Healthy aging	Bone health	Weight management	Skin health
UNITED STATES	4	0	227	0
UNITED KINGDOM	0	1	118	3
JAPAN	18	17	95	14

TABLE 3.4 ▶ ▶ ▶ WHITE SPACE INNOVATION ANALYSIS: NUMBERS OF NEW PRODUCTS LAUNCHED IN HEALTH BENEFIT-FOCUSED CATEGORIES, DELIVERED THROUGH A YOGURT PLATFORM, BY COUNTRY.

This simple fictive analysis immediately makes clear that weight management is a benefit area where the market is crowded. It may be challenging to obtain attractive profits from offering another weight-management proposition based on yogurt, unless there is compelling evidence to the contrary. In addition, the table shows that Japan has a dynamic, innovative yogurt-based market in all benefit areas. This suggests Japanese consumers are more involved in buying health benefit-related yogurts than consumers living in the US or the UK. In addition, it shows that in both the US and the UK, health concepts in the yogurt category other than weight management have not yet taken off. Otherwise, more innovations would have been launched. The table suggests that either the US and/or the UK offers potential for launching such concepts or that the American and British consumers have no interest in the concepts. Other parties may have tried earlier, failed and stopped. Additional data will be needed to determine whether 'absence of innovation' indeed is a proxy indicator for 'presence of opportunity'. Even when that is the case, the next even more relevant check that still needs to be made is whether 'presence of opportunity' equates to 'presence of opportunity to our company'. The strategy department may identify a white space market for our company. The identification as such does not by default mean that serving that white space market can be done profitably given a company's capabilities and competitive edge.

THE ROLE OF THE STRATEGY DEPARTMENT IN COMPETITOR PRODUCT PORTFOLIO ANALYSIS

The strategy department may easily accept the end responsibility for preparing a competitor product portfolio analysis, provided it has the means/resources to outsource sub-tasks to specialists (e.g., trademark registration analysis, communication analysis). As in operating other analysis tools, the strategy department will play the role of the lead violist of a chamber orchestra: ensuring all other specialist musicians stick to their specific timings and notes to in good harmony deliver a common performance, for the audience (read: principals) to enjoy. *Table 3.5* summarizes the application of product portfolio analysis as a tool.

DIMENSIONS	DESCRIPTION
What use does this tool have?	Product portfolio analysis allows us to assess the 'white spaces' in a market (geo/product/channel) to target future innovation launches into blue oceans. It may also enable us to assess the value of a brand/product portfolio in support of M&A activity. Finally, it may inform R&D and marketing plans on what the market of the future will look like in terms of competitive (or customer or supplier) offerings by extrapolating historic and current new product launches linked to past, current and possible future technological developments.
When to apply this tool?	Product portfolio analysis is a critical input to R&D and innovation/marketing plans. Brand and innovation capability value assessments serve M&A target valuations.
Who to involve when applying this tool?	Product portfolio analysis is a team sport. For a strategy department, it is recommended to liaise closely with brand registration specialists, probably within the legal department and with R&D and marketing staff. In addition, third-party specialists may need to be consulted/involved, such as an advertising agency or specialized innovation analysis boutiques such as Mintel.

TABLE 3.5 ▶ ▶ ▶ **APPLICATION OF PRODUCT PORTFOLIO ANALYSIS AS A TOOL**

INTERMEZZO: GLOBAL NEW PRODUCTS DATABASES

In the Fast Moving Consumer Goods (FMCG) industry, the 'F' for 'fast' is critical. This equally applies in other industries where innovation rates are high, e.g., the high tech sector. For an individual player in the FMCG industry, keeping track of the physical products that competitors launch across multiple countries in the world is impossible.

Specialized service providers have stepped in to pre-competitively offer the permanent watch on global new products as a service to all sub-scribing FMCG industry players in all thinkable FMCG categories. The global market leader in this service is the UK-based, privately owned

Mintel with its GNPD service. Other players offering a similar product include Innova.

With Mintel's larger customers, every individual employee at any location in the world has unlimited access via an intranet portal to all subscriptions that are bought. The process consists of the following steps:

Collection

Mintel operates with a team of 'shop visitors' in more than 50 countries in the world that represent close to 90% of the globe's GDP. The shop visitors regularly (e.g., monthly) check the various FMCG-categories in various channels. They buy any innovation they spot. They fill in an elaborate form (including selling price) with product details. Any product packaging (after emptying) is physically sent to London to Mintel's back office where more than 20,000 products arrive each month or more than c. 1,000 per working day for inclusion in Mintel's database, GNPD, access to which is offered to its subscribers.

Databasing

The database, in principle, records anything that reasonably can be recorded on a newly launched product, including pack photographs. Details include the product's ingredients list, packaging materials used, on-pack claims, pack-type, price point, brand, producer, shelf life and country of purchase. The details form the product metadata in multiple dimensions.

Customer interface

The product metadata are the basis for allowing subscribers to install tailored search alerts in the database. A user can, for example, install a permanent personalized search for any new product launched by company XYZ in Latin America in category ABC. Every new product that matches the provided metadata profile will be emailed to the user.

Similarly, a user can do a tailored search on all new products that have been launched in the US containing sucralose in the drinking yogurt category. The latter is a powerful tool to B2B ingredient players that want to keep track of how their ingredients are really used by customers around the world – to potentially inspire new customers.

Beyond the database

Companies like Mintel increasingly aim to sell services over and above the new product launch database subscription to their customers. Mintel thus offers consultancy projects in the field of their expertise – new product development and innovation – featuring not only the use of the database, but also assisting customers in making sense of the myriad of new innovation launched and facilitating them in new product development workshops.

For some countries, a separate subscription allows not only to observe newly launched products but also to follow actual sales data of the innovations, provided by Mintel's partner IRI. The latter service allows one to estimate market success. Market success is very different from market launch. Generally up to 75% of all FMCG-products launched have been delisted say two years after their launch. Regardless of all the consumer research that usually preceded their launch, all too often the consumer simply didn't buy the innovation in sufficient quantities to justify its continued production. Table 3.6 below summarizes the pros and cons of outsourcing new product launch monitoring and the related use of such subscriber services.

+	-
- Convenient. - Early alert, assuming the first launch market of a global adversary innovation was covered by the subscriber service. - Searchable database in multiple dimensions with large historic records to develop a view on e.g., an competitor's brand or category strategy over time. - Nearly global scale. - Multiple categories covered. - Access to neutral, global category analysts/specialists in innovation as sparring partner, either included in subscription fee or as add-on.	- Not avoiding surprises, only when the product is 'in the shop' it is picked up, registered and displayed. - New products do not equal successful products: sales data are limited to single-digit number of countries. - Not too relevant for local marketing and sales teams, that has usually picked up the innovation (long) before Mintel, as it has its channels (e.g., sometimes forewarned by the trade prior to an upcoming competitor launch). - No competitive advantage versus competitors that use the same tool: the facts available to all players are the same, an advantage can only be obtained by extracting and then using superior insights in the own firm.

TABLE 3.6 ▶ ▶ ▶ PROS AND CONS OF OUTSOURCING NEW PRODUCT DEVELOPMENT MONITORING

In conclusion, for FMCG players, subscriptions to new product launch databases are recommended, as there is no way the scale advantages of the supplier will ever be matched by an individual FMCG player. Earning back the subscription cost requires ensuring a service like Mintel is fully embedded in NPD – and consumer marketing processes in B2C and in sales and marketing efforts in B2B companies.

 3.5

COMPETITOR PATENT ANALYSIS

Patent analysis requires both a permanent shallow and broad monitoring process, as well as project-based deep-dives.

NEW PATENT APPLICATION MONITORING IS A CONTINUOUS PROCESS

The monitoring process consists of steps that resemble that in common market intelligence collection and analysis:

- Definition of key technology (and company) interest areas to monitor.
- Permanent collection of new patent applications, to monitor (like a RADAR) all new news on the defined technology areas and or competitors/supplies/customers; the collection proceeds by selecting new patent applications (one-by-one) based on a match of technology fields or of the relevant inventor company or inventor.
- Selection of the most relevant patent applications for a more detailed review (by experts in the respective technology fields covered).
- Analysing the potential business impact of new patent applications to a company's current and future business interests – including screening potential infringements that new patent applications may have with existing intellectual property a company possesses.
- Decide whether or not to start an opposition against a new patent application.
- Periodically review whether the key technology (and company) interest areas are still up to date and, if not, adapt these.

A permanently installed 'new patent application' review team that has the responsibility to carry out the above process in most companies is part of the R&D organization or closely connected to the R&D organization. The role of the strategy department in such review teams may be in assessing the patent position choices of other companies in the broader context of how market intelligence monitors these other companies. Such other companies may be suppliers, customers and, of course, competitors. A more in-depth involvement of the strategy department is common in the case of focused 'deep-dive' patent analysis projects.

PATENT ANALYSIS PROJECTS MAY FOCUS ON TECHNOLOGIES OR COMPANIES OR BOTH

New patent application monitoring in principle is a reactive activity. Patent analysis is generally proactive: it provides input to, for example, R&D plans, marketing plans and/or to the valuation of a patent (intellectual property) portfolio of an acquisition target. In preparing R&D plans, a patent analysis may be used to provide the 'free room' for a company to file its own future unique intellectual property that it can protect. The latter is a critical way to earn back costly and time-consuming R&D investments. There is no point for a company to do extensive R&D work in a field that is so well covered by other companies' patent positions that bringing the output of the R&D work to the market in the form of superior products is next to impossible.

Marketing and communication plans may be built on the uniqueness of the functional benefits a company's products offer. Patent analysis may illustrate supplier, competitor and (B2B) customer activities, even in cases linking future technologies to competitor brands. The latter may provide an insight into a potential future competitor's brands' innovation roadmap. A patent analysis may assist in identifying open-innovation partner selections. Parties that through patent analysis prove to be working all too closely together with direct competitors may be less likely partners for your firm. *Table 3.7* provides an overview of different scopes for patent analysis.

	INDIVIDUAL COMPANY	MULTIPLE COMPANIES
INDIVIDUAL TECHNOLOGIES (OR PROCESSES, COMPONENTS, ETC.)	Deep-dive on a single company's patent portfolio in a particular technology: usually done to check 'room-to-move' for your firm's R&D projects and/or operations.	Patent landscaping on which players (companies, universities, inventors) are active in a specific technology, possibly illuminating links between sub-fields, inventors and co-innovating companies. This analysis should reveal the intensity of competition (through patent frequency) in some areas and the absence of patents in others (where no patents have been filed).
MULTIPLE TECHNOLOGIES	Patent landscaping on a single company's complete patent portfolio is usually carried out to assess the economic value of the portfolio.	A broad scope, multiple technologies, multiple companies analysis may be needed to assess, for example, the upcoming technology trends in a particular (consumer) product category, e.g., yogurt.

TABLE 3.7 ▶ ▶ ▶ FOUR COMMON SCOPES IN PATENT ANALYSIS

SPECIALIZED SOFTWARE HAS BEEN DEVELOPED FOR PATENT ANALYSIS

Patent content analysis, like other 'unstructured document analysis', is based on natural language processing. In the context of patent analysis, natural language processing is also referred to as 'text mining'. Text mining depends on complex algorithms in specialized software to identify patterns of the frequency and interrelationship of key terms occurring together in multiple documents. Relations between different key terms, be they the names of inventors, companies, universities, substances, processes, etc., may be revealed by advanced word count programmes. Such programmes subsequently visualize the output of the analysis in 'patent topographies'. Like geographical maps, such topographies describe a so-called patent landscape. The more patents have been filed with particular combinations of key words, the darker the colour on the map becomes. Just as on geographical maps, mountains have a different colour than meadows.

PATENT ANALYSIS REQUIRES PATENT ATTORNEY AND/OR SUBJECT MATTER EXPERT INPUT

Patent analysis consists of three dimensions: process, content and context. The process part is best judged by a patent attorney. The attorney is best suited to answer questions like:

- The status of an individual patent's application process.
- The jurisdictions where the patent is filed – and most of all, where it has not been filed.
- How opposition may have to be started.
- What partners may be identified to join in an opposition.
- What the (legal) angle and approach of an opposition may have to look like.
- What claims may be disputed and how, etc.

The content analysis of an individual patent or a patent family is a specialized (R&D) activity for which a subject matter expert is required. The subject matter expert should be qualified to answer questions like:

- What is the invention?
- What is the technological process or functional product benefit compared to current technologies or products?
- Who is the inventor?
- To whom is the inventor related/connected (think of: LinkedIn, citation indices, universities, large technological institutes, co-members of boards of scientific associations)? This type of network analysis, not unlike how law enforcement agencies map terrorist networks, may illuminate hidden yet relevant links.

THE ROLE OF THE STRATEGY DEPARTMENT IS TO UNDERSTAND THE CONTEXT

The strategy department is needed for the company context and the normal mild paranoia. Patent analysis-related questions (not exhaustive) for a strategy department include:

- Why did the company or the inventor choose to apply for a patent?
  - o To provide recognition to a vain in-house inventor, as a personal reward. When is the next conference this inventor will deliver a speech? Vain people love to impress others: they may say more than is good for their company's interests.
  - o Because there was no harm in publishing this patent, as the technology that is patented proved to be economically useless anyway.
  - o Because this new patent (or this newborn member to a company's patent family) builds or adds to a company's existing and possibly future competitive edge by monopolizing advantageous technologies or products (think of pharmaceuticals), in doing so stretching the period that patents' related high profits can be sustained.
  - o Because the company needs cash for future R&D and hopes through license fees from other companies on its existing patents to obtain new funding.
- What does this patent say about future company strategies (think xeno-centrical)?
- What B2B or B2C offerings (under what brands) may in the future be connected to the technology/product/benefit/claims described in this patent?
- What impact may this patent have on the company's strategy/positioning?

Always remember that the paradox of a patent application is that it provides protection by opening up (trade/technology) secrets. Many companies tend not to file patents in advance when it is clear that patent infringement by other companies will be impossible to discover. When thinking xenocentrically about patents and the logic of the companies that applied for them, remember that other companies want you to know what is in the patent. Companies may either do so because the other party believes your knowing it does no harm or because they believe your knowing it will not provide you with a competitive advantage. This may be because infringement is easy to discover and related rights are easy/cheap/reliable to enforce in the jurisdictions where the patent is (to be) filed. Taking a xenocentric view requires a strategist first to think why a company allows competitors to read a patent application prior to thinking of hiring/involving expensive subject matter experts to answer other questions regarding that patent. *Table 3.8* summarizes patent analysis as a tool.

DIMENSIONS.	DESCRIPTION
What use does this tool have?	A patent analysis typically provides input for R&D plans, possibly for marketing plans and at all times for M&A target valuation (and/or the related due diligence).
When to apply this tool?	Patent analysis is, or better should be, a proactive tool. The tool should be applied prior to assigning substantial funds to future R&D plans or marketing/communication plans and, most of all, prior to agreeing on the valuation of a to-be acquired (or sold) business.
Who to involve when applying this tool?	Patent analysis is a craft: it requires specialists to complement strategy. When for a strategy department patent analysis is part of the responsibility portfolio, ensure the analyst responsible for this is up to the job. When the strategy department has to in-source patent analysis, ensure the person 'procuring' an analysis either understands the subject matter sufficiently well to both provide a good brief and be able to judge the quality and usefulness of the output. Another option for a strategy department is to assign an in-sourced (i.e., third party) specialist at the strategy department's side to source a patent analysis from another third party.

TABLE 3.8 ▶ ▶ ▶ APPLICATION OF PATENT ANALYSIS AS A TOOL

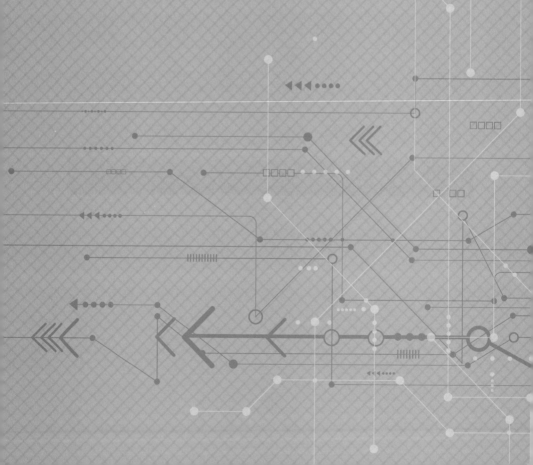

CHAPTER 4

COMPETITOR MANAGEMENT ANALYSIS

4.1 INTRODUCTION

Competitor management analysis usually boils down to preparing a competitor executive profile. Creating such profiles is neither a routine nor a frequent task of a strategist or market intelligence professional. Profiling a senior leader of a competitor may, however, be a powerful tool for assisting to predict a competitor's next steps. History provides great examples of what happens when an adversary's leader is either not profiled or misunderstood. Think of the UK and French misreading of Adolf Hitler's intent in Munich in 1938. Another classic example of underestimating a competitor's leader has been documented well. Western and Israeli intelligence in the late 1960s had to profile the successor of the Egyptian leader Gamal Abdel Nasser. His successor, Anwar Sadat, was believed to have been a yes-man to Nasser (Shalev, 2014a):

The assessment was that Sadat was a weak man and incapable of leading and making tough decisions, and that he would therefore not remain in his position for the long term.

In 1973, this Egyptian leader stunned Israel and the world by starting the Yom Kippur War. A few years later he again stunned the world by signing a peace treaty with Israel, which earned him the Nobel Peace Prize. Not quite the weak character he had been expected to be. Misreading Sadat as a person is still perceived to have been the key reason for the surprise of the Yom Kippur War: one of the intelligence history's most famous failures. Former US Secretary of State Henry Kissinger concluded (Shalev, 2014b):

> *What literally no one understood beforehand (before the Yom Kippur War) was the mind of the man. The boldness of Sadat's strategy was in planning for what no one could imagine.*

In business, a competitor CEO profile – implicitly or explicitly – typically forms input into assessing a competitor's behaviour in M&A bidding wars or negotiations. It may also be used to anticipate the reactions of competitors that may be provoked by a company entering into one of their markets. The questions that a competitor executive profile aims to answer include:

- Who is the poker player at the other side of the table?
- What is their personal style?
- How will their personal needs and preferences translate into a company's next steps?

PROFILING EXECUTIVES MATTERS MOST WHEN SINGLE EXECUTIVES MAKE KEY DECISIONS

The logical model underpinning the preparation of an executive profile when predicting a company's next steps is:

- Data collected from a range of sources allow an executive to be profiled.
- An executive with a particular profile will behave in a particular *predictable* way when facing particular circumstances.
- The company led by this executive is a shadow of this executive; i.e., the executive facing particular circumstances will make their *predictable* call on the decisions to be taken at a company level.
- By implication: knowing the circumstances and the executive's profile allows predicting the company's next steps within a certain level of accuracy.

A word of warning should be given here. Assessing the intent of another company is much harder than assessing the other company's more tangible capabilities. Typical outputs of competitor profiling are given below. Competitor executive profiling may, for example, shine a light on the fact that a family company will not be offered for sale until the founding grandfather has passed away, as he is known to reject the idea of a sale. The family, even when it comes at a price, cannot close a deal as long as grandpa is still alive. These sorts of details emerge when the broader personal and psychological context of a company's owner/director are taken into account. These types of detail do not automatically result from a plain economic analysis of the owner's interests.

Another similar example is that a company with a wide portfolio may not be interested in divesting a poorly performing unit, if that unit happens to have been the unit in which the current group CEO has made his fast-track career. The moment a new CEO gets in, the unit's divestment may suddenly be on top of the corporate agenda. Similarly, a top executive who lost a job earlier in their career at another company, due to destructing value with an acquisition, may be reluctant to entertain the thought of doing acquisitions in his current company, even when business logic would be compelling enough for the company, looking from a distance, to do so.

Similarly, in an M&A bidding process, a company's current owners, especially when it is a family, may not always choose the highest bidder if a cultural connection lacks. Understanding what the cultural connection is that the family seeks and where possible acting upon it may provide a unique advantage. To do this, some sort of competitor executive profiling – even in a rudimentary form – may make the difference.

This is why even as indirect a model as that of competitor executive profiling may still be used fruitfully – often as part of a broader analysis – even when several factors may affect the accuracy of a competitor executive profile.

The sections below discuss in more detail how to profile a competitor executive, as well as what factors may affect the accuracy of such an exercise.

4.2 THE WORKFLOW OF COMPETITOR EXECUTIVE PROFILING

Diagram 4.1 summarizes a possible workflow for preparing a competitor executive profile. This workflow is entirely positioned within the responsibility area of a company's strategy or market intelligence department. The critical first step in the workflow is shown in the top-left box in *Diagram 4.1*. It is imperative to secure the commitment of the decision maker so they will accept competitor executive profiling as an instrument in support of their choices. With that commitment in place, chances are high that the decision maker will indeed use the output of the analysis (i.e., the prediction of the next move by a competitor).

It is not recommended to profile a competitor executive for the sake of it. A strategist is to be careful when picking up an assignment that is not demand-driven. There may be good reasons to do unsolicited proactive work, such as analysing the implications of new news to a company but, overall, demand-driven work is to be preferred.

In competitor executive profiling, the first step is usually to define the decision the competitor company's executive is to take. Afterwards, competitor executive profiling is generally supportive to predicting future competitor moves that are preceded by key competitor decisions.

Defining the decision or decisions enables a definition of the ingoing market intelligence needs. This will allow the collection phase of market intelligence to focus on getting the need-to-have or *critical* data. Moreover, it will allow identification of which competitor executive is mostly or completely in charge of taking the decision. It is the key decision maker of the competitor that should be the focus of the profiling. Profiling teams of executives is possible but, subsequently predicting not only the team members personal preferences but also the intra-team dynamics, may be too speculative to deliver useful output.

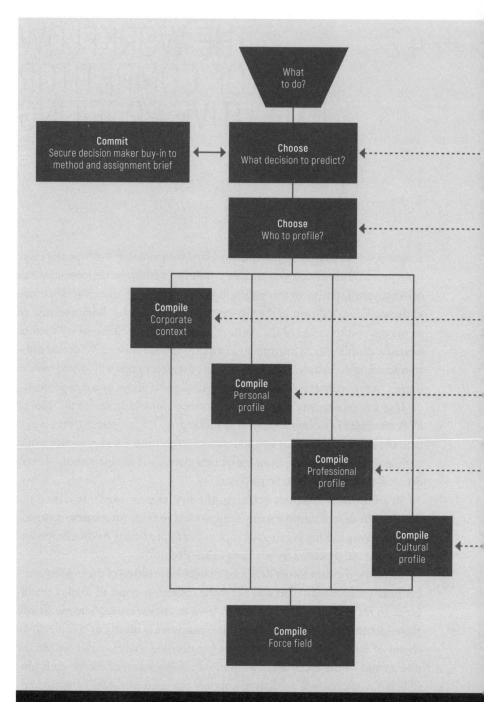

DIAGRAM 4.1 ▶ ▶ ▶ WORKFLOW FOR PREPARING A COMPETITOR EXECUTIVE PROFILE

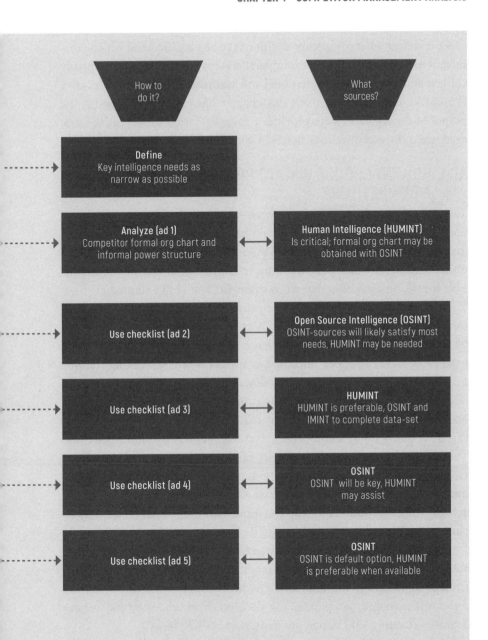

How to
do it?

What
sources?

Define
Key intelligence needs as
narrow as possible

Analyze (ad 1)
Competitor formal org chart and
informal power structure

Human Intelligence (HUMINT)
Is critical; formal org chart may be
obtained with OSINT

Use checklist (ad 2)

Open Source Intelligence (OSINT)
OSINT-sources will likely satisfy most
needs, HUMINT may be needed

Use checklist (ad 3)

HUMINT
HUMINT is preferable, OSINT and
IMINT to complete data-set

Use checklist (ad 4)

OSINT
OSINT will be key, HUMINT
may assist

Use checklist (ad 5)

OSINT
OSINT is default option, HUMINT
is preferable when available

HUMINT: intelligence from human sources
OSINT: intelligence from open source; public domain data
IMINT: intelligence from studying imagery (static or moving) e.g. interviews

Once it is clear what competitor decision is to be predicted and which executive is to be profiled, the next four parallel steps are to compile a company context and a personal, a professional and a cultural profile of the executive (Philips, 2009; on whose work this chapter has partly been based). The output of these parallel steps provides a 'force field' that the executive faces, even when the executive may not even consciously experience this field.

AD 1. HOW TO CHOOSE WHO TO PROFILE WITHIN A COMPETITOR?

The first step to take is to determine whom to profile. This sounds like an open door, but especially in large companies, *informal* power structures may not always resemble formal organization charts. What is needed is an understanding of which person is most influential in or exclusively responsible for taking a decision that we as strategists would like to predict.

In a multinational (FMCG) company, matrix organizations are common. When predicting business choices in a country, the question will be whether the local managing director calls the shots or whether some head office-based category director has the last word. Collecting the formal organization chart from public domain sources will normally not be difficult. Understanding who within a company really takes the decisions on matters, however, almost certainly requires *recent* insight views on what exactly is going on at a competitor. Power structures by nature are fluid. This means that data may have a short validity, to be measured in quarters rather than years. Managers tend to be as powerful as their unit's last strong quarterly results. Identifying legally and ethically acceptable and reasonably actually informed sources to map the inside world of a competitor may be challenging enough.

Such sources are less relevant when a company, for example, has a single autocratic shareholder/owner/director and the decision is believed to be sufficiently significant to warrant that the owner themselves will take it. In truly top-down managed companies, any decision, from choosing the Winter Season's Greetings card design onwards, may be '*Chefsache*'.

Do not proceed with competitor executive profiling when any of the below three conditions is met. When …

- It has not been determined with sufficient accuracy who the decision maker actually is that has clear authority to take the decision we aim to predict,
- A well-informed source on the current dynamics in the competitor is not available,

- In advance it is obvious that the decision at the competitor that we aim to predict will be taken by a large committee.

AD 2. HOW TO COMPILE A RELEVANT CORPORATE CONTEXT?

The relevant corporate context collected about a competitor should relate directly to the competitor decision that we aim to predict. Avoid drowning in 'nice to know' data on the competitor that does not get to the core issue: what decision will the company take through this particular executive on their issue at stake? Questions that may be helpful to ensure to collect (only) *critical* data include:

- What are the overall targets the company has communicated to its owners?
- How would the decision to be predicted by us as strategist fit in the overall narrative the competitor's top management has told its shareholders?
- How consistent would a decision be within a corporate overall journey the competitor is taking? When, as an example, earnings before interest and taxes (EBIT) margin growth for years has had a higher priority than topline growth, what does this fact mean for this particular decision? If we as strategic analysis department assess a decision that will likely dilute EBIT margins, how is the competitor's top management going to 'spin' this decision to at least make it *look* consistent with their margin growth strategy?
- What is the formal responsibility and authority of the executive?
- What are (or are expected to be) their (personal) targets? Personal targets are secrets that are usually well kept: do not expect to get them just like that. An executive, however, may communicate personal targets indirectly in interviews. As Peter Drucker has advised: "The most important thing in communication is to hear what has not been said." When executives sketch their priorities, they also implicitly mention which topics are not their priorities.
- What was the assignment this executive got when they were appointed? Quite often, interviews with senior leaders when they are appointed reveal what their (initial) priorities are and why. Indirectly the person's profile at the moment they were selected for the job may show the intent a company's board or top management had with the business when appointing this particular individual. No board would normally appoint an executive with a marvelous track record in cost cutting and restructuring to work in a high-growth market, unless that company's business first needed to be turned around prior to be able to return to profitable growth in line with the market it operates in.

AD 3. HOW TO COMPILE AN EXECUTIVE'S PERSONAL PROFILE?

Prior to going into details on this, it should be emphasized that profiling a person's psychological self is expert work (Clark, 2007a). Admit to yourself that you are not an expert. When I had to prepare a profile the other day, I benefited significantly from hiring an outside expert to make sense of executive profiling. As a strategist, you may either choose to recruit an expert in this field or identify a good partner – internal or external – to work with when psychological profiling needs to be done.

A psychological personal profile should at least cover the following four dimensions:

- Concept of self – the conscious ideas of what a person thinks they are, along with the frequently unconscious motives and defences against ego-threatening experiences such as withdrawal of love, public shaming, guilt or isolation.
- Relation to authority – how an individual adapts to authority figures.
- Modes of impulse control and of expressing emotion.
- Processes of forming and manipulating ideas.

These profiling dimensions link to six basic needs of individuals (AchieveGlobal, 2010). These needs often drive behaviour, just as the above four dimensions.

- Recognition
- Achievement
- Control
- Power
- Affiliation
- Safety

Assessing which combination of these psychological needs mainly drives the behaviour of an executive in general may be useful to assess what choice an executive may take for the decision we as strategists want to predict. An executive with a high safety need is less likely to consider a high-risk acquisition than an executive with a strong recognition need who constantly wants to make headlines in the papers with their next big deal. Even though personalities may change over time, historical behaviour (what the executive did to satisfy which of their needs) is likely to predict the future. A control-oriented executive will not likely entertain the thought of buying a minority stake in a joint venture (JV) in a business in a new market on a new continent, unless the JV-contract explicitly provides binding clauses toward a majority ownership with clear valuation formulas in the term sheet. As so often in strategy, executive profiling is also all about probabilities.

Together the four dimensions mentioned by Clark and the six needs compiled by AchieveGlobal do not collectively exhaust all there is to know about the psychological make-up of a personality; rather, both sets form a checklist for inspiration. *Diagram 4.2* summarizes how a model of the psychological 'self' profile of a competitor executive can be filled by interpreting the behaviour of that executive, leading to predictions of that executive's behaviour in particular circumstances. All models are wrong, but some models are useful. Modelling competitor executives is no exception.

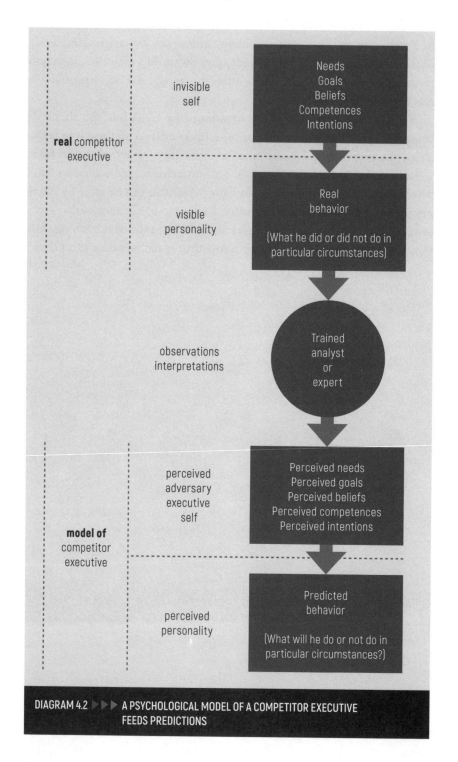

invisible
self

Needs
Goals
Beliefs
Competences
Intentions

real competitor
executive

visible
personality

Real
behavior

(What he did or did not do in
particular circumstances)

observations
interpretations

Trained
analyst
or
expert

perceived
adversary
executive
self

Perceived needs
Perceived goals
Perceived beliefs
Perceived competences
Perceived intentions

model of
competitor
executive

perceived
personality

Predicted
behavior

(What will he do or not do in
particular circumstances?)

DIAGRAM 4.2 ▶ ▶ ▶ A PSYCHOLOGICAL MODEL OF A COMPETITOR EXECUTIVE
FEEDS PREDICTIONS

In psychology, multiple psychological profiling methods have been described to ensure comprehensive models of personalities can be made. Some of these methods have been developed for 'remote' analysis, i.e., without direct participation of the subject. This is the case in strategy work (Weber, 2004). The most common profiling method is probably the Myers-Briggs Type Indicator (MBTI). Dimensions of functional preference variables in MBTI are (Weber, 2004):

- Extroversion – introversion → self-energizing preference
- Sensory – intuitive → information processing preference
- Thinking – feeling → decision-basing preference
- Judging – perceiving → self-organizing operational preference

Using a questions-based methodology, like Myers-Briggs, it is possible to remotely profile another person. The question, however, remains whether there are enough data available to xenocentrically and meaningfully profile another individual. After all, it remains remote work: access to the individual to be personally profiled may be limited or may even be totally lacking. The exercise will thus remain one of remote profiling based on *interpretation* of information from open sources. The following questions and sources may be helpful to 'populate' a chosen psychological profile/model that is to identify **what drives a person in their decision-making** in his corporate and cultural environment (based on Weber, 2004):

- **Style**
  What are the key observable elements in their business approach?
  What aspects of this leadership or management role do they emphasize?
  What areas of their responsibilities do they seem to ignore or to avoid? Why?
  Where do they delegate, where do they hold the reins?
  What body language do they show when interviewed by the press?
  What characterizes their communications style?
  What behaviour do they fall back into in stressful situations?
  What network do they have within the company?
  What network have they built outside the company (e.g., sports, industry associations, non-executive boards they are a member of, charities, non-governmental organizations)
  What sports do they do/have they done? At what level? Team or solo?

- **Motivation**

  What needs (recognition, etc.) are driving their behaviour?

  What repeatable patterns of behaviour can be identified? Do these behaviours link to their apparent personal need pattern?

- **Personal background**

  In what environment did they grow up?

  What family background do they have? What standards did they have to meet to satisfy implicit or explicit family norms?

  What values did they inherit from their social environment/family?

  What education did they have? At what schools/universities?

  What if any long-term friendships did they make?

  What family do they now belong to (married, divorced, children)?

  What (personal) defining experiences did they have? How did they handle those?

- **360° view**

  What do others say about them and why?

  What if anything does the press say about them?

  What do or did (former) mentors say?

Exceptional executives may have become exceptional because they have all their lives been successfully living up to exceptional (family) expectations. For example, General Douglas MacArthur – the architect of many daring military campaigns for the US Army between 1942–52 – has long been overpowered by his dominating and demanding mother (Manchester, 1978). Former Danone CEO Franck Riboud realized the unusual achievement of succeeding his father Antoine as CEO of Danone even when the company was listed and the family did not hold a large stake. Franck, in the course of his tenure, even outperformed his father's strong corporate track record. Franck had a lot to live up to – and he did.

One of the most valuable avenues to explore in profiling executives is to identify areas where the behaviour of the individual is not or has not been rational. Such behaviour may, for example, be displayed by executives that have to live up to self-set or family-set high expectations (Weber, 2004):

> *Individual idiosyncrasies and highly subjective personal proclivities play a much larger role than is typically recognized or acknowledged.*

For each of the answers on the above long list of questions, it is essential to have solid evidence; sentences that start with "I think" usually do not qualify. Next to interviewing sources that have interacted with the individual to be profiled, indirect sources of evidence may include:

- A LinkedIn/Facebook page.
- Transcripts of interviews.
- YouTube interviews as these also offer body language, facial expression, etc.

The most valuable approach to sourcing data is to meet the individual to be profiled in person, as this would enable to test hypotheses 'on the fly'. This, however, will usually not be feasible. It should be re-emphasized that answering all questions in the above checklist is neither mandatory nor essential. The answers to only a few questions may already provide enough evidence and thus *critical* data for the problem to be solved. Always operate need-driven; do not collect data for the sake of completeness.

AD 4. HOW TO COMPILE AN EXECUTIVE'S PROFESSIONAL PROFILE?

Aspects of an executive's psychological personality also may become visible in how a person approaches his work. This may be called a 'professional profile'. The boundaries between a psychological and a professional profile are neither closed nor rigid. This is not an exact science. The questions below may assist in mapping a competitor executive's professional profile. The psychological and the professional profile together make up who the executive is and what their input to and choice in a competitor decision likely will be.

- **Ambition**
  How does the individual want to go into history?
  What success story are they currently aiming to add to their resume?
  What repeatable success models may they wish to reapply?
  Who do they have to watch out for: who may compete for their job?

- **Strategy**
  Are they more comfortable as a strategist or as a tactician?
  Are they flexible or rigid? Thoughtful or forceful?
  How are their priorities expressed operationally? Choosing what channels?
  What stories are their favourites to tell to a new hire or contact? What

does this reveal about their preferred strategy?

What does their company need now in terms of strategy?

- **Strengths and weaknesses**

  What talents do they have?

  What is their competency comfort zone?

  What capabilities do they have to develop?

  What knowledge areas do they depend on others for in their current role?

  What mistakes did they make that they will never want to make again?

  What business success have they been responsible for? How can they repeat that?

- **Team**

  How do they work with their team?

  Who have they appointed since they joined and who did they dismiss?

  How did they do this? What message did they send in doing this?

  What where the previous jobs/organizations of their new team members? How many have been former trusted 'inner court' members?

  How do they use their team?

- **Decision-making and execution**

  How do they approach decision-making?

  Who do they involve? From whom does he seek input?

  How much information do they normally seek?

  How many alternative courses of action do they normally consider?

  How open are they to negative input or feedback?

  How predictable/logical have past decisions been, given their profile?

  How have they developed in their decision-making style over time?

  What challenges do they face in execution? How do they tackle them?

  What is probably on top of their 'to do' list? Why?

Having profiled the company context and the executive's professional and psychological profile, there is a final dimension left that still needs to be covered to complete the overall profile. This is the societal cultural dimension.

AD 5. HOW TO COMPILE AN EXECUTIVE'S RELEVANT CULTURAL PROFILE?

No man is an island. A person lives and behaves in a cultural setting. In the psychological profile, the personal and cultural background of an executive has been covered by referring to the environment the executive grew up in.

Similarly, a company is operating in a cultural setting. Culture should here be read in a broad sense (Courtney, 2009):

> *You can't evaluate any large strategic moves GM or Ford might make without considering the interests of the United Auto Workers and how those interests might check or facilitate such moves. The importance of non-owner stakeholders in driving a company's strategy varies by country of origin too. If you compete with a Chinese company, the Chinese government is often a critical stakeholder. In Europe, environmental organizations and other nongovernmental stakeholders exert more power over corporate decision-making than they do in the United States.*

Another example of culture relates to behaviour. Shouting at co-workers, to name just an example, is never a good idea. Doing so in South East Asia as a foreign executive will render you ineffective in a remarkably short period of time – without a single complaint or comment ever being uttered by a co-worker as feedback to you. At the risk of overgeneralizing, the norm in most of Asia is that shouting at others makes you lose face – and a person who has lost face cannot be taken seriously anymore. Anyone is free to ignore such norms. Expatriate contracts, however, tend to stipulate that cultural misbehaviour may be a reason for dismissal, so doing this is at a person's own risk.

The above implies that an executive will at least have to partly respect the cultural norms and stakeholders of the society they operate in when taking decisions. Questions that may assist in identifying such cultural norms may include (list not exhaustive):

- What political/societal norms set (implicit) borders to an executive's decisions?
- What stakeholders may implicitly or explicitly influence this decision?
- Which religious norms must be respected?
- What is the role of a private company in a society? The different answers to this question between, for example, France and the UK, two Western democracies that by global standards are a narrow (English) Channel apart, are already significant. What does this mean for the real 'room to move' for the company and its executive?

DEPICTING THE 'FORCE FIELD' AN EXECUTIVE HAS TO OPERATE IN

Having completed this culture check, the 'force field' within which the executive operates in a simplified form looks like the figure depicted in *Diagram 4.3*. The four profiles (company context, psychological profile, professional profile, cultural profile) together (hopefully) deliver as output the critical 'what' data.

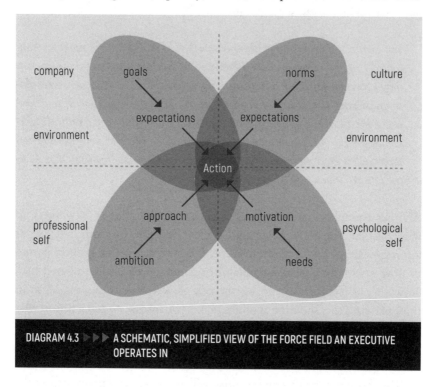

DIAGRAM 4.3 ▶ ▶ ▶ **A SCHEMATIC, SIMPLIFIED VIEW OF THE FORCE FIELD AN EXECUTIVE OPERATES IN**

It is up to the strategist, assisted by psychology experts, to determine the 'so what' related to these 'what' data. The 'so what' is the prediction of the executive's action or decision. Based on the 'so what' analysis, a 'now what' recommendation to the principal of the profiling assignment is the ultimate output of the analysis. Below, several factors are shared that may affect the predictive accuracy of a competitor executive profile.

⫸ 4.3   FACTORS AFFECTING THE ACCURACY OF A COMPETITOR EXECUTIVE PROFILE

The accuracy of profiling a competitor's executive is not to be overestimated. Here's why:

- **Intention does not equate ability**
  Wanting to take an action, for a competitor executive, does not equate to being able to take that action. In a larger company setting, a single executive, including a CEO, may not be able to turn their preferred *personal* course of action into an identical company course of action (Vella, 2000). Compromises are common in corporate life, as multiple stakeholders have their say. In more complex contexts, a strategist aiming to predict a company's intent and subsequent actions may not only have to analyse the profiles of *all* the key executives in a company, but also the group dynamics of their interaction that leads to their company's decisions. The outcome of such analysis is usually too speculative to justify the efforts. Profiling thus has the highest accuracy when companies are led by relatively autocratic leaders or decisions are to be predicted that are assessed to be taken within a company by a single individual.

- **Sources may lack**
  There is definitely beauty in profiling but, *"the trick is to get (psychological) test results on the target individual."* (Clark, 2007a). Even when in step (i) above all imaginable (legal) sources have been identified and used, a profile may still be too incomplete to be accurate enough to predict an executive and thus a company's next steps.

- **Actions are taken for multiple reasons, not just to affect our company**
  In our analysis, an executive's actions that have led to their profiling may have been assessed from too narrow a perspective. Competitor executive actions, especially in times of intense competition between a competitor and your company, are naturally perceived to be related to competing with your company (and yours alone). This may at times be a correct interpretation but, more often than not, the overall agenda of the competitor and thus of its executive is not *only* related to competing with your company (Heuer, 1999a). Rarely will a competitor predominantly be focused on competing at the cost of us, rather than on winning in its markets. The latter may indeed affect your company, but normally as an indirect consequence. When taking a xenocentric view of the competitor, the executive's actions have to be interpreted in the context of the full agenda of the competitor, not just the part of the agenda related to your company.

- **The relevance of the competitor's culture may be overestimated**
  When the CIA profiled the Soviet leader Mikhail Gorbachev, it believed he had to be a hard liner. The CIA couldn't accept the thought that Gorbachev was a reformer, given the well-known hard-liner mentors that groomed him (Hoffman, 2011). No matter how strong a culture, an individual may make a difference. Gorbachev clearly did not have the intent to abolish the Warsaw Pact: that happened to him as the reform got out of control. But he did have the unanticipated intent of trying to reform the Soviet Union and to end the Cold War.

- **Press releases express a corporate truth, but not a CEO's personal views**
  In profiling a company's CEO, multiple sources for a CEO's views are to be reviewed. It is common practice that in corporate press releases, CEOs are quoted. These quotes are rarely authentic: they originate from the minds of corporate communication or investor relation staff. The CEO at best may have approved them. For profiling a CEO, these quotes are useless or even misleading. An analyst tasked with profiling a CEO needs to exclusively look for original material. Such sources may be the answers to questions given by the CEO *personally* at a press conference or the full transcript of a CEO's investment analyst briefing. The most preferred sources are video footage of interviews, as such coverage also offers the nonverbal communication of the CEO when facing awkward questions.

- **Effective executives are all over the map in terms of personalities**

  The assumption behind profiling is that knowing the profile of an executive and the circumstances that this executive faces will allow us to predict with minimum accuracy what the executive will (want to) do next. Peter Drucker reflects on his 65-year consulting career in *Harvard Business Review* with a sobering introduction (Drucker, 2004):

  Some of the best business and non-profit CEO's [...] were all over the map in terms of their personalities, attitudes, values, strengths and weaknesses. They ranged from extrovert to reclusive, from easygoing to controlling, from generous to parsimonious.

  Drucker describes a wide spectrum of personalities that can all effectively lead corporations. In other words, there is no preferred personality type for an effective executive. As so often in strategy, preparing a profile should thus most of all be need-driven. The question to be answered is not "who is this executive?", as that may generate a lot of data that is not *critical*. Data abundance does not equate to data relevance.

  When the abundant data on an executive's personality do not contribute to a meaningful answer on the question "what will this executive, regardless of his overall personality traits, **do** in particular circumstances and why?" the data are still noise, as personalities as such are not a proxy indicator for effectiveness of behaviour.

- **The complexity of executive profiling is easily underestimated**

  Executive profiling is not rocket science. That is a pity, because it may be equally complex, but it lacks the reputation of complexity that is proverbial of rocket science. No amateur would attempt to build and operate a rocket, yet many an untrained person feels comfortable in profiling another person. A strategist should refrain from feeling qualified to do executive profiling when he has not had solid specialist training, e.g., in anthropology or psychology.

  Anthropologists look through a different lens that allows them to see a different perspective. In a particular business context, the next action of a major competitor had to be assessed in preparation for a company's strategic choices. A data set on the competitor's CEO formed part of the preparations for this decision. In order to ensure nothing was overlooked, it was decided, without particularly high expectations in advance, to ask a

PhD. in cultural anthropology (who worked in the company's R&D department anyway, so would not introduce out-of-pocket cost) have a one-day look at a competitor's executive data set that the market intelligence department had collated. The anthropologist came up with insights on the CEO that even experienced, long-term strategy analysts who had watched the competitor's leadership for years had not generated.

The anthropologist recognized behavioural patterns that were strong and thereby possibly predictive, but that had proven to be invisible to the untrained eye. Years later, the analysis proved to have been highly accurate in most of the predictions. This experience carried a clear lesson: humility as to the strategist's real competences pays off. Hiring an expert is a sign of strength, not of incompetence.

- **A person's statements may not reflect a person's real intentions**
  In May 1912, the French ambassador to Germany characterized the autocratic German Kaiser Wilhelm II with the following quote (Clark, 2013):

  It is a curious thing to see how this man, so sudden, so reckless and impulsive in words, is full of caution and patience in action.

  There is plenty of evidence in social science – I haven't illuminated specific examples here – that people say they will do things that they in reality do not intend to do; and do things they will deny they intend to do. This phenomenon also affects market intelligence analysis and in particular executive profiling. As a rule, market intelligence analysis will have more predictive value when it reviews what CEOs *did* in particular circumstances than how they *say* they will act in these circumstances.

⋙ 4.4 CONCLUSION

EXECUTIVES' PERSONALITIES MAY NOT MATTER TOO MUCH FOR STRATEGIC CHOICES

The last section of this chapter should be seen as a word of warning. There are and will always be limits to how much difference an individual executive can make, especially in a large, established company. As a result, competitor executive profiling should only be applied when it may indeed lead to those insights that enable your company to take better decisions.

Friedman points out that in what he calls a 'strategic intelligence model' for a country and a political leader, the personality of the individual is not mapped. A strategic intelligence model describes the sets of constraints a political leader faces and identifies the imperatives the leader has to pursue to survive (Friedman, 2014). The logic is similar in business. A CEO, no matter who they are, faces constraints, starts with a given asset base and will be held accountable to deliver predefined results: think of sales growth and profit growth. Friedman thus remarks:

A psychology of power in general is more useful than a psychology of individuals.

Applying Friedman's reasoning to business means that, for modelling the strategic moves of a company, the focus should be on both the company and its assets and constraints, as well as on the leader. When time pressure is high, focus on the company more than on the individual. Finally, *Table 4.1* summarizes the key messages regarding competitor executive profiling.

DIMENSIONS	DESCRIPTION
What use does this tool have?	A competitor executive profile, provided it correctly models the key decision maker in a competitor for a particular decision, assists in predicting that competitor's next steps. Knowing the competitor's next move in advance allows our company to stress test and, where needed, improve our plans – and thus prepare our company better for an upcoming commercial challenge.
When to apply this tool?	Competitor executive profiling is neither simple nor cheap, nor 100% accurate. This means that the upside potential of correctly predicting a competitor move ahead of that move being taken, must be substantial prior to considering profiling a competitor's executive. Competitor executive profiling is an instrument that is typically applied once every few years. High upside-potential decisions may include M&A bidding strategies or M&A negotiations. New market entry strategy plans where a competitor will be strongly affected by your company's launch may also qualify, as executing such plans may also involve high stakes. Pre-empting competitor intent and their anticipated actions in such cases is critical.
Who to involve when applying this tool?	Competitor executive profiling is a specialist subject. A strategic analysis department that does not have specialist competencies in this field needs to involve an outside expert to ensure the output meets minimum quality standards. There are several steps to take, each introducing potential inaccuracies, from profiling an executive to predicting the decisions taken at the company within which this executive serves. The prediction route is quite indirect. It is therefore critically important that the decision maker buy-in has been secured for using the outcome of an executive profiling exercise-based decision-prediction. When this indirect method of prediction has not obtained the decision-makers' trust, the decision-makers will not use the intelligence, no matter how high-grade and no matter what efforts have gone into the exercise. Gaining your company executives' trust may after all well be the hardest part in applying this tool.

TABLE 4.1 ▶ ▶ ▶ APPLICATION OF COMPETITOR EXECUTIVE PROFILING AS A TOOL

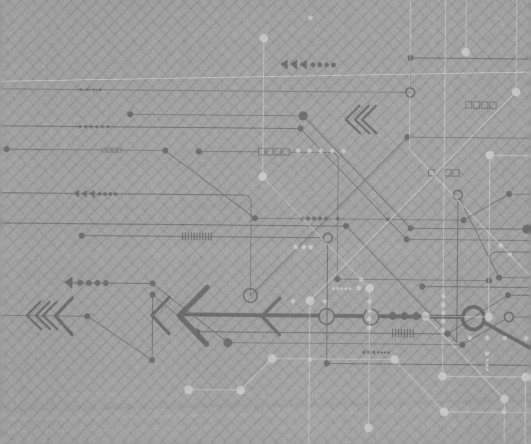

CHAPTER 5
COMPETITOR FUTURE MOVES ANALYSIS

5.1 INTRODUCTION

From the outside, military and business problems look rather different; however, military tools may have value in business. In the military, war-games have earned a solid reputation as a decision-support tool. With only slight adaptions, military wargame methodologies are directly applicable in business. It is remarkable that wargame use in business is still modest. A reason for this may be unawareness in the business community of how to successfully apply wargames. This chapter provides a manual, based mainly on empirically obtained evidence, to close this awareness gap and assist in successfully applying wargames.

⋙ 5.2   WHAT IS A WARGAME?

Military wargaming expert Peter Perla has defined (military) wargaming as (Perla, 1990):

> *A wargame is a warfare model or simulation that does not involve the operations of actual forces, in which the flow of events affects and is affected by decisions made during the course of those events by players representing the opposing sides.*

The aim of running a military wargame is to train for battle without exposure to hostile fire. This aim easily translates to a business setting. A military maxim is that 'it is better to sweat in training than to bleed in battle'. Insert the word 'cash' after the verb 'to bleed' and the maxim applies to business. Paradoxically, a wargame is neither a war nor a game. Rather it is (Gilad, 2006):

> *A rigorously structured, analytical role play of selected players in one's industry, aimed at creating a strategy based on expected moves and countermoves of these players.*

A wargame is not only a simulation. It is by its nature also a project with a beginning and an end. Once it has been decided to run a business wargame, a project should be defined, with a principal who assigns a project leader to run the business wargame project. The latter requires all the skills that other intracompany multidisciplinary project leaders have. There is a budget to be managed, there are stakeholders to be involved in various stages of the project, there is an objective to be met, a deliverable to be produced, etc. The project planning side may be time-consuming, but it is critically important to the success of running a wargame.

A WARGAME IS NOT A COMPUTER SIMULATION

Now that we defined what a wargame is, it is equally useful to point out what it is not. A business wargame is not a computer simulation (Schwarz, 2013). In advanced business wargames, computer-model-based tools may be used, but computer models are better not relied on too much to predict a competitor's intent. Moreover, computer models can never replace the human interaction and learning experience that a wargame setting normally delivers.

BUSINESS WARGAMING STARTED IN THE 1950S AND TOOK OFF IN THE LATE 1980S

In 1957, the American Management Association (AMA) was the first commercial entity to not only offer wargaming on a commercial basis, but also apply the tool in business (Schwarz, 2013). Twenty-nine years later, Ries and Trout attempted to popularize wargaming in business (Ries, 2006).

The adoption of wargaming as a tool in business proceeded slowly. In 2008, 77 European companies were questioned on wargaming (Schwarz, 2013). Only about 10% of this sample regularly used the tool, with another about 30% using it occasionally at best. Fifty years after the AMA pioneered business wargaming, the tool had not yet become a common instrument in strategy design and execution. The next section discusses why wargaming in business should get more management attention.

 5.3

WHY RUN A WARGAME?

A wargame is run to prepare a company for winning the business war it may wish to start or is being confronted with. The implicit thinking behind running a wargame is that in doing so, a company's team can enter so deeply into the minds of their competitor that it enables the team to predict their competitor's next moves with minimum uncertainty. A company, having properly played a wargame, taking the perspective of their competitor's competencies (assets and capabilities) and intent into account, minimizes the competitor's power to surprise when the real battle starts. Being able to predict a competitor's next moves with minimum uncertainty will not ensure victory. It may, however, at least allow one to minimize the damage done by this competitor move, or, even better, render the move useless. The latter is most elegant. A recurring series of competitor moves that in execution prove useless to them may contribute to achieving the ultimate objective in military as well as in business competition: to frustrate the competitor's willingness to fight against your interests.

WARGAMES SUPPORT ATTACK AND DEFENCE PLANS

Wargames may be used both in attack and defence planning, or in business parlance, proactively or reactively. *Table 5.1* summarizes the dynamics of both options.

	PROACTIVE	REACTIVE
COMPETITIVE SETTING AS INPUT TO WARGAME	A company's move that may or will trigger moves by competitors (be they suppliers, customers, competitors). Examples: – A company entering a Product Market Combination where an competitor has a leading position. – A company's bid in M&A.	Real or imagined competitor move that may or will affect a company's business. Examples (based on Sandman, 2003): – A competitor entering a product-market combination where a company leads. – A competitor bidding for an asset in an M&A process. – A competitor introducing a new technology or channel approach. – A new regulatory environment that will apply, affecting both competitors and a company.
DRIVER FOR WARGAME	– Stress test a company's draft plans by imagining the competitor's moves and their impact.	– Imagine details of the competitor's plans and subsequently use these to stress test a company's current plans.
TIMING FOR WARGAME	Timing matches a company's agenda.	Timing matches a company's agenda for anticipating imagined competitor moves or business environment changes. Timing is imposed by outside changes when these changes are to occur or have occurred.
OUTPUT OF WARGAME	– Defining and possibly choosing a company's course of action that maximizes success at minimum vulnerability to competitor actions. – Define and subsequently monitor early warning indicators to timely detect anticipated competitor moves.	– Define and implement own action plan. – Define and subsequently monitor early warning indicators to timely detect anticipated competitor moves.
FOCUS (UNDERWOOD, 1998)	Learning	Implementing

TABLE 5.1 ▶ ▶ ▶ PROACTIVE AND REACTIVE SETTING OF BUSINESS WARGAMES

Next to tangible business objectives like achieving the targets set in a launch plan of a new product, running a wargame may also have less tangible objectives, like participants' learning (Heilmann, 2013):

Tell me and I forget. Teach me and I remember. Involve me and I learn.

The next section covers what objectives to set for wargaming, showing the relative importance of less tangible objectives.

5.4

WHAT OBJECTIVES TO SET FOR WARGAMING?

Wargaming enables the achievement of team- and result-driven objectives simultaneously.

RESULT-DRIVEN OBJECTIVES FOCUS ON BUSINESS TARGETS

Put simply, a wargame is run to simulate the defence of an existing market position or the capturing of a new market position. In both cases, clear-cut business targets need to be defined in advance. The overall business target is, in military parlance, referred to as the 'Commander's Intent' (Zook, 2012):

A small number of simple statements that outline the purpose of a mission and the key principles that must be followed.

A Commander's Intent is provided to drive and coordinate all parallel activities executed toward a commonly desired outcome. The overall strategic aim is centrally determined. Through the Commander's Intent, the various functional departments involved in the execution are connected. In warfare, an Allied Second World War Commander's Intent could have been, 'Get the Nazis out of power in Germany'. The Commander's Intent summarizes the 'what' but does not specify the 'how'. A one-on-one translation of Commander's Intent to business strategy has its share of translation issues.[1] In wargaming, especially in wargames that focus on a single competitor, single product or single market combination battles, a Commander's Intent is a useful criterion to test any new business idea against.

In commercial battles, the 'how' in execution is limited by the need to comply with legally enforced constraints such as Competition Laws, just as in warfare the Geneva Conventions define parts of the laws of war. The constraints that define the limits to a wargame have to be kept in view at all times. These limits are captured as 'Rules of Engagement'.

As a principal, when considering running a wargame, it is imperative not only to set a clear and unambiguous Commander's Intent, but also to set clear Rules of Engagement. These rules include at minimum full compliance with any applicable (competition) law.

A business target for a wargame needs to be SMART: specific, measurable, actionable, realistic and time-linked. An example of a SMART target description for a wargame is:

> To define, by November 2016 at the latest, *our actions* to, where possible, neutralize competitor X's anticipated actions in response to our February 2017 launch of product Z in market Y, enabling us to reach our strategic objective of 10% value market share with product Z in market Y by January 2018.

TEAM-DRIVEN OBJECTIVES FOCUS ON CREATING CAPABILITIES TO WIN

Wargaming is not a solitary activity. To the contrary, the team dynamics are among the critical success factors in running a wargame. When a principal considers running a wargame, the following team-driven objectives may be helpful to consider as targets.

CREATE A STRONGER TEAM

A good wargame designer plans to create a stronger company team. The military equivalent is called 'unit cohesion'. Team strength may be built by the wargame contributing:

- To building a **shared confidence** in a company's strategy. It is hard to underestimate the relevance of morale in battle. A military maxim is that 'wars are usually not lost due to loss of men, but due to loss of hope'. This equally applies in business.
- To develop a **common team language** on the business environment and/or the competitor. In a high-intensity competitor review in a company's unit, the segmenting of the unit's competitors was as follows:
  - Flushers (dumpers in the market),
  - Surrogates (producers of inferior lookalikes) and
  - Rabbits (innovative players that were deemed too small to survive

stand-alone in the ongoing industry consolidation: they were expected to be served at some Christmas dinner in the next years).

Ten years later, these terms were still not only used to segment competitors, but also to define this unit's competitive moves opposing them. Such is the power of framing. A wargame may offer the platform to create such a vivid experience for a team.

- To develop a **common enemy** worthy of fighting against as a team. Colleagues in different departments may discover in a wargame setting that they are in the battle together – with aligned mutual interests.

- To build **stronger intra-company connections**. A wargame setting may resemble that of a holiday. This is especially true when the wargame takes place at a fancy venue and the rooms used are moderately decorated with military paraphernalia. Many people meet their future spouse in a holiday setting. A holiday setting apparently takes down people's natural defenses. Similarly, a wargame may allow colleagues to work with each other and connect to each other in a setting that is less formal than the regular office meeting rooms. Breaking down functional boundaries and building trust and personal links between staff members from different departments that participate together in a wargame may not be the leading objective, but the resulting network may add substantial future value. Especially the syndicate work (see below) is critical to network building both across functional disciplines within a business and across businesses in a holding.

- To build the **participants' library of patterns**, ready for recognition when a similar business challenge appears in another context. This makes a wargame resemble one of the objectives of case-based studying in business schools.

CREATE A PLATFORM FOR DATA-TO-INTELLIGENCE EXCHANGE AND SHARED INSIGHT BUILDING

A wargame is a setting for learning. Running a wargame may serve the following learning objectives, as it facilitates:

- Everybody in the participants' team has the **same understanding** of the business environment dynamics a company is facing. This is true both for the analysis (what is the matter?) as well as for the actions (what have we agreed to do now?). A wargame setting offers a platform, especially in the syndicate work sessions, to allow the various participants' to exchange tacit knowledge and, in doing so, discover commonly shared but also market insights held by only one or two participants. The market insights that had not been known to most of the group before and are unlocked during the wargame are the most important. Such insights generally have disproportional value in the later decision-making process because their being shared broadens the view of all other participants (Sunstein, 2015a). Given their value, it is critical to capture such tacit knowledge. To do so, assigning participants a scribe role during the syndicate work and during the plenary work is essential.

- **Busting some myths** about the competitor that may affect staff morale. A wargame should create a realistic competitor picture, emphasizing not only what they may be capable of doing, but also what they may not be capable of doing.

CREATE A PREPARED TEAM

The output of a wargame is either a stress-tested strategy or an action plan to counter a competitor's strategy. Both the execution of the proactive strategy and of the reactive action plan needs to be done by the team. The wargame facilitates:

- The whole team, not just the designer or the principal, to **understand**, **anticipate**, **test and train** for the upcoming battle (Lauder, 2009).
- To **prepare** the best thought-through and played-out options to minimize the damage or maximize the gains in the upcoming competitive endeavour. As the team has been instrumental in the preparation of the plan, buy-in will also be easier.
- To **discover** real-life sensitivities in potential outcomes. Doing so should direct further market intelligence work: what are the most critical elements or parameters in a company's and in its competitor's courses of actions? To stay in military parlance, to set the right RADAR frequencies (Kodalle, 2013).
- To **define and agree on a 'crisis planning script'** where applicable (Schwarz, 2013).

When creating a prepared team, the physical presence of the participating team members is critical. Once a Europe-based team running a half-day wargame had a single member based in Singapore. To save travel cost, it was decided to have the Singapore colleague dial in on the game. Their time was wasted. Having all participants attend in person is the only way to capture the atmosphere and the experience.

Running a wargame generally serves a mixture of the above-mentioned result and team-driven objectives. Literature provides a real-life example of business targets that were set in a wargame operated at Henkel (Keutmann, 2013):

- How probable is a further consolidation in the beauty care market?
- What consequences would such a consolidation have?
- How would our (i.e., Henkel's) competitors like to develop?
- What is the capability of our competitors to develop?
- Which strategies will our competitors choose?

No matter how useful a wargame may be to address some business challenges, it is not a universally suitable tool. The business objective to be achieved should be leading in choosing the appropriate tool. Once the choice to run a wargame has been made, the antecedent success factors given below may help maximize the chances of success.

CREATE STRONGER TEAM MEMBERS

A wargame not only may offer the opportunity to build and share insights, it may also be a venue to practice skills and allow team members to develop capabilities. A wargame set-up as we discuss later is often interactive, involving several moments to present syndicate work results in plenary (pitch with impact) and to practice critical and creative thinking. Even though a wargame is not a capability training per se, offering team members a platform to practice and demonstrate 21st century soft skills may have merit in itself.

 5.5

ANTECEDENT SUCCESS FACTORS

Nine antecedent success factors are mentioned below in the sequence when they matter most to the success of the wargame project. Each is important in its own right, even when in some settings, some factors may be more important than others. When, however, at least one of the success factors is not met, do seriously consider not proceeding with the wargame project. A failed wargame wastes a lot of precious time of many executives. It may also hurt the wargame principal's reputation.

First, a staff member needs to have an issue that is suitable to be resolved by wargaming. They need to:

(I) SELECT A GOOD, SUITABLE TOPIC

A suitable topic of a wargame has the following attributes. The topic is:

- **Close to reality** and not too far-fetched. Unlikely, low-credibility challenges will result in the sales staff present being distracted first – usually within a minute.
- Related to an industry with a **moderate level of uncertainty** (Horn, 2011). When the industry's uncertainty level is too high, planners cannot offer enough guidance to come to reasoned decisions. In such cases, scenario planning may be a better tool.
- Related to an industry with **meaningful competitive dynamics** (Horn, 2011). When the only objective is to understand whom the competitor really is, choose a competitor profiling session.

The topic that is gamed in the wargame should at all times justify the investment of time and money. This is to be determined by the wargame's principal.

(II)   ENSURE A GOOD COMMITMENT OF THE PRINCIPAL

Business wargames that are not driven by the principal usually fail. It is critical that the scope of the wargame links perfectly with the scope of the principal's responsibilities and authorities. A principal that expands the scope of a business wargame into territories they have no authority to drive change in may end up with a demoralized team. Frustration may result when a team's most preferred action cannot be executed because the principal cannot turn the lever. A marketing director of a business unit may be a great principal for a wargame. They may, in their management team, even get the informal support of their functional peers of sales, HR, finance and operations by the latter assigning their staff to participate in the wargame. When, however, the unit's managing director feels bypassed and therefore blocks the execution of critical actions defined in the wargame, a lose-lose situation has emerged for all involved. This is to be avoided.

A good principal should:

- **Contribute** their own team's resources and where applicable budget.
- **Persuade nay-sayers** to participate or buy-in to the use of this tool.
- Be **present**, at least during the wargame's kick-off and debrief session.
- **Deliver** the company's strategy in summary as input in the game.
- **Trust** the participants to think in the company's interest. Only when a principal gives this trust they will unlock the full creativity and imagination of their team.
- **Lead** the conversion of the wargame outcomes/ideas into tangible actions session.
- **Act upon the outcome** of the game, even when conclusions may not fully align with current views or choices.

Given the principal's commitment, the next step is to define the roles in a wargame.

(III)   DEFINE THE ROLES

There are at least seven roles in a wargame setting:

- The **project leader**, who manages all aspects of the wargame: the venue selection (including arranging projectors, flip charts, etc.), setting the date, inviting the participants, staying within budget, buying competitor products where applicable, arranging any special wishes the designer or facilitator may have regarding venue or agenda, ensuring the outputs are properly captured and later disseminated, etc.

- The **principal**, who selects the topic, the project leader, the facilitator and the designer, and who approves the budget.
- The **designer**, who designs the flow of the wargame, including possibly the templates used during syndicate work. The role of the designer and that of the facilitator may be the responsibility of a single person.
- The **facilitator**, who 'runs' the wargame itself, managing the flow, the agenda (including time management), stimulates discussions, etc.
- The **strategic analyst**, who contributes the market intelligence that pertains to the issue to be gamed, both in a pre-read to be distributed in advance and during a live presentation. The analyst must also be present during the wargame or be 'on stand-by' to answer market intelligence questions during the wargame.
- The **scribe(s)**, who per syndicate group and for the plenary session ensures all ideas that are expressed, are captured. The importance of this role is not to be underestimated. When vivid discussion develops during a wargame, a lot of tacit knowledge is shared. It is often this tacit knowledge that underpins ideas or actions that are being proposed. When the tacit knowledge is not captured, the ideas or actions will make less sense when the conclusions are worked out after the wargame – and the actions may, as a result, be less easy to defend to senior managers who did not attend the game.
- The **participant**.

For a successful wargame, it is critical for all participants to understand these roles. The roles and responsibilities of all involved should be communicated, e.g., by the project leader and preferably personally with all participants prior to the start of the game. Role confusion may negatively affect participants' energy level during the game, so role communication should be properly managed in advance.

Organizing a wargame should be a single project leader's responsibility. The project leader reports to the principal. The latter usually is a senior business leader. The project leader should be up to the job, especially when it comes to possible stakeholder management (e.g., politically sensitive matters like how to split the total group in syndicate groups and who to invite). For the project leader, the exposure to a senior business leader as principal may be attractive, as it gives them the opportunity to interact with the principal. This may, in day-to-day business, not be the case. The project leader should preferably be part of the business unit that faces the pro- or reactive challenge to be gamed. It is not recommended to have the market intelligence department, when the latter is for example part of a corporate staff entity, to own and organize the project. When a business that may be interested in running a wargame is not prepared to offer to run the project on their cost and with their human resources, double-check whether enough commitment is present in the business for this initiative. In the absence of the willingness to commit resources, the wargame should not be run. It may lead to new market intelligence and to unknown insights but, sadly, a lack of commitment will negatively affect the wargame outcomes. With a leader in place, the timing needs to be set right.

(IV) ENSURE GOOD TIMING

Timing is everything. In wargames, two timings matter. First, the timing of the wargame matters in relation to the issue being gamed. There is no point closing the door once the horse has bolted. A wargame is no post-mortem analysis. Holding a wargame too early in relation to the issue to be gamed also has its risks. When a competitor announces the building of a new factory, ready two years from now, a wargame may be a great instrument to identify what actions with a long lead time need to be identified. Two years in the corporate world is a long time. Managers may change jobs. Markets may have developed and technologies may have changed. Holding the same wargame a few months before the competitor factory really starts its production may deliver additional value. This is true both for the participants who were already around two years ago, but also those that joined the business after the wargame had been held.

The second piece of timing relates to the corporate agenda. A corporate planning cycle has its peak workload periods. Planning a wargame in September, when all line-businesses are fully engaged in preparing next year's budget, is not a good idea. The principal sets the date. Wargaming is a team sport. We thus need to have the right participants to be successful.

(V) ENSURE YOU HAVE A GOOD TEAM OF PARTICIPANTS

Participants make or break a business wargame. A key participant is the market intelligence analyst. The analyst preferably delivers the brief (see later). The analyst should know all the facts of the pre-read by heart (Gilad, 2006). As in any responsibility an analyst has, their objectivity and integrity should be known to all.

Participants in general should originate from as many functional business disciplines as needed. This is true both to have lively and all-encompassing plenary discussions, as well as to obtain good syndicate-work-group outputs. Planning the syndicate team assignments and the composition of the syndicate groups must be done in advance. The group composition is preferably chosen by the principal. Unless there are very good reasons to do it differently, the syndicate group compositions should be non-negotiable to the participants. Ideally the composition has been chosen to have as diverse a view as possible in these work groups. Preferably a participant group has a mix of job levels to ensure different responsibility perspectives, e.g., ranging from a junior brand manager to a marketing director.

Syndicate groups typically consist of 3–7 staff, with the overall group of wargame participants consisting of 9–21 staff. Syndicate groups are recommended to appoint a scribe, a chairperson, a timekeeper and a reporter, depending a bit on the culture of the organization. Preferably the whole team, as well as the syndicate groups, should consist of thinkers, doers and leaders. Good experience has been obtained by inviting knowledgeable staff from suppliers (e.g., advertising agencies) or customers (e.g., exclusive distributors). Especially the latter may contribute fresh and highly original insights and viewpoints to a wargame. Moreover, as the distributors are part of the deliberations of what to do next, their buy-in to the execution of the commonly agreed actions in the wargame usually also is guaranteed.

A good facilitator is critical to successful wargaming. Attributes of a good facilitator include:

- Knowledge of and **experience** with wargame processes.
- At least **basic knowledge** of the issue that is gamed, such that their interventions will not only be made on process, but possibly also on content matters.
- **Respected character** that naturally brings opinionated people to shared conclusions.
- **Objectivity** toward all players and regarding the issue at stake.
- Having **no vested interest** in the outcome of the wargame (e.g., getting budget for an activity they are responsible for).
- **Innovation**, recognizing creative ideas when they emerge and facilitating these ideas to be built upon and nurtured toward the final action planning.
- **Action-orientation**, ensuring high-quality outputs are created during syndicate work groups and a clear action list is delivered as final output, linked to the wargame objectives.

(VI) ENSURE THE WARGAME HAS A GOOD FOCUS

A wargame should have a focused, clear scope. In advance it should be clear what is out-of-scope. Generally, the more focused a wargame, the better the output will be. Both the issue at stake and the objectives set for the wargame should also be defined in advance. It is recommended to game only a limited number of discrete options, like a team playing "we increase price" and another team playing in a parallel group "we maintain prices as is". The more clear the discrete options, the more applicable and enlightening the outcome.

(VII) ENSURE YOU HAVE A GOOD STRUCTURE

It is imperative for the facilitator, in cooperation with the principal of a wargame, to ensure the structure of the wargame is well understood by all participants at the start. In general, a more simple structure leads to better output. Wargames are mainly played in syndicate groups, as we will see below. Ensure the assignments given for the syndicate work are easy to understand, unambiguous and do not lend themselves to corporate hobbyhorse riding or confusion. The structure of the wargame leads to an agenda and thus to a duration of a wargame. The duration of a wargame is generally a single day, but it can stretch to a maximum of two days. The duration should match the width of the scope of the game. A broader topic may require gaming in several dimensions.

It is essential that the width of the scope and the duration of the game are such that a high 'strategic intensity' is achieved and maintained. Distracted participants who start to talk about other matters or simply start to cater to their emails are to be avoided.

The templates format of the output for the syndicate work and the final session should be designed in such a way that an easy transfer is possible to the real-life business action planning cycle, into which the wargame outputs should be integrated.

(VIII) ENSURE A GOOD ORGANIZATIONAL CULTURE

Culture is not a factor that is easily influenced. When, however, some of the cultural factors mentioned below are not in place in an organization, chances diminish that a successful wargame exercise can be run. A wargame benefits from a culture where all participants understand that:
- There are **no enemies** within the room. Different participants may have different business objectives. This is especially true in larger organizations that operate in matrices. The matrix staff and the operational line

may at times have conflicting agendas. Even so, a wargame is not focusing on what keeps colleagues apart in different parts of the organization, but what unites them in outperforming a common competitor. The latter shared belief among all participants is essential to run a successful wargame. It is up to the principal – possibly delegated to the project leader or the facilitator – that at all times prior and during the wargame all participants share and work for the same overall objective.

- **Everybody's opinion** counts. A successful wargame depends on the contributions of all participants. When in advance the opinions of some participants are not rated high, these participants should not be invited. This means that all participants should care about all other participants' opinions. The facilitator is to elicit and include everybody's opinions, especially during the syndicate work. A wargame is a setting where established views must be questioned. Some of a company's choices may in advance be 'off limits' for discussion in a wargame setting. The principal or the facilitator needs to ensure no time is wasted on discussing them.

- **Strategic intensity** is imperative. Strategic intensity is achieved when the sharp brains of the participants all simultaneously and vividly discuss ideas for and options of the competitor and later of their own company. This intensity is not achieved when participants are allowed to be distracted by email, social media, phones, etc.

- **Internal competition** between teams within a wargame does not create a positive learning environment (Lauder, 2009). The word 'game' may stimulate participants to think of winning a competition. There is a battle to be won, for sure. But the battle is not *between* teams *within* the wargame, but between a company and its competitor that is being gamed against. A competition element may be useful in, for example, a sales training context; it is less commendable in a wargame setting.

- **Compliance** is imperative. The language used during a wargame may cross the line of what within companies should be said about other companies. Competition legislation in many countries is strict and is strictly enforced. Any utterings, especially in writing but also jokingly in formal sessions, that suggest what may be understood as anticompetitive behaviour ('we kill the bastards') is absolutely off-limits. Compliance also requires ensuring that no actions are being proposed or taken that may not comply with competition law like, for example refusing to sell to an existing distributor that is considering selling a competitor's product (Sabin, 2013). It may have a merit to have the action-list output of a wargame checked by a competition lawyer, prior to taking the actions into formal execution. Lawyers may have a reputation to tend to err on the safe side, but the alternative is less attractive. Personally, as executive spending time in jail for violations of competition law is no fun, not even when during the wargame the executive had had a jolly good time killing the competition for now and for good.

- **An overly military style** should not be embraced. The number of participants in business that easily identifies with the military profession may be limited. Moreover, some participants may reject violence all together, making them reluctant to participate in an overly bravado-filled atmosphere. In such a case, rather than benefitting from the learnings of serious military methodologies, a prejudice-based kill-kill-kill atmosphere based on recollections of violent war movies may emerge. This negatively affects the seriousness that running a wargame requires. Participants constantly throwing plastic hand grenades at each other do not contribute to a wargame's success.

- **Ethnocentric biases** affect the judgments of even the best trained staff. The wargame module in which the competitor is being played by definition needs to be xenocentric. Being xenocentric is easier said than done. A good company culture is one in which principal, facilitator and other participants recognize that the other company really is different in some dimensions (Underwood, 1998).

  The worst principal is the one who, in advance, arrogantly postulates they really understand the competitor (except maybe when they worked there for the last two decades), so they already know what they will do anyway. Firstly, this demotivates the participants; secondly, their views may well be flawed.

  Anticipating all the competitor's thoughts may be a stretch, but it needs to be attempted. When time permits in a wargame agenda, the facilitator may need to build in an exercise to ensure all participants understand the risk that an ethnocentric bias may flaw your view of the competitor. Such flawed views may lead us to predict different actions for the competitor than the competitor will take in real life. This obviously forms a bad start for a business stress test.

- **Confidentiality** needs to be respected. Strategy is and should be secretive. As wargames are often run in venues outside the formal office setting, all participants should be made extra aware that confidentiality is another wargame imperative. As the facilitator, ensure that:

- Participants do not use social media to reveal what they are doing. A negative social media post against a competitor does not do a company's reputation any good and may even be perceived as violating competition law.

- Neither in-house nor outside venues are to communicate the purpose of the meeting on sign screens: 'Our company's wargame *Operation Frustrate the Frogs,* Ballroom 3.' Apart from the fact that the title is, from competition law perspective, already questionable, matters really go awry when this message catches the wrong eyes. It may be on social media and beyond your control before the actual wargame has even started. Moreover, it strongly hurts a company's reputation for competition law compliance and even more importantly for decent ethics.

- When hiring outside venues, the neighbouring meeting rooms should either be empty or be hired by non-competing parties. Nothing is so embarrassing as finding the competitor that is being gamed against actually being in the room next door. This may sound like too much of a coincidence but, especially in emerging markets, the number of suitable venues (often five-star hotels) is limited. Speaking from bad experience, running into competitors is more likely than you may think.

- The meeting room door is always closed prior to starting the discussions, either in the plenary room or in the syndicate rooms. Preferably the snack and coffee and tea buffet is placed within the plenary room and not in the corridor. When convenience butts heads with confidentiality, convenience wins, hands down, every time. Loose lips sink ships!

- The discussion materials (flip charts, competitor product samples, posters, etc.) are not left behind when the wargame has finished.

- The competitor stimuli materials are taken in at the end of the wargame and do not diffuse with the team of participants through the organization after the wargame. In some wargame settings, caps or shirts with competitor logos are used to stimulate the xenocentric thinking in the 'competitor round' of the game. Such stimuli may have a value to create the right atmosphere, although that value should not be exaggerated. A simple sticker with a competitor logo for the participants to put on their shirt is often more than enough. It is also cost-effective.

- When, however, shirts or caps are being made, the project leader and/or the facilitator should ensure that all shirts or caps are returned before the end of the wargame.
- The participants should not communicate their participation in a wargame, the objective of the wargame, etc. to other company staff who are not involved. The pre-read should stress the need for confidentiality.

(IX) ENSURE GOOD PREPARATION

A wargame needs to be prepared well. The principal decides on the budget and the budget partly determines what preparations for the wargame will exactly be taken and at what level of detail. For most wargames, the project leader needs to consider taking at least the following preparations:

- Send out a 'warning order'. A warning order is military parlance for an invitation of the selected participants. The privileged staff who are invited are informed of the venue, the timing, the objective, the need for confidentiality, etc. The warning order should preferably be sent out some six weeks ahead of the wargame taking place, to ensure most participants either are available or have enough time to make themselves available.
- Send out a pre-read. A good pre-read is a real timesaver in a wargame setting. Moreover, there is strong evidence that sending out a pre-read (provided it is being read by the participants) contributes to the quality of the decisions made in the wargame. I will now first discuss the time-saver and content part of the pre-read and will later get back to the role a pre-read may play in improving a group's decision-making.

Time saver:
Getting a large group of senior company staff simultaneously together is not only a logistical and agenda challenge but also involves serious cash and possibly opportunity costs. You save valuable executive time by limiting the wargame duration to the minimum, restricting the agenda to what has to be done together. The time the participants are together should be used as effectively as possible. Any matter pertaining to the wargame that does not need to be shared in plenary in the group, should be shared in advance in the pre-read. To allow participants to prepare properly, a pre-read needs to be sent at least one week in advance. Having the pre-read sent out by the principal of the wargame accompanied by a personal letter is a common way to motivate participants to prepare for the upcoming wargame.

Content:

The timely issuing of the pre-read is the responsibility of the project leader, but the responsibility for the content of the pre-read preferably is with the analyst. The pre-read should be as complete as possible. It is a waste of time when, for example during syndicate work, facts lack and time is lost on collecting them. Even worse, facts that are quickly collected may subsequently become a topic of discussion within the wargame. When facts do not match what is expected, or worse what is politically needed by some participants, the source of the new facts may be disputed or the definition may be different than what is needed, etc. There are better ways to derail a wargame, but not too many. As shown below, data that appears late in the process has a less than proportional impact to their relevance.

Well-prepared pre-reads are critical to a wargame's success. The target audience experience, knowledge and capabilities should be central in the choice for *how* to report. A pre-read with exotic jargon that is, for example, only known to and understood by the R&D community, is not conducive to the pre-read being read by all the participants.

The balancing act in preparing a wargame pre-read is to avoid overloading the participants with too much 'hard to absorb' information, making them skip reading altogether, and being too brief, thus missing *critical* data. What works well is to provide a 'reading guide'. The reading guide informs the participants that some 20 slides make up the must-read summary fact book. In addition, five appendices are provided with selected deep-dives on mentioned topics. The choice of what to cover in these appendices depends on the topic chosen. In wargames, include at least the following topics (Hoyer, 2013):

- Key competitor facts
- Key channel dynamics in a market and related competitor positions
- Key competitor product-market combinations (including where needed recipe and/or product cost analysis, marketing mix, brand positioning, etc.)
- Key consumer data (usage and attitudes regarding the category, trends, etc.)
- Relevant demographic, socioeconomic, political, regulatory and technology data

Decision-making:

Fascinating psychological research shows that under circumstances quite similar to that during wargame preparation and execution (Sunstein, 2015b):

- Groups base their decisions on data that *all* group members had *prior* to the wargame.
- Relevant data that had not been shared before the wargame and that only a few members have will probably *not surface* in plenary discussions. Data the individual holds, after all, is only shared voluntarily. There is no punishment for not sharing them with other participants. After all, nobody else knows you as a participant have the data. By implication, nobody can ever blame you for failing to share relevant data. So if sharing (new) data is perceived by a participant to involve a personal risk (i.e., is seen as less than conducive to that individual's career prospects) sharing likely will not happen.
- Even when relevant data surfaces during plenary discussions, these data will *not have an impact* on decisions made *proportional* to their relevance.

To an analyst or project leader preparing a wargame, these insights may be turned into actions in the following way:
- Ensure a good pre-read is being prepared and sent out timely.
- Ensure the pre-read captures the data that all participants should know prior to the wargame, to ensure wargame decisions are based on all data.
- Consider, when time permits, to collect data only single participants may have as tacit knowledge and compile it into the pre-read. In doing this you avoid relevant data not surfacing or, if it surfaces only during the wargame's plenary session, not being used.

- **Order physical stimuli** related to the competitor. When the principal is comfortable with or encourages the use of physical stimuli (polo shirts, caps, pens, stickers, paper with competitor logos, etc.) these need to be ordered timely. Separately, a range of competitor products that are relevant to the gamed topic need to be present at the game. There is no limit to creativity. For a good effect, cheap stickers to be worn during the competitor round in a wargame may be sufficient. A project leader is well advised – when the budget permits – to involve a creative (advertising) agency to truly build an competitor atmosphere for some time, assisting the xenocentric thinking process and also the quality of the wargame output. Do not take this over the top. It may only add to already existing negative perceptions by some on wargames, like wargames being an excuse of adults refusing to grow up to play with adolescent toys at other people's cost (Sabin, 2013).

- **Manage various stakeholders**. The principal and/or the project leader need to talk to several of the invited participants, especially those higher up in the organization, to ensure their buy-in of and input to the wargame. This is time-consuming, but it is time well spent (Horn, 2011). When those senior executives who are involved understand well in advance what this wargame can and cannot do for their future business success, the corporate immune system – which can never be fully neutralized – may at least be less active during the execution of the actions resulting from the wargame. People love to change *themselves*, but most resist being changed *by others*.

- **Book a suitable venue**. The venue for a wargame is preferably outside the office to avoid participants being tempted to multi-task in their office environment, at the cost of achieving the required strategic intensity in the wargame. The venue preferably has a main or plenary room and adjacent breakout rooms for the syndicate work. Participants who are not based in the city where the wargame is held preferably stay in the hotel where the wargame is being held to avoid time lost due to commuting problems, etc. In the plenary room, and in all breakout rooms, flip charts and a projector with a screen must be present. The rooms should be large enough. Ideally the plenary room has (some) daylight. The venue should have good cooks. Good (really good) food and snacks and a continuous flow of coffee, tea and refreshments do contribute to the quality of a wargame's output.

  A buffet lunch is recommended – if only to spend the expensive time together on the topic of the wargame and not on lunch networking.

- **Define good templates** for the various activities during the wargame. Most of a wargame's time is used in syndicate teamwork. Templates to be used in syndicate work should be tailored to match the objectives set for the wargame. All companies have their own jargon. The templates should be based on the company's jargon in order to minimize the risk of confusion or lack of clarity on what the assignment, during the syndicate work, is about. A syndicate assignment may be, for example, to define the actions of a competitor over the next three years (for a product group or category in a given geo-market) in sales and distribution. In such case, it is helpful to indicate that the competitor strives to increase distribution from their current estimated base of 5,000 stores to 15,000 stores and how the competitor will do this. Generally, however, detailed figures and modelling are counterproductive. Asking too many details in a template tends to take a group too much time, distracting the participants in the syndicate group from giving a complete picture at headline level, rather than details on one topic only. Any template should at least list the 'what' and the 'how' of:

- The overall syndicate work objective
- The relevant sub-objectives (in time, by channel, by product
- line/category, etc.)
- The relevant anticipated competitor (or your own company's) actions per objective (where needed, including substantiations or links to consumer trends, etc.)
- The relevant resource and capability needs to execute the actions listed and, where applicable, gaps with the current situation.

If anything, the templates used should ensure that the output of the wargame is 'ready to use' as input in management decision-making.

- **Purchase and distribute pen and paper** for use during the wargame. Every participant at the start of the wargame in a small ceremony receives a special pen (not expensive, but distinctive) and a small notebook. Preferably the notebook has a sticker with the title of the wargame, e.g., Operation Clausewitz and a dotted line to fill in the participant's name. The participant will be asked to make extensive notes, both during the briefing and during the syndicate and plenary sessions. In providing pen and paper, the facilitator may, where needed, ask participants to read aloud what they have written, if only to ensure all participants remain focused on gathering and remembering insights gained together.

The nine antecedent success factors discussed above show how much of the success of running a wargame depends on preparation and communication. With all preparatory steps having been discussed, the next section covers the flow of a common form of wargaming.

5.6 THE FLOW OF A COMMON WARGAME

A wargame is tailor-made. The flow of a wargame is determined by the objectives set for the game (see the intermezzo at the end of this chapter for a real-life wargame example). In wargame design, structure or flow follows strategy. Even when the duration of a wargame may vary from less than a day to two days or even more, most objectives can be met with a more or less common flow. *Diagram 5.1A* depicts this common flow of what may be termed a three-round wargame. The upper diagram depicts the introduction phase and the first round of the game. This is the part where a team plays the competitor. In a one-day wargame, the steps shown in the upper diagram take about four hours. It is advisable, when playing a one-day game, to play this first round in an afternoon, break for the evening (or even better have a participants' team dinner) and the next morning play the rounds two and three (shown in the lower diagram). Doing so allows the facilitator, where needed, to do some stakeholder management. In addition, it allows the facilitator in the evening to prepare a comprehensive summary of the work of the first round, to be shared the next morning. If necessary, the market intelligence analyst can collect data in the evening that proved to be missing. In *Diagram 5.1B* it is assumed that the segmentation of the syndicate groups is by functional discipline (here: sales, marketing and supply chain). The segmentation of the groups should be determined by the objective of the wargame. It may also be one group playing the competitor's B2B and the other the B2C activities, or one group playing Europe/Africa, one group Asia/Pacific and one group the Americas within the competitor portfolio.

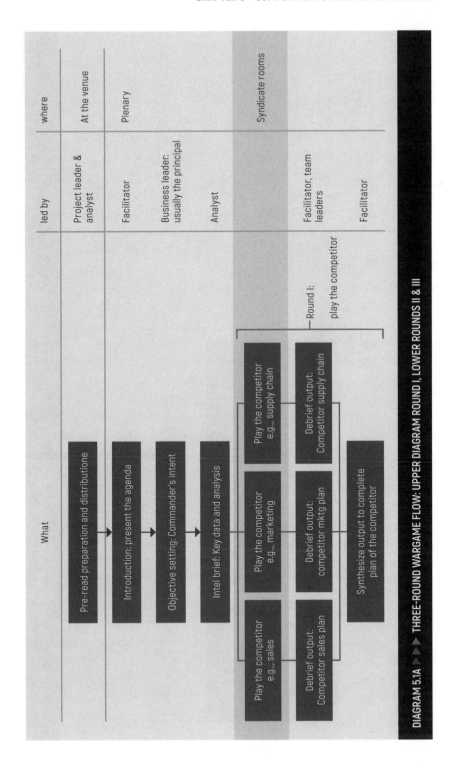

DIAGRAM 5.1A ▶ ▶▶ ▶ **THREE-ROUND WARGAME FLOW: UPPER DIAGRAM ROUND I, LOWER ROUNDS II & III**

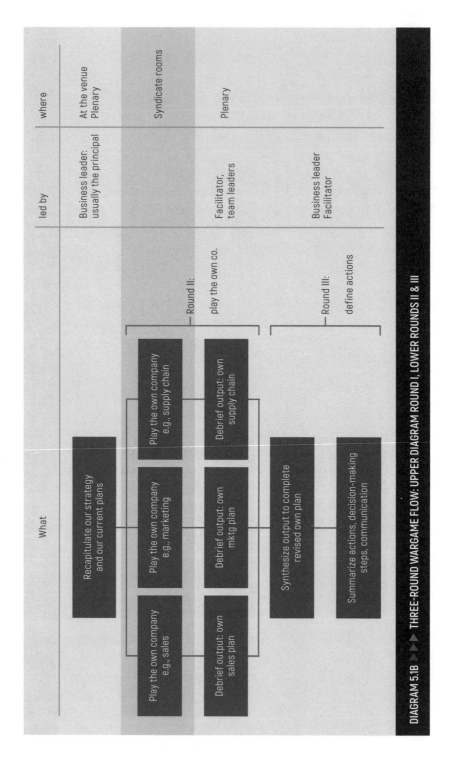

What			led by	where
Recapitulate our strategy and our current plans			Business leader: usually the principal	At the venue Plenary
Round II: play the own co. — Play the own company e.g., sales / Play the own company e.g., marketing / Play the own company e.g., supply chain			Facilitator, team leaders	Syndicate rooms
Debrief output: own sales plan / Debrief output: own mktg plan / Debrief output: own supply chain				
Round III: define actions — Synthesize output to complete revised own plan			Business leader Facilitator	Plenary
Summarize actions, decision-making steps, communication				

DIAGRAM 5.1B ▸ ▸ ▸ THREE-ROUND WARGAME FLOW: UPPER DIAGRAM ROUND I, LOWER ROUNDS II & III

There are multiple instruments to enrich a wargame. Below a few are mentioned.

- **Play the competitor's CEO**. After the intelligence brief and prior to the start of Round I, the facilitator may give an oral five-minute pep talk briefing, pretending to be the representative of the competitor's CEO. This brief highlights and summarizes for extra effect, preferably in no uncertain terms, what the CEO expects the local team to achieve. Using this instrument enables participants to feel the pressure the competitor team faces. This instrument is particularly useful when a reactive wargame is played, where the initiative for the market disruption lies with the competitor. For this instrument to be effective, the facilitator or the analyst must have studied the competitor in great detail and must be sure the brief is balanced and matches what a real brief in the competitor would look like, given the publicly stated competitor priorities.

- **Appoint a competitor board member in each syndicate team**. This instrument resembles the previous instrument. In this case, the project leader or the principal appoints an individual participant for each syndicate team in advance who will play the competitor's board member during the game. This participant will get the assignment to make an in-depth study on the competitor, assisted by the strategic analyst. During Round I of the wargame, the participant has to ensure that the defined competitor plans are sufficiently xenocentric. This instrument works particularly well when each syndicate group plays a different competitor, rather than all playing different geo-zones, product mixes or functional disciplines of the same competitor.

- **Visualize the competitor's intent**. This is an instrument that may also assist in a team of participants to develop the right xenocentric view (and a bit of gaming spirit as well). Prior to the step in Round I to develop the competitor's plans, the participants are requested to make a collage of the competitor. This collage – based on clipping pictures from magazines or from downloading and printing net-based materials – should depict the competitor's intent. In the debriefing, the team should present both the collage and their competitor plan. As making a collage takes some time, using this instrument requires a wargame duration to be a of minimum 1.5 days.

- **Wear competitor logo stickers**. At the start of Round I of the wargame, the facilitator may distribute competitor logo stickers (or baseball caps with the logo, or polo-shirts, etc.). Sticking to the stickers, the facilitator may inform the participants to wear the sticker at their shirts as long as playing Round I. It is the facilitator who informs them when the stickers may be removed and thrown away. From that moment onward, the facilitator may correct participants when they talk about 'they' that they must be talking about their own company because, being the competitor, as long as the participants are wearing the stickers, means the participants refer to themselves being the competitor as 'we'. Enforcing the use of 'we' for the competitor and 'they' for their own company assists in thinking xenocentrically. At the end of Round I, the facilitator may in plenary ask attention for the magical moment of pulling off the stickers, with all participants in one strong pull returning back to their current employer. The emotional charge of all participants simultaneously pulling off and crushing the stickers assists in the team-building element.

- **Use mathematical decision-models**. Companies may have developed econometric market models that provide, for example, market share outputs when certain inputs are fed. When such models exist and the results are trusted by the wargame participants, the principal may consider using such models to evaluate different proposed actions against each other. As long as the models are used as a tool within a tool and do not become an aim in itself, using such models may be considered.

- **Stimulate creativity through competition**. The principal may in advance present a symbolic award that the most creative syndicate team in Round II will win for 'the most original idea or action proposal'. After the Round II syndicate team debriefs, the principal may hand over the award to the winning team. This instrument is preferably not used in a proactive wargame, as the competition element may affect the learning atmosphere. In a reactive wargame, winning the award for the idea that best defends your company's market shares from some competitor initiative is better suited.

- **Define 'friendly forces'**. Both in Round I and in Round II of the wargame, the template format may contain the assignment to the syndicate group to define friendly forces. Friendly forces in military terms are allies. In business, as in the military, 'the enemy of my enemy may be my friend'. When the planned move of a competitor not only threatens your company's market share but also that of your distributor, that distributor is a natural ally. When the competitor is, for example, a surrogate producer (e.g., vegetable fat vs butter), other dairy companies may also be affected by the planned competitor's move. As long as compliance with applicable competition law is ensured, such companies may be approached to 'fight with us'. A 'friendly forces analysis' is thus suitable in both rounds of the wargame to ensure that no battle dimension is overlooked.

- **Create 'fog of war'.** Fog of war in the military is formed when at the battlefield so many explosions cause dust and smoke to disperse in the air that neither the competitor nor our command knows exactly what is going on. Apart from poor visibility, conflicting situation reports may also come in from various sources, adding to the confusion at the command centre. Business may experience the equivalent of fog of war. Rumours in the market on competitor initiatives may prove to be incorrect. Deals that competitors conclude with trade partners may be misunderstood. In short, confusion may hinder adequate situation analysis and thus decision-making. A wargame may simulate this real-life confusion experience in business. One way to do this is for the facilitator during Round I (e.g., after one-third of the playing time and again after two-third of the time) is to provide 'press releases' or 'rumours' about the competitor or the market situation that need to be taken into account. The use of this instrument should remain focused on delivering a better output of the syndicate group work. It may not result in attention distraction or syndicate team frustration. The facilitator may prepare fog of war instruments in advance but may need to watch the output and performance of the syndicate teams, prior to deciding whether or not to use this instrument.

EX-POST SUCCESS FACTORS

Running a wargame is an instrument to achieve a business objective. When the fog of war at the end of a wargame session clears and all participants leave the venue to go back to their day-to-day responsibilities, a successful achievement of the business objective is not yet assured, no matter how well the wargame was run. To contribute to further increasing the chances that a wargame results in business success, the following factors must be taken into account by the facilitator and the principal:

- **The wargame output report should be unambiguous**. In military parlance, the output report is referred to as an 'After Action Report' or 'After Action Review' (AAR). The report should contain the key outputs of the syndicate work in Round I and Round II (this is where the well-structured templates come in). In addition, the report should give a clear action list and participants' recommendations to the business leadership. Compiling an AAR is preferably the role of the wargame project leader, provided the latter is part of the business that is to take action. US General Patton once stated (Axelrod, 1999):

  Plans are made by those with the responsibility and authority to execute them.

  It is the role of the facilitator to ensure the outputs during the wargame meet the predefined standards. It is the role of the business to compile and act upon them.

- **The wargame should be integrated in business strategy and planning**. The output of the wargame needs to be integrated in the existing business strategy and planning cycle rhythm. Businesses tend to have budgets, specifying both top-line and bottom-line targets. By implication, the expenditures that are incurred in between top and bottom line also have their limits. These limits have usually either been agreed upon between the management and the owners of the company or between the unit's management and its hierarchical superiors, e.g., in head office. Running a wargame does not tend to change these limits automatically. For a unit's management, integrating the output of the wargame in the existing business may thus be a 'zero-sum game'. What is spent in money or in human resources on intensifying a particular course of action may need to be withdrawn from another, already existing course of action. Advertising may, for example, need to be cut to pay for a drive to expand weighted distribution. It is the sole responsibility of the unit's management to find the new balance between supporting existing initiatives and supporting ideas born in the wargame. It is recommended for a unit's management to put working out this new balance on the agenda of the unit's first management team meeting after the wargame (or the first meeting after the AAR has become available).

Once priorities have been redefined and agreed upon within the management team, the next important step is to communicate the actions made based on the wargame and how these actions may affect staff priorities.

- **Communicate, communicate, communicate.** The management team preferably tasks the wargame project leader with sharing the following with all participants after the wargame:
  - The AAR
  - The action list agreed by management and integrated in the business planning
  - The initiatives to monitor the progress on these actions (plan-do-check-act) related to these actions

The participant team will be motivated to see the output of the wargame being used to build a better business. Whenever the wargame tool may be used again, the next time getting participants to free up their agenda may be a lot easier when not only the wargame experience had been valuable to them. It is also helpful when participants see management taking the output highly serious, leading to business success.

5.8 COMMON PROBLEMS IN SETTING UP AND RUNNING A WARGAME

A wargame is a powerful tool and yet it doesn't always deliver a good output. Below some problems are listed that the project leader should watch out for and should preferably prevent from hindering the quality of the wargame or of the post-wargame execution.

- **Poor representation of reality**. An incomplete picture of reality may emerge from simply not knowing or sufficiently understanding a competitor or a market. This may be due to lacking specialists who understand the market or the competitor being played against. The future at large may also be simply too uncertain to usefully apply the wargame tool. In the former case, a better preparation leading to a better pre-read file is the way to mitigate this risk. In the latter case, the question is whether a wargame is the right instrument to use. In highly uncertain environments, tools like scenario planning may work better.

    A special case of a poor representation of reality is that during Round I of the wargame, inadvertently, the ethnocentric bias manifests itself. US Second World War Admiral Chester W. Nimitz, who was among the leaders of the Allied navies in the Pacific Theatre, after the war reflected on the value of wargaming:

    "The war with Japan had been re-enacted in the game rooms at the War College by so many people, and in so many different ways, that nothing that happened to us during the war was a surprise – absolutely nothing, except the Kamikaze tactics toward the end of the war – we had not visualized these."

In other words, as long as the Imperial Japanese Navy behaved according to standard US naval operating procedures, surprises could be prevented. This quote again illustrates the heavy responsibility of the intelligence department and especially the analyst being present during a wargame to stress to think xenocentrical. It is great to succeed taking market share from a competitor, but when you succeed, what will they do? When pushed between a rock and a hard place, the Japanese invented kamikaze actions. What dramatic actions may a competitor take when feeling under severe pressure? Nobel Prize laureate Schelling summarized it well (Büchler, 2013):

The one thing you cannot do, no matter how rigorous your analysis or heroic your imagination, is to make a list of things you never thought of.

Xenocentric thinking aims retrospectively to make that list as short and harmless to business as possible.

- **Politicized (hidden) objectives**. Unit managers or functional discipline managers (e.g., a marketing director) may drive for running a wargame not to test their initiatives objectively, but to get buy-in for a choice they have already made in their mind. The wargame is planned to confirm rather than to challenge plans. The airline Swissair, for example, held a wargame in 1999. The outcome was ignored, as the CEO had already made his choices. Two years later, the airline, having executed choices that tested poorly in the wargame, filed for bankruptcy (Schwarz, 2013).

  A wargame will not by its nature change established opinions of the various participants. More often than not, a few different courses of actions to handle an issue are already on the table prior to the start of the wargame. These courses of action tend to have a leading spokesperson – and as all leaders, these leaders may be defined by having some followers. Thus, prior to a wargame, participants may already be split into different factions, one favouring course of action I, another group lobbied into favouring course of action II and a third being yet undecided. The courses of actions I and II may not overlap or, even worse, may differ significantly. This is why the key role of the facilitator is to run the wargame strictly as per the templates for the syndicate groups (Gilad, 2006). A lack of formal structure or a loosening of the reigns may lead to an unproductive 'shouting match' between participants in the plenary of whether or not to favor course of action I or II.

Rather, a well-run wargame should enable the participants to together discover and agree to the smartest course of action, which may well prove to be different from both the courses of actions I and II.

- **Poor timing**. There is a risk of running a wargame too long in advance of the expected event to be gamed (Strother, 2006). In such a case, there is usually a limited need for immediate actions. This takes the sense of urgency out of the wargame. Urgency normally is a driver for good ideas. Even worse, both participants and the principal(s) may change jobs before the event happens, leading to a loss of tacit insights built up during the wargame experience.

-

- **Mismatch between authority and wargame scope**. It has been emphasized above that the principal and the facilitator should well align the business scope within which the wargame should and should not be run. A mismatch, with the scope of the wargame extending outside the authority of the principal, may lead to action proposals that never lead to implementation and thus to future participant frustration.

5.9 CONCLUSION

A wargame is a useful tool in business, provided it is well prepared. The above manual offers a checklist to facilitate the preparation and running of a wargame in business and for ensuring after wargame action. When a wargame is properly prepared, it has proven in many businesses to be a great tool to unleash the creativity and imagination of a company's staff to define and substantiate strategic decisions, based on truly thinking through future competitor moves.

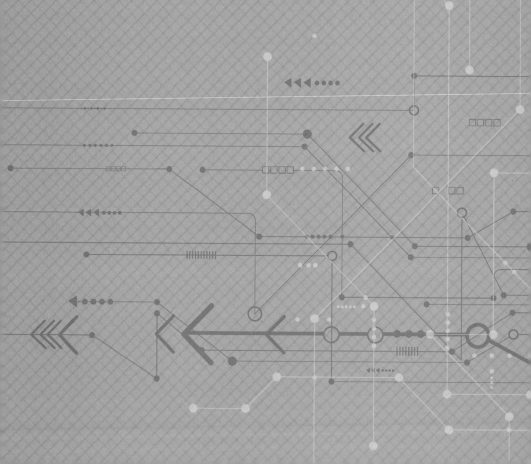

CHAPTER 6
MARKET ENVIRONMENT ANALYSIS

>>> 6.1 INTRODUCTION

Any company operates in a market environment – and that environment changes ever more rapidly. To understand and, where possible, pre-empt such change, this chapter discusses four commonly applicable tools in strategic analysis. In the following section, we discuss how to map a country that may be the target for new business development initiatives. We then briefly cover what questions to ask when aiming to understand the changes in technology a company may be facing.

Many companies face volatile markets. We discuss the phenomenon of volatility and how to map it. Finally, we look at the market environment at large and review a method to discover and act upon societal, consumer or other trends that may change a company's playing field or fields.

6.2   COUNTRY PROFILE

A country profile is defined here as a document offering a description of a country as a political/national entity. Such profiles are meant to provide context to management on the country in which they may contemplate doing or actually do business. Country profiles usually cover dimensions such as (list not exhaustive):
- Economy (growth, gross domestic product, main sectors, import/export, etc.)
- Population (growth, ethnic groups, age distribution, etc.)
- Climate (rainfall, temperature, etc.)
- Infrastructure (roads, airport, harbors, etc.)
- Healthcare
- Political/governmental systems and stability
- Competitor assets (factories, market positions, brands, etc.)

Country profiles, no matter how rich the data sources available, should only provide need-to-know data for decision-making. When looking for facts, the CIA's *World Fact Book* (www.cia.gov) is a great start.

Country profiles may support strategy design (market entry), strategy execution (e.g., identifying and funneling M&A candidates) and even strategy monitoring processes. In the latter case, a country profile may be, for example, an input to a corporate business risk assessment. In support of strategy execution, e.g., to underpin and provide context to an acquisition proposal, country profiles may need inputs from other tools such as (but not limited to) country market sizing analysis, competitor profiles and profit pool analysis.

A report on, for example, the structure and dynamics of a country's retail market requires both an in-depth description of retail outlets and chains, but also has to cover a regulatory review of retail shop opening permit policies. Similarly, such analysis may justify looking at the country 'city by city', when as in many emerging markets, the vast majority of the economy and thus the market for many products is concentrated in the top 10 cities. In such countries as, for example, Russia, the cities are islands of economic activity in a sea of land that is economically irrelevant (perhaps except as source for agricultural or mineral products-based value creation).

Entering such an emerging market with consumer products usually only requires securing distribution and brand awareness in the top cities. A country profile may in such case end up being a collection of city profiles.

Preparing a country profile is a typical desk research activity of a market intelligence or strategy department, provided there is a solid brief and a decision maker committed to act upon the key data in the country profile.

Decision-makers may request their analysts to prepare numerous profiles in one assignment, for example, as preparation for writing a new geo-mix strategy (e.g., for all African countries). In such case, my recommendation is to gently push back. Don't just start. Do not boil oceans. Ensure that only the parameters of the different countries that *matter* are collected and reported. Begin these sorts of assignments with the end in mind. What criteria will be used to determine a country's attractiveness for a company's business? Where does the company we work for have a competitive edge? How can that edge be capitalized upon in a new geo-mix? What is need-to-know? It is essential to keep thinking critically. For example, in judging the market attractiveness of countries in Africa, a country with a harbour that serves other countries as well may rank differently in, for example, import statistics than the local country justifies. The country with the harbour, for example, Gambia, may be irrelevant as a market, but the harbor may be a critical point-of-entry for a West African business development plan. To conclude this section, *Table 6.1* summarizes the application of the tool of country profiling in strategic analysis.

DIMENSIONS	DESCRIPTION
What use does this tool have?	A country profile provides the context and directional data for decision-making in multiple occasions in strategy design, execution and monitoring.
When to apply this tool?	A country profile is usually an input document in strategy: it should be there before the strategy is to be designed, the investment or deal is to be decided upon or the business risk profile is to be assessed.
Who to involve when applying this tool?	A country profile is typically a desk research-based product. There is usually no need for stakeholder management within a company. The market intelligence or strategy department may involve human intelligence sources where needed.

TABLE 6.1 ▶ ▶ ▶ **APPLICATION OF COUNTRY PROFILING AS A TOOL**

 6.3

TECHNOLOGY ANALYSIS

Technology analysis is an umbrella term. From a strategy perspective, the objective of technology analysis is to analyse current or future sources of competitive advantage of competitors/customers/suppliers based solely on technologies and technological changes and to advise your company's management on implied technology strategies for your firm's brands, production processes, supply chain choices and so on.

In this book, technology analysis covers those elements of competence- and technology-related tools that are not covered in the sections on product portfolio and on patent analysis. *Table 6.2* summarizes the positioning of technology analysis in this book.

	PRODUCT PORTFOLIO ANALYSIS	PATENT ANALYSIS	TECHNOLOGY ANALYSIS
SOURCES	(physical) products or offerings and/or the communication related to these products	patent applications and patents filed	scientific literature business news human networks
LEAD PARTY IN ANALYSIS	strategy department with specialist input (e.g., advertising agency or an R&D lab for analysing competitor products)	patent specialists with strategy department input	R&D subject matter experts possibly with strategy department input
COMMON ORGANIZATION	strategy or R&D in the lead	R&D in the lead	strategy department or R&D in the lead

TABLE 6.2 ▶ ▶ ▶ **THE POSITIONING OF TECHNOLOGY ANALYSIS**

Table 6.2 shows that, similar to the case of patent analysis and product portfolio analysis, a strategy department may not be in the lead in technology analysis. In some companies, technology analysis is executed within a technology or R&D department, ultimately reporting to a senior vice president of technology or R&D. When an organization combines corporate strategy and technology, possibly including market intelligence, combining patent analysis and technology analysis into one department is logical. When the two are not combined, a close cooperation is essential to align views on business environment trends in markets and technologies and in doing so ultimately inform a company's top management with a single voice and view.

Technology analysis, similar to strategy and market intelligence at large, as well as patent analysis, has two distinct responsibilities. Firstly, it is in charge of a permanent news monitoring role, in the case of the scientific literature, on technological changes that may affect the company. For this role it may utilize all legal information collection methods. The relevance of human sources should not be underestimated. Human experts in technology may greatly assist technology analysis efforts by offering periodical summaries of recent key developments in their field of technological expertise.

In doing so, they minimize the time and effort of the in-house technology analysis team to read and digest the underlying literature. Deutsche Telekom (DT), for example, has set up a network of such technology scouts, being experts themselves in their respective fields and based outside DT, to permanently monitor a range of DT predefined topics (Thom, 2010). DT rewards their sources on a pay-per-contribution basis.

In principle, technology news distribution within a company may be operated along the same lines as the news on the market environment is distributed: by collecting, tagging, filing and disseminating news by technology area, by company, by relevant product category and so on.

Secondly, a department responsible for technology analysis is to provide periodical and one-off project-based deliverables on specific technology deep-dive topics. Deliverables may, for example, be technology-, company- or category-specific. For the former two, some questions are provided for inspiration.

PERIODIC TECHNOLOGY-SPECIFIC UPDATES

Such deliverables should, for each technology, provide answers to questions like (list to be tailored to match the interest of a specific company/technology combination):

- What is new?
- What regulatory dimensions are relevant related to the new technologies?
- What are new or breakthrough insights in technologies?
- How could these new technologies affect the way our company produces or distributes products?
- What could applying the new technology mean to our company's current and future's position in manufacturing, in brands and products, in supply chain?
- Who worked or works on the new topics (scientists, universities, companies, scientific institutes)?
- What future actions are in relation to a more detailed assessment of the technologies proposed by the technology analysis department and by whom, ready by when, at what cost?

PERIODIC COMPANY-SPECIFIC UPDATES

- What literature or technology-related news have company-affiliated staff published in scientific literature or in the business press or on their LinkedIn profiles?

- What new open innovation partners has the company connected to recently?
- What company announcements have featured the R&D or technology portfolio?
- What has been reported on R&D efforts in annual reports (both budgets spent and achievements realized)?
- When is the next conference when a company's scientist delivers a presentation? Who, if anybody, from your company will attend?
- What are patterns of umbrella themes that emerge when reviewing all scientific work done in a company? What could be the (future) value of working on these themes for the company? How could the company turn these themes into competitive edges?

Company, category and technology-specific update reports that are addressed to senior management (R&D, marketing) may of course combine the outcomes of patent analysis, new product analysis and technology analysis in a single deliverable.

A technology analysis department may consider empowering all (need-to-know) company staff by offering access to an intranet-based permanently updated knowledge management repository. To conclude this section, *Table 6.3* summarizes the application of technology analysis as tool.

DIMENSIONS	DESCRIPTION
What use does this tool have?	Technology analysis typically provides input for R&D plans, possibly for marketing plans and at all times for M&A target valuation (and/or the related due diligence).
When to apply this tool?	Similar to patent analysis, technology analysis is or better should be a proactive tool. The tool should be applied prior to assigning substantial funds to future R&D plans.
Who to involve when applying this tool?	Technology analysis requires specialists to complement the usual market intelligence and/or strategy analysts. When, for a market intelligence department, technology analysis is part of the responsibility portfolio, ensure that the analyst responsible for this is familiar with all relevant technology fields that need to be covered and has a strong personal network with various internal and external technology experts.

TABLE 6.3 ▶ ▶ ▶ APPLICATION OF TECHNOLOGY ANALYSIS AS A TOOL

6.4   VOLATILITY ANALYSIS

Next, to unpredictable government regulation changes, volatility is one of the biggest nuisances in business. Volatility occurs especially, though not only, in commodity markets. Volatility may, for example, have variable weather conditions as root cause, with currency fluctuations being a good second. It should not come as a surprise that agricultural commodities display among the highest price volatility among globally traded commodities.

The origin of volatility in prices usually is that supply and demand in commodity markets both change, but do not do so at the same time. Supply meets demand at a price. As supply and demand change, so do prices. The amplitude, however, of the price swing often is a multitude of that of the change in supply or in demand. As an example: a drop in the global supply of raw milk of 1% may lead to 30–40% higher raw milk prices within three to four months. In response, moderate supply and demand changes may alter a buyer's market into a seller's market and vice versa. Major product price changes in volatility-prone markets often hurt or boost the profitability of companies producing for or trading in these markets. This is caused by the fact that such fast raw material price changes may not be passed on to customers and consumers as quickly as the input prices change. The resulting lack of predictability of earnings and cash flows is despised by investors. These are the sorts of external environment surprises a market intelligence or strategy department is paid for to prevent.

The implication of the above discussion on volatility is twofold. Firstly, volatility is there to stay – it cannot be prevented. Secondly, it is the surprises that need to be prevented, not the phenomenon as such, as the latter is clearly quixotic. A strategy department may take two types of steps to assist a business facing inherently volatile (raw material) markets. The first step relates to the strategy design phase. The second step relates to continuous or at least frequent strategy execution monitoring:

- To support the business in **defining strategies** to mitigate volatility-related risk by changing the product portfolio; this usually means moving toward value-added offerings where commodity cost form a lower part of total production cost.[1]

- To **develop** econometric supply-demand **models** with, where possible, forward indicators that allow the business – within a certain accuracy – to prepare for commodity price swings by predicting them in advance.

Outputs from market sizing analyses (see *Chapter 8*) are logical inputs to volatility-related models. Quantitative predictions may also require a remarkable lot of qualitative inputs. A diverse mix of qualitative and quantitative inputs from a multitude of sources has to feed into the prediction model, for the model to deliver an accurate output. In *Table 6.4* below, the focus is on econometric models as a tool for analysing volatility.

DIMENSIONS	DESCRIPTION
What use does this tool have?	Preventing (raw material) price fluctuations from surprising business management – allowing the latter to prepare the business properly for a rollercoaster before it hits.
When to apply this tool?	Modelling a supply/demand business environment to predict future commodity prices is a permanent activity. The output of the activity should be a periodically updated 'commodity price outlook'. The required frequency of the update is determined by the *potential*, not by the recently *observed* speed of commodity price changes.
Who to involve when applying this tool?	Modelling future commodity price predictions is among the most challenging activities in strategy and market intelligence, as some uncertainties like the weather are fundamentally unpredictable. Building and operating models requires the best and brightest (probably econometrically trained) analysts. Even these minds are useless when management is not prepared to act upon the predictions of the models. Therefore, the most important condition for success in volatility analysis is that management needs to *believe* that commodity prices are sufficiently predictable through modelling – at least for the next six months – to justify the cost of doing so. In the absence of that condition, starting modelling may still be done, but a lot of strong evidence may need to be delivered to management prior to them starting to act on the outputs of predictive modelling work.

TABLE 6.4 ▶ ▶ ▶ APPLICATION OF VOLATILITY ANALYSIS AS A TOOL

6.5 TREND ANALYSIS

Trend analysis is a tool that typically provides input for strategic plans. The word 'trend' may have as many definitions as there are trends. In this context, a trend is defined as a change in the business environment of a firm that either relates to the (ultimate) consumers of the firm's products or to a development that may affect the attractiveness of an industry segment or a market as a whole. Trends are almost by definition changes that are beyond a firm's control, although some companies may consider themselves trendsetters. The latter, however, are the exception. Examples of trends include:

- Regulatory changes affecting the business model or profit pool of an industry. A historic example is the trend that, in the US, major companies were forced to break up because they had gradually built monopolistic positions, e.g., Standard Oil. This trend could have been called 'trust busting'.
- Consumers being increasingly reluctant to buy food products that contain excessive amounts of refined sugars because of the associated long-term health problems (type 2 diabetes and other syndromes). This trend may be referred to as 'sugar is the new fat'.
- Companies adapting to consumers shifting their purchasing behaviour from 'high-street' retail to on-line retail. This trend may be referred to as 'e-commerce'.
- Citizens in democracies where voting is not mandatory increasingly refrain from using their right to vote. This trend may be called 'government losing legitimacy'.

Examples of phenomena that should not be referred to as trends are, for example, individual governments enforcing new legislation, unless that legislation is eventually adopted by other governments as well. As such, the government of Thailand enforcing legislation that demands locally sold food products to contain a percentage of locally produced food raw materials, prior to permitting food producers to import raw materials, is not a trend. It would become a trend if neighbouring ASEAN governments would be inspired by this legislation and adopt legislation with a similar philosophy.

As there are so many trends in the business environment of a company, it is not a problem to dream up trends in a brainstorm session. A quick search on the internet or a call to a friendly management consultancy firm may easily deliver a long list of generic trends. Trend watching reports, and especially the authors of such documents, i.e., futurists or trend watchers, may also be a source of inspiration (some more than others; there's a lot of hot air in this business).

The implication is that getting a long list of (generic) trends is not the problem. The trick is first to select those trends that directly or indirectly (look to) matter most to the future cash flows of the company. Secondly, the aim is to define appropriate risk mitigating strategies for those trends that pose risks to a company. This is normally done in a strategy design phase. For the trends that may offer opportunities, the strategy design phase should allocate future company resources to harvest this upside. Such resources should be proportional to the upside potential the trends (look to) offer. Truly innovative companies, however, create rather than embrace trends.

In summary, trend analysis in strategy design is probably at all times useful as a defensive tool. In this role, trend analysis is an input in a process that allows the strategy department to ensure the firm is prepared for potentially unfavourable changes in its business environment. Market intelligence staff should monitor the first weak signals and determine the potential impact of the emerging trend, to determine whether or not the firm should choose to revisit its managerial choices. Trend analysis as a tool is also often used to discover opportunities: as input for R&D or innovation.

As with other strategy analysis tools, applying them is useless unless decision-maker commitment is secured that decisions will be based on the output of the analysis. An interesting interactive way to do so is discussed below.[2]

ORGANIZING TREND ANALYSIS AS A GAME MAY UNLEASH CREATIVE AND CRITICAL THINKING

An elegant model to short-list trends ranked on impact and probability is to use a self-made card game in a workshop setting. In the card stack, each card describes one trend. The total stack equals about 100 different trends. Colour coding distributes trends in some categories, e.g., consumer trends, regulatory, channel, demography, economy, etc. Split the top 20 to 30 executives of a business (unit) who have been invited to a trend analysis workshop up in three to five groups. Give each of the teams one hour to select the ten most relevant trends to their business – no matter whether the trend offers an opportunity or poses a risk. Make them also select the next ten trends in terms of relevance. This implies they also have to ignore 80 or so other trends as less relevant *to their business as they know it.*

After each team has selected the trends, the facilitating strategy department takes stock of how many times each trend has been selected (if at all) by all the groups together. To come to a prioritization, the strategy department allocates two points for a top-10 trend per group and 1 point for a top 11-20 trend. In doing so, the ten trends for the whole team that have obtained the most points emerge. For each of these trends, the business team is invited in a plenary session to identify matching actions for the to-be-defined strategic plan. This crude action list, inspired by the trend analysis, helps shape future business strategic moves beyond doing more of the same. Such trend analysis allows not only to pick up 'weak signals' of change, but also to make the relevant decision-makers familiar with them and eager rather than resistant to act upon them. The whole exercise only takes three hours. Due to the game element, engagement tends to be strong. This assists in building the team's commitment to later act upon this in day-to-day business.

Trend analysis may be included in the overall responsibilities of a strategy or market intelligence department, to ensure delivering useful business environment input to corporate plans. When operating in the game set-up discussed above, the design and facilitation of a workshop is typically a strategy department responsibility. Acting upon the outcomes is the responsibility of the management team that participates in the game. *Table 6.5* summarizes the application of trend analysis as a tool in strategy design.

DIMENSIONS	DESCRIPTION
What use does this tool have?	The output of trend analysis feeds into strategy plans. Trend analysis assists in identifying future risks to mitigate, and opportunities to harvest for a company.
When to apply this tool?	Trend analysis is preferably used preceding the design phase of strategic plans; it may also be used as input for updating existing strategic plans.
Who to involve when applying this tool?	Trend analysis requires decision-makers' commitment to turn the outputs of the analysis into actions with a deadline and an owner with enough authorities/resources to make a difference. Selecting the most relevant trends to act upon is a task that shall be carried out by the business team that is responsible for the design, but most of all for the execution of the strategic plan.

TABLE 6.5 ▶ ▶ ▶ APPLICATION OF TREND ANALYSIS AS A TOOL

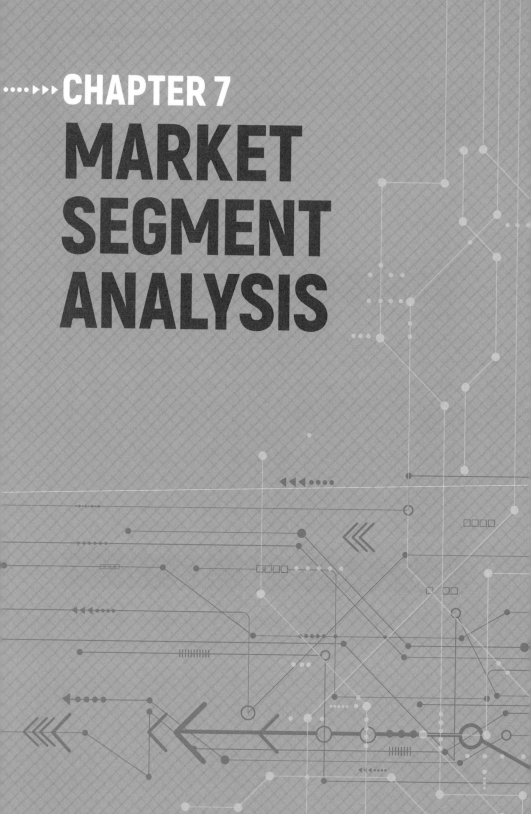

CHAPTER 7

MARKET SEGMENT ANALYSIS

INTRODUCTION

In many industries, costs determine profits, but market circumstances determine profit pools. In this chapter, we first discuss a classic concept to map a company's position within its industry when it comes to its cost base. This concept is called the 'industry cost curve'. It is not a quick and dirty analysis but, when carried out diligently, it may be a truly helpful tool both in improving the quality level of strategic management conversations and subsequently in driving the quality of strategy decision-making.

The second tool is called the 'profit pool analysis'. This tool enables you to map the attractiveness of a market or an industry. In the absence of a decent profit pool, any business will turn into what's known in some business schools as a 'five-star crappy' business. So a profit pool analysis is among the first tools that, as a strategist, I apply to get myself acquainted with a (new) business.

7.2   INDUSTRY COST CURVE

The main purpose of preparing an industry cost curve is attempting to predict a competitor's future steps by understanding their (and other players in the same industry) cost positions. No matter what industry a company competes in, being a cost leader is almost by definition a competitive advantage (Bales, 2009):

> *A strong competitive cost advantage is a versatile and often decisive strategic asset.*

To determine the strength of a company's cost position versus its competitors, the industry cost curve tool has been developed. Industry cost curve analysis first and foremost informs strategy designs, such as strategic or marketing/sales plans. In strategy execution, a cost curve may be input prior to taking capital expenditure or M&A decisions.

This tool finds its origin in strategy consultancy, just as the profit pool analysis tool that is discussed later in this chapter. The idea for this tool has been published in an internal staff paper in October 1981 within McKinsey & Company. The idea was later released in the public domain (Watters, 1981):

> *The industry cost curve is really just the standard microeconomic graph that shows how much output suppliers can produce at a given cost per unit.*

The tool aims to link profits in an industry via product prices to product demand, installed capacity required to produce the product by all industry players together, and the cost each of these producers incur in each of their facilities to make the product.

Diagram 7.1 schematically displays the cost curve for an industry. In this industry, three companies operate five factories, with a fourth company considering entering the industry. Assume that all the factories operate in an imagined island country, Island Nation, which knows no imports or exports of the products produced in the three companies. The factories all produce a commodity e.g., whole milk powder. Installed capacities for each of the factories can be seen at the horizontal axis:

Player A	factory A-1: 70 kt/y	factory A-2: 17 kt/y (idle)
Player B	factory B-1: 30 kt/y	factory B-2: 17 kt/y (idle)
Player C	factory C-1: 25 kt/y	
Player D	investment plan for factory D-1: 20 kt/y	

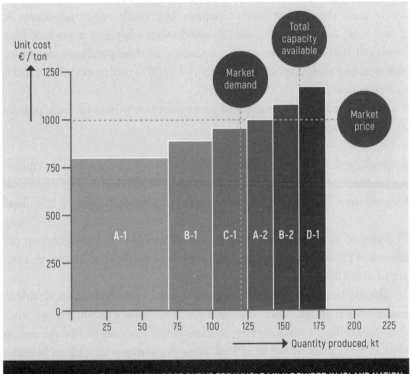

DIAGRAM 7.1 ▶▶▶ THE INDUSTRY COST CURVE FOR WHOLE MILK POWDER IN ISLAND NATION

At present, the market demand for whole milk powder in Island Nation is 120 kt/y. Given that the total installed capacity for whole milk powder is 159 kt/y, the industry utilization rate thus equals -75%.

PRICE IS WHERE SUPPLY AND DEMAND MEET

Provided the market for whole milk powder in Island Nation functions well, a market price of (just below) €1,000/ton will normally establish itself. The moment the price becomes higher than €1,000/ton, producer A may start up its facility A-2, as when above €1,000/ton doing so would become attractive. In a simplified world, A and C would subsequently start to compete for customer orders to load their factories C-1 and A-2. Producer A would no longer do so when the price of whole milk powder sinks below €1,000/ton, as marginal returns on whole milk powder would become less than zero for producer A when operating facility A-2. The moment the price sinks below €950/ton, marginal returns for producer C would become negative, removing producer C's incentive to produce whole milk powder. C discontinuing whole milk powder production would leave the market undersupplied. As a result, when producers A, B and C all act purely rational, demand meets supply at a price of (just below) €1,000/ton. In that market situation, all three producers are profitable utilizing their respective facilities A-1 (100% utilization), B-1 (100% utilization) and C-1 (80% utilization).

In this situation, the margin or profit pool (see below) for milk powder in Island Nation equals:

for producer A: 70 kt x €1,000 net sales/ton - €800 cost/ton = €14   million
for producer B: 30 kt x €1,000 net sales/ton - €875 cost/ton = €3.75 million
for producer C: 20 kt x €1,000 net sales/ton - €950 cost/ton = €1   million

The sum of all margins (or the profit pool) equals €18.75 milllion on net sales of €120 million, suggesting this ingredient market has an average margin of over 15%.

The implicit message is that an industry cost curve is most applicable to commodity markets, where customers switch between producers, as products from different producers are exchangeable. This may not be the case in FMCG B2C markets (or so at least most marketing staff wish to believe), but this exchangeability is common in many B2B markets, so the tool is quite widely applicable.

HOW TO PREPARE AN INDUSTRY COST CURVE

As with many tools, prior to deciding to apply them – with all the work that may entail – securing management commitment to use the output of the work in their decision-making is key. When management is committed to use the outputs of the analysis, for preparing an industry cost curve, the following steps are logical:

- Define the scope of the industry cost curve: what market, what country or countries.
- Define the cost types to use (see below).
- Ensure cost type definitions are aligned for competitors and your own company to allow comparisons to be made on an apples-to-apples basis.
- When the analysis has been completed, define with management actions/ measures that management can influence (e.g., factory efficiency: yes, energy unit cost: no, or not easily) to change the *relative* position in an industry cost curve, should they wish to do so.
- Assess the impact that such measures may have on your firm's *relative* position.
- Determine the strategic implications of taking the measures – how does taking all feasible measures affect your *relative* competitiveness as a company versus your competitors? What does that tell you on the (future) value of executing your strategy?

Preparing an industry cost curve for a commodity requires an almost limitless use of sources to create the data set that is needed to come to conclusions. It takes time and effort to obtain a data set for an industry cost curve that is both sufficiently complete and correct to base significant management decisions upon. A market intelligence department with an experienced staff should be able to integrate all sorts of primary market intelligence methodologies in collection and analysis to independently be able to take full responsibility for preparing a cost curve.

ALL COST DEFINITIONS ARE EQUAL, BUT SOME ARE MORE EQUAL THAN OTHERS

In this section so far, costs have been called cost, without further elaborating on the definition of cost. In the whole milk powder example in Island Nation, for the sake of simplicity the vague term 'margin' has been used to predict industry players' behaviour. For an industry cost curve to really be useful, more explicit definitions may be needed.

Normally, cost may be split up in several categories for a commodity production unit:

- Variable cash costs that are incurred when an extra unit of product is produced: e.g., energy, raw materials, shipment cost to the customer when applicable.
- Fixed cash costs that are incurred directly related to production, but that do not immediately change when an extra unit of product is produced: e.g., labour, allocation of interest related to debt incurred for the investment in production assets.
- Non-cash costs that are incurred directly related to production: e.g., depreciation of production assets.
- Overhead cash costs that are not related to production, but that are allocated anyway: e.g., sales, marketing, R&D, general & administrative cost and other overheads.

Good market intelligence work may provide in sufficient detail the insight into what these different costs look like for a commodity producer, even per unit of production. So far, so good. The real challenge now is to predict how the competitor's management will *act* given these costs when markets change. Addressing this challenge is partly discussed in the next section.

CHALLENGES IN APPLYING AN INDUSTRY COST CURVE

Using an industry cost curve in business decision-making has two fundamental challenges:

- Will the market intelligence work be able to *really* calculate the cost of production of a competitor? Does market intelligence work really ever reveal fundamental inputs to cost like energy prices, labor cost, etc.?
- Even when market intelligence delivers these outputs accurately enough for decision-making on the first challenge, will you as a strategist and your management really be able to xenocentrically think through what *the competitor* would do in *their* situation, rather than, possibly unconsciously, stick to imagining what *your company* would do in *their* situation?

The above set of tasks may be time-consuming to carry out and has to deliver a result with a sufficiently high accuracy to base management decisions upon it, but it is do-able.

More challenging is to predict how the competitor's management may act when markets or external factors change.

Recently an industry cost curve has been applied to assess the potential impact of a carbon dioxide-related charge on energy cost on the *relative* cost position of different aluminium producers (Lemarre, 2009). Given that aluminium production is highly energy-intensive and that some producers, e.g., in Norway, use hydroelectricity with zero carbon dioxide impact, this single potential change in the business environment could upset the global aluminium industry's mutual relative competitiveness. An industry cost curve is thus a tool that may inform e.g., scenario analysis.

To assess the management choices of an individual competitor, the recommendation is taking as broad a perspective as possible on the competitor and to prevent taking your own company's logic as implicitly affecting your view. Usually, understanding the cash position of a competitor, rather than just the profit position, adds a valuable dimension. A question that is always relevant is: what options does the competitor have when they do not get (for example) this commodity tender? Or what other options do they lose when they do get this tender? What is the value of such options to them? What would therefore be their real cost tipping point for them to take a particular decision?

Another tool that may be useful to apply is either a wargame or a pre-mortem analysis. What if two years from now the competitor had this new facility built and up and running? What would the competitor's management have had to believe two years earlier to have taken this major investment decision? How would that fit the company culture of the competitor? How would that fit the competitor's executive style? What, if anything, could our company do now to influence a competitor's decision in a favourable way for our company – while remaining compliant to anti-trust legislation?

A truly xenocentric view, coupled with a solid industry cost curve fact base, is a powerful tool to inform a company's management on an investment and pricing decisions in commodity markets. The most important element is probably to *document* the logic of what we as strategists believe. In writing it down with the objective to inform others, one often discovers the flaws of one's own logic, prior to others pointing it out. A written assessment also facilitates a regular post-mortem analysis, which assists in further building a truly xenocentric view of a competitor: What did we believe they would do? What indeed did they do that we anticipated? What did they do that we did not anticipate? What didn't they do that we had anticipated them to do? Why? What does this tell us for future predictions? In conclusion, *Table 7.1* summarizes the industry cost curve as a tool.

DIMENSIONS	DESCRIPTION
What use does this tool have?	The industry cost curve informs management on the relative cost position a business has versus its competitors. The implications of a correct assessment of a business's cost position is critical input to taking decisions that are strategically sound for a business.
When to apply this tool?	The industry cost curve tool is preferably used prior to or as part of making longer-term strategic plans or prior to taking major capital investment decisions.
Who to involve when applying this tool?	The industry cost curve is among the most complicated deliverables to produce, given the multiple dimensions of cost for several competitors that need to be assessed and ultimately objectively compared. An industry cost curve requires experienced market intelligence and strategy analysts to be in the lead and a management that understands the remaining uncertainties that making the curve cannot resolve. Such uncertainties may include potential inaccuracies in cost estimates for various competitors. Much more importantly, the leading uncertainty will be to assess how competitors will act in the market given their starting position in the curve. Assessing the intent of a competitor – i.e., what they will do given their competences – is much harder than assessing their competences as such – i.e., their relative cost position. Even when a perfectly accurate industry cost curve is available, the output still must be used xenocentrically to ensure good predictions of a competitor's future steps.

TABLE 7.1 ▶ ▶ ▶ APPLICATION OF AN INDUSTRY COST CURVE AS A TOOL

PROFIT POOL ANALYSIS

The relevance of analysing profit levels in an existing industry can hardly be underestimated. Next, to market size and market growth, an assessment of an industry's current profit levels features among the most relevant deliverables market intelligence can provide a strategist with (Bradley, 2013):

> *Real strategic insight [...] rests on [...] a thorough understanding of how and why a company, its competitors, and others in the industry value chain make money. Absent dumb luck, a strategy that doesn't tap directly into such understanding will underperform.*

To analyse what profits players in an industry value chain really make, the concept of profit pool analysis has been developed (Gadiesh, 1998). The objective of a profit pool analysis is to discover in sufficient detail the sources and distribution of profits within an industry. In this book, the profit pool scope is not limited to a sector within an industrial value chain, as the original authors have proposed this tool to be used for, but it also includes potential other sectors of the industry's value chain, even when technically this should be called a value chain analysis. As profit pool and value chain analyses have similarities from a methodology perspective, the two are covered together in this section. Both the sector profit pool and the value chain analysis are illustrated using a simple example.

THE PROFIT MARGIN DISTRIBUTION WITHIN A VALUE CHAIN

Our imagined country, Island Nation, knows no imports or exports of dairy products. The dairy industry in Island Nation exclusively produces three consumer products: cheese, yogurt and drinking milk. The farms that supply the industry are self-sufficient in feed, so no cattle feed is bought from a feed industry, which otherwise would have formed an extra value chain step. The value chain therefore consists of three sectors:

- **Farming**, resulting in the production of raw milk to be delivered to a dairy processor;
- **Processing**, turning the milk into consumer-packed goods;
- **Retailing**, selling the finished consumer-packed products to end-consumers.

A profit pool analysis covering the entire value chain (farming, processing and retailing) in this island country aims to identify:

- How much profit all dairy farms together generate in this country (absolute amount) and what profit margin (i.e., EBIT margin) these farms generate in average.
- How much profit all processors make together in turning milk into cheese and/or yogurt and/or drinking milk (both absolute and average EBIT margin).
- How much profit all retailers together make on their sales in the dairy category (absolute and average EBIT margin).

This part of the analysis shows which sector within the value chain generates the highest profit margins. When an assessment is being made of how much capital is being employed per sector, the analysis can also show the return on capital employed (ROCE) per sector. The latter is just as relevant to do. ROCE analysis often delivers extra insights that profit analysis do not provide.

Such an insight may, for example, be that an efficient private label producer generating 2% ROS actually delivers a higher ROCE than an A-brand producer that generates 8% ROS.

HOW TO CALCULATE AN INDUSTRY SECTOR'S PROFIT POOL?

A four-step approach is common to determine a sector profit pool. The first step is to define the scope of the sector pool. The second and the third steps are to be taken in parallel. In these steps, a top-down and a bottom-up estimate of the sector's profit pool needs to be made. The final step is to reconcile both estimates and finalize the analysis.

As sources for the top-down analysis, it is proposed to review industry market reports that may indicate the total size of a market (in net sales). This net sales quantity may be multiplied by a typical industry EBIT margin factor, which may be extracted from financial analyst reports such as investment banks or specialized sector consultancies produce.

The bottom-up analysis starts with identifying who are the players in a sector. For each of these players, individual data are sourced (where possible) and added up to create one industry sector overview. A data set with sales, profit and possibly even capital employed data should be compiled for the various players in the dairy industry sector in Island Nation, just as well as for the various retail players operating there. The data set may be filled with public sources, such as financial statement filings of players, and human sources: people knowing the profit engines of players in an industry. An experienced market intelligence department should take the full responsibility for preparing a profit pool analysis, which a strategist may order or co-produce.

In summary, the four steps are:

- Define the pool: Which value chain activities need to be in scope?

- Top-down estimate of the pool size: Look for sources that give a top-down view.

- Bottom-up estimate of the pool size: Source the data and make the analysis: where what profit is being made in the chain and by whom.

- Reconcile the estimates: Use bottom-up and top-down approach to finalize the analysis.

In contrast to the Island Nation example, a profit pool in reality may be less easy to construct. Import/exports do happen, blurring, for example, processors and retail category sales margins. Companies' financial statements may relate to multiple categories. Nestlé's corporate profit and loss account is the result of an aggregation of thousands of product/market combination results, giving no insight into individual business positions' profitability. It is recommended to start building a bottom-up sector profit pool analysis by focusing on 'pure play' players. Pure play companies' results relate exclusively to the sector under review. The more pure play financial results are available as a percentage of the total industry sector under review, the more reliable the calculation of the total profit pool will probably be.

Strategies and often also financial performances of different players in the same industry converge – provided the players all apply the same business model. For Western passenger airlines, most full-service airlines have approximately the same business model and indeed similarly weak financial results. Low-fare airlines in the West, as well as elsewhere, however, operate with a fundamentally different model – and as a result also show markedly different financial results.

The extrapolation of data from the results of one or two players in an industry sector as proxy for other comparable companies in the bottom-up analysis is sometimes needed and possible. Do not, however, do this to estimate the results of other companies when the other companies are not well enough understood. Unknown companies may operate other business models, with fundamentally different profit margins.

COMPETITIVE ENTRY BARRIERS TEND TO CORRELATE WITH A SECTOR'S SLICE OF A PROFIT POOL

Usually, the sector that generates the highest margin in the value chain is the sector with the highest competitive entry barrier. Consider the food retail sector. In most Western countries, governments are not influencing the number of retail outlets that get permits to operate in certain territories. This makes the entry barrier to start or, more importantly, expand a chain of retail outlets relatively low: facing a government unwilling to give that extra permit is not too common. As a result, retail chains may expand until overcapacity emerges in the sector as a whole. Once overcapacity exists, the profit pool in that sector of the value chain gets under pressure, as the different players start to fight for market share to cut unit cost and load their part of the underutilized total industry sector's capacity. This rarely proceeds without putting pressure on the margin of the sector as a whole.

In a market where retail margins get under pressure, retailers will understandably aim to push part of that margin pressure up the value chain to their suppliers, for example, dairy processors. When the latter have secured fixed raw milk volumes from their farmers and have no other (more) profitable markets to serve, the processors will have to give in to at least some of the retailers' pressure. This lowers the profit pool of the dairy processors. Retailers may now either increase their slice of the industry profit pool or, more often, given the market circumstances they are operating in, pass on part of the profit pool to consumers, e.g., in the form of lower prices. The lower prices are to attract more consumers at the cost of their retail competitors' market share (possibly, due to price elasticity, lower prices may also create a higher demand). When elasticity is low, both the retailers and the dairy processors have now seen their sector profit pools shrink. In such markets, dairy farmers will ultimately also face margin pressure, as processors will be less eager to buy raw milk that doesn't have a profitable market but does have a high price. In the end, no sector in the chain makes attractive margins any more. Now they together have become a 'five star crappy industry'. Full service Western European airlines, facing tough competition from Gulf States-based competitors with lower fuel cost bases, tend to also be 'five star crappy industries'.

Retail doesn't need to be a crappy industry at all. In high-growth emerging markets, organized retail may be highly profitable. Consumer demand exceeds the speed of retail growth, leading to capacity constraints rather than overcapacity. Moreover, governments may limit the number of new shops that are allowed to be built, further strengthening scarcity for as long as it lasts. Another example concerns, for example, a city like Hong Kong. In this city, capital is an entry barrier to build and operate shops, as real estate is exceptionally costly per square meter floor surface. As a result, Hong Kong has one of the world's most concentrated grocery retail industry structures. The two largest chains thus have a strong negotiation position. Every grocery producer *must* get a listing in at least one and preferably both of the two major chains to be able to advertise their products to the end-consumers; there is no point advertising a product that is not for sale on the shelf. Understandably, in Hong Kong the large retail chains are believed to command a significant part of the industry profit pool – in spite of their high costs of operations due to the high real estate costs. Retail consumers, of course, pay the ultimate price for the real estate scarcity, as all players in an industry profit pool will all try to pass on high costs down the chain.

PROFIT POOLS MAY BE VISUALIZED TO PERSUASIVELY SHOW PROFIT DISTRIBUTIONS

There are at least three ways to visualize the results of an industry profit pool analysis:

- Showing the aggregated EBIT margin for each of the sectors in a value chain.
- Taking a granular view, showing the EBIT margin for each of the business lines – in our example: cheese, yogurt and drinking milk – within a sector.
- Taking an even more granular view: showing for each of the players within a sector and a business line their profit share.

Diagram 7.2 shows all three visualizations. In the top diagram, the value chain EBIT margin distribution is depicted. This diagram shows that, in this example, the dairy processors realize the highest EBIT margin in the chain.

In the middle diagram, the vertical axis shows the EBIT margin split within the dairy processing sector by business line. The horizontal axis shows the net sales split by business line. In Island Nation, about 40% of the dairy industry's net sales are realized in drinking milk, 10% in yogurt and 50% in cheese. This middle diagram shows that the margins in the yogurt sector are the highest per unit of sales. Multiplying EBIT margins with net sales realized (horizontal axis) gives the absolute EBIT profits realized by business line. The absolute profit pool of the cheese business line is larger than that of the yogurt business line, in spite of the yogurt EBIT margin being higher, as the area of the cheese profit pool rectangular figure is larger than that of the yogurt profit pool. The profit pool split for the dairy processing industry in Island Nation is approximately 30% in drinking milk, 20% in yogurt and 50% in cheese. *Table 7.2* summarizes these conclusions that are displayed visually in *Diagram 7.2*: yogurt is small, has an attractive profitability but a small profit pool. Drinking milk has a weak profitability, but still a larger profit pool than yogurt. The cheese business line performs as the industry average: the profit pool share is proportional to the sales share. The strategic question that, based on this analysis, may now be answered is: which profit pool is your company best suited to capture, and why? To answer this question, an extra layer of granularity needs to be added: this is shown in the bottom section of *Diagram 7.2*.

	Net sales as a percentage of total market pool	EBIT as a percentage of total market pool	*Relative* EBIT margin vs total industry
DRINKING MILK	40%	30%	0.75
YOGURT	10%	20%	2.0
CHEESE	50%	50%	1.0

TABLE 7.2 ▶ ▶ ▶ THE DAIRY INDUSTRY SECTOR PROFIT POOL BY BUSINESS LINE IN ISLAND NATION

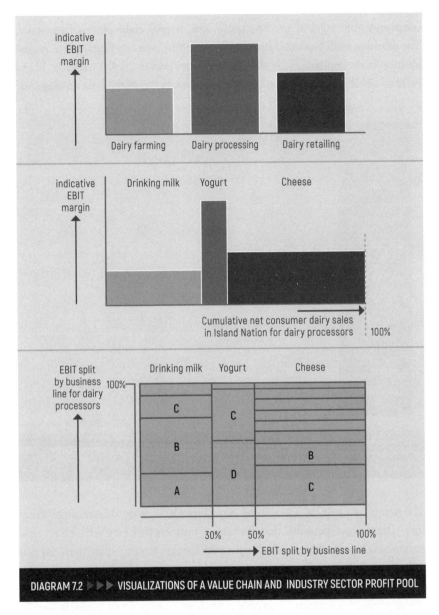

DIAGRAM 7.2 ▶▶▶ VISUALIZATIONS OF A VALUE CHAIN AND INDUSTRY SECTOR PROFIT POOL

In the bottom diagram, the letters A, B, C and D refer to the four most relevant dairy processors active in Island Nation. The diagram immediately shows the differences in industry structure between the different business lines. Yogurt is a highly consolidated line: 95% of the business line profits are harvested by the top two players in the line, with the top two being challenged by only one smaller player. In contrast, cheese is a fragmented business line: the top two players command only 50% of the line profit and in total eight players participate. The drinking milk business line is neither concentrated nor fragmented. Across business lines, company C is the dairy industry sector (profit) leader in Island Nation. *Table 7.3* provides the quantitative data shown in the bottom diagram.

COMPANY	DRINKING MILK	YOGURT	CHEESE	COMPANY TOTAL
A	8	0	0	8
B	14	0	8	22
C	6	8	17	31
D	0	11	0	11
8 OTHERS IN TOTAL	2	1	25	28
BUSINESS LINE TOTAL	30	20	50	100

TABLE 7.3 ▶ ▶ ▶ **DAIRY INDUSTRY PROFIT DISTRIBUTION IN PERCENTAGE BY LINE AND BY PLAYER IN ISLAND NATION**

The results in *Table 7.3* allow some general predictions on this industry structure. The first prediction is that the yogurt business line may well attract new entrants. It is profitable and the largest profit maker is a pure-play that may not wish to retaliate in milk or cheese, as such entry, would likely dilute company D's margin levels. The second prediction is that company A's position may be under pressure. Company A is only a weak no. 2 in a single business line, in contrast to B, C and D each being clear no. 1's in one of the three business lines, with B being strong no. 2 in cheese and C being strong no. 2 in yogurt, next to having a meaningful no. 3 position in drinking milk. Another prediction is that the cheese business line may consolidate. Also overall, the dairy industry in Island Nation is already moving toward full consolidation: the top two dairies harvest 53% of the industry's profit pool and the top three (25% numeric;

3 out of 12) harvest 64%. In a fully consolidated industry, Pareto's rule may be useful as a rule of thumb: 20% of the companies (numerically measured) harvest 80% of the profit pool. The above lines show that a profit pool analysis may provide multiple insights as input for a company's strategy making.

IN VOLATILE INDUSTRIES, LOOKING AT A SINGLE YEAR'S PROFIT POOL MAY NOT BE ENOUGH

A single year's profit pool analysis still only delivers a one-off view on an industry. In an industry where at least part of the segments are exposed to highly volatile pricing dynamics, such one-off views may deceive rather than inform, as volatility-related effects may constantly shift margins across the value chain. In a year of tight dairy supply, farms tend to be more profitable than in a year of milk being supplied beyond demand. The opposite is true for a retail chain. When dairy is tight, product prices go up. In some markets, increasing retail prices may be difficult, given consumer buying power constraints. Some of the raw material price increases in such markets may have to be absorbed by the retail chain at the cost of their profitability on the category in that given year.

To conclude this section, *Table 7.4* summarizes profit pool analysis as tool.

DIMENSIONS	DESCRIPTION
What use does this tool have?	Profit pool analysis is among the most prominent tools to turn data from multiple sources into intelligence. The analysis delivers insights into the structure of an industry. Both who in the value chain commands most of the profits, as well as who within an industry sector does so and in what business line.
When to apply this tool?	This tool is preferably applied in longer-term corporate strategy making.
Who to involve when applying this tool?	This tool necessitates the deployment of experienced market intelligence analysts with a good insight into strategy making or possibly strategy consultants, working with a good data set and/ or a good market analyst. For interviewing human sources to obtain missing data to reach the right level of granularity in data collection, experienced market intelligence collection skills are a must.

TABLE 7.4 ▶ ▶ ▶ APPLICATION OF PROFIT POOL ANALYSIS AS A TOOL

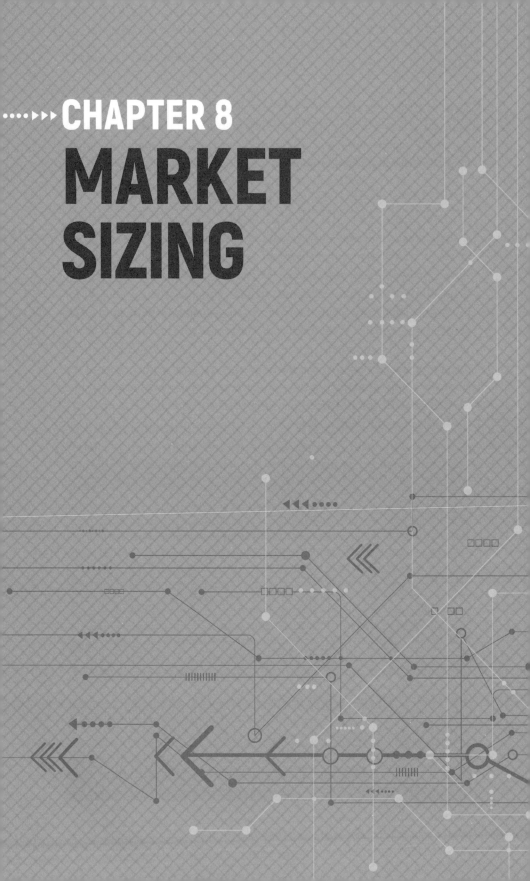

CHAPTER 8

MARKET SIZING

8.1 INTRODUCTION

Market sizing analysis is among the most common tools in strategy and market intelligence. Market size estimations are input to almost all business development and investment-related management decisions. Given the relevance of good market size estimations, a whole book could justifiably be dedicated to market sizing. To manage the size of this book, however, in this chapter only a broad introduction to market sizing will be provided. This introduction aims to be a guide on how to execute common market sizing assignments.

A MARKET'S SIZE IS THE FIRST PROXY INDICATOR OF A MARKET'S ATTRACTIVENESS

Market sizing is commonly applied in support of different business development strategies. A market size is generally the first (proxy!) indicator of a market's attractiveness. When a market is sizable, there is a chance it is attractive. To make it attractive, other conditions have to be met. Secondary conditions that need to be met may be that the market has an attractive and stable profit pool and that a market shows an attractive growth rate. When, however, a market is small, other parameters do not usually have to be looked at. When a market is small, most businesses tend not to bother, unless a still-dormant market potential is looming and growth is already strong. In general, however, a too-small market is a market that is most often rightly ignored. *Table 8.1* uses a classic Ansoff-matrix to schematically indicate how market sizing supports business development (Ansoff, 1957).

	Existing product	New product
NEW MARKET	**Market development** Market sizing to be used for: - Prioritizing market opportunities - Acquisition target assessments - Business case substantiation	**Diversification** Market sizing to be used for: - Acquisition target assessments - Prioritizing innovation opportunities and related R&D budget allocation
EXISTING MARKET	**Market penetration** Market sizing to be used for: - Sales target setting and monitoring - Competitor assessments - Market share analysis	**Product development** Market sizing to be used for: - Prioritizing innovation opportunities and related R&D budget allocation - Acquisition target assessments - Business case substantiation

TABLE 8.1 ▶ ▶ ▶ MARKET SIZING SUPPORTS DIFFERENT BUSINESS DEVELOPMENT STRATEGIES

Market sizing has multiple other applications in business. It may, for example, inform a company's procurement department how big the market share of a particular supplier is in a strategically relevant raw material to your firm. When such share is or becomes too high, a procurement department may well wish to diversify its sourcing to mitigate the risk of becoming too dependent on a single supplier.

Market sizing analysis may either be applied one-off or periodically. One-off analyses tend to relate to business development work. Such analyses by their nature should not just give the size of the market as a figure, but should also address qualitative features of a market, like the usage and attitudes of buyers (consumers/customers) related to a product. The analysis is to elucidate not just how much is being sold today, but also why. In business development, market size and an understanding of current and potential future customer needs together form an indication for market *potential*. In periodic – for example, bi-monthly – market sizing analyses, the emphasis is on numbers. In this case, monitoring and reporting is the aim of the work. It is great to have a plan. It is better to deliver it in execution: what gets measured, gets done.

8.2 MARKET DEFINITION

To come to a market size estimation for a product, it is first required to dissect the term *product market sizing*. Three questions come to mind:
- What is the right measure of size?
- What is a market?
- What is a product?

These three interdependent questions are discussed in more detail below.

MARKET SIZES SHOULD BE EXPRESSED IN THE INDUSTRY'S MOST COMMON UNIT

GIA (now M-Brain) defines a market size as (Misund, 2014):

> *The total sales by a defined group of companies that together can address a market.*

The mentioned group of companies together make up an industry sector. Each party of the group qualifies to sell. This means that each party meets legal or other standards to compete. In the case of zinc metal, each seller either is able to procure or to produce zinc ingots that meet all standards to allow sales thereof on the London Metal Exchange. By meeting the standards, a company – following GIA's definition – can address a market. In market sizing, an accessible size is sometimes defined as the market that a firm can transact in.

Butter in Europe may offer an example to elucidate the concept of accessible market. The European butter market includes the market for butter in Norway. For an EU member-state based dairy seller, the Norwegian market is virtually impossible to access, given the import barriers with which Norway protects its domestic dairy industry. Even when the market for butter in Europe includes Norway, the accessible market for an EU-based butter seller is smaller, as it in reality excludes Norway. Similarly, a company that exclusively sells products online cannot access a market in bricks-and-mortar retail outlets. It is essential to define a strategy or have a market intelligence department work with the customer of the analysis to decide *what* market should be sized and how to define the current and/or future scope of the term *accessible*.

It is recommended to report a market size not per se in sales value but sometimes also or even only in the unit most relevant to the industry sector. This unit may be a billion kg of raw milk in dairy, single units (cars), barrels (crude oil), hectolitres (beer), bushel (grain), passenger-kilometers (airlines) or whatever indicator is common in the market that is sized.

When knowing and using the appropriate indicator for the size and the definition of the size, the question that follows is how a market is to be defined.

A MARKET IS DEFINED BY TRANSACTIONS, BUYERS AND SELLERS

A narrow definition of a market has been provided (Misund, 2014):

> *A market is a group of customers buying a certain product or service from the same sellers.*

GIA thus defines a market by the characteristic that a transaction takes place: a good – either tangible or intangible – is exchanged for another good. The exchange takes place between a buyer and a seller. The other good may be money but, in barter trade, does not need to be money. In the above definition, the market may still be worldwide and may cover a large range of products. For most managerial and thus strategy applications, this is not practical. For practical decision-making purposes, markets are segmented.

MARKET SEGMENTATION IS A CRITICAL INPUT TO MARKET SIZING

There are multiple ways to segment markets. Most common in business are five different ways: a geo-mix, a channel-mix, a product-mix, a category-mix and a split between existing and new products. The next section discusses the details of how to come to proper market segmentation in market sizing.

In the above section, the questions: "Why should we do market sizing?", "What is a market?", "How to express its size?", and "What is a product?" have been covered. In summary:

- A market size is the best proxy indicator for a market's current or future attractiveness to a company.
- A market is characterized by the fact that transactions take place.
- Market sizes are best expressed in the most common industry metric for sizes.
- Markets can and need to be segmented in
  o Different geo-territories
  o Different channels
  o Different products (new or existing) and, when relevant,
  o Different categories

Prior to moving toward the discussion of how to segment and to size a market, a final word of warning: market sizing needs to be demand-driven. When, however, a customer requests a strategy or market intelligence department for sizing the market in 12 countries for six products (each with three quality specs) in four channels over the next four years, something is going wrong. Blindly meeting this customer's expressed request means to assess almost 3,500 different market sizes (12x6x3x4x4). This is not to say that the customer's request is ridiculous: to the contrary. When a business development director is tasked to develop a plan to enter a new continent with an existing product line, the above example easily gives the number of different market opportunities that may emerge. It is the strategy or market intelligence department's responsibility to develop an efficient analysis method to spot the 10–20 largest geo/product/market/channel combinations first. When those are estimated, the question is whether the other 3,400 g/p/m/c-combinations still need to be looked at. *How* to come to a market segment and later size will now be discussed.

 # 8.3

MARKET
SEGMENTATION

In market sizing, five different market segmentations are common: a geo-mix, a channel-mix, a product-mix, a category-mix and a split between existing and new products. In the Appendix, segmentation dimensions and definitions are discussed in some detail.

GEO-MIX: DEFINE THE RELEVANT GEO-TERRITORY, WHICH IS PREFERABLY HOMOGENOUS

A geo-mix defines a geographical region within which the market transactions took place. Nestlé, for example, until mid-2014 reported sales of most of its businesses divided over three geo-segments: Asia-Oceania-Africa, Europe and the Americas. In Q3 2014, Nestlé announced it would change the segmentation to Asia-Oceania and Europe-Middle East-Africa. Segments make most sense when the sub-markets, aggregating to form a segment, have the same market dynamics in common. Whether that was the driver in the case of Nestlé is less clear. For the dairy industry, the EU is a market that knows virtually no internal barriers between the member countries, so summarizing dairy sales in the EU as geo-segment makes sense. Talking about the European market makes less sense because countries like Norway and Switzerland are part of Europe but not part of the EU. Tariff barriers exist, e.g., for particular dairy products that are traded between the EU countries and these countries. The markets thus have limited similarity. For an EU-based dairy producer, different strategies for success in selling dairy products will apply within the EU as compared to, for example, Norway. A single commercial approach may thus not be advisable. Segmenting into homogenous markets is preferable, prior to starting a market sizing project.

CHANNEL-MIX: ENSURE NO INDIRECT OR HIDDEN CHANNELS ARE OVERLOOKED

A sales channel may be defined as the sub-market where the transaction takes place. A traditional trade channel may consist of a producer that sells its consumer-ready, finished product to an importer. The importer sells the product to a city-based distributor, which then sells it to a local wholesaler. The wholesaler sells it to a small shop owner, who then sells it to a consumer. In this example, the product reaches the consumer after five different transactions took place in the chain. The producer may, however, also directly sell to a large modern chain of retail stores that subsequently sells the product to consumers. In this case, only two transactions take place. Increasingly, producers sell directly to consumers via on-line web-based ordering systems. The above three different channels, all featuring a business-to-consumer (B2C) transaction, are complemented by a producer selling its product to another producer. The latter may process the product prior to it reaching a consumer. This is an example of a business-to-business (B2B) channel.

It is imperative in market sizing to define not only the geo-mix, but also the channel mix that is in scope. When estimating, for example, the Dutch-type cheese market in Uruguay, it is relevant to estimate the size of the transactions in a given year in *all channels* together. Cheese sold through modern retail stores leaves measurable traces: scanning data at the cash machine. Companies like IRI and AC Nielsen collect such data and offer it to whoever is interested (alas at a hefty price). Cheese may, however, also be sold to restaurants for use in desserts, quick service eateries as a key ingredient in a cheeseburger, hospitals and schools for sales in canteens and it may be sold to retail pizza producers as an ingredient. The list is endless. Imagination is also in market sizing the key to prevent surprises.

Prior to starting a market sizing project, it is essential to both define the channels into homogeneous segments as such and define which of these pre-defined channels are in and out of scope of the project. Missing relevant but less visible or obvious sales channels may well be among the most common reasons for inaccuracies in market sizing projects.

A peculiar channel is the captive channel. Captive sales are sales that take place between units within a large(r) company. One unit within a company may produce steam and sell this steam to another unit of the same company. This transaction realizes an intra-company-sale. Unfortunately, intra-company sales are rarely reported in detail in the accounts most companies publish. Consider a company that aims to sell anti-corrosive compounds for steam boilers. When this company – for market sizing purposes for their compounds' sales plan – wishes to know the market size of steam production, all channels, including the captive channel, need to be assessed. Steam is, of course, an extreme example. Steam can hardly be transported cost-efficiently. Steam production and consumption are thus inevitably physically connected. What is true for steam is partly also true for salt (to name another example). In the case of salt, the cost price of production per unit is low e.g., between €0.05–0.10/kg, but shipments are expensive in comparison to production cost. Salt usually doesn't travel far. A lot of salt producers, especially those operating evaporation processes, use the salt at the same location and often intracompany, to produce chlorine, caustic soda and its derivatives. Although there is a large 'free' market for salt, where salt does change ownership in an intercompany transaction, a large part of the global salt volume that is produced is used in captive applications. When it is required to assess the total market of a good, ensure that when there is a captive market, it is properly assessed and not overlooked.

PRODUCT-MIX: PRODUCT SEGMENT BOUNDARIES MAY BE DETERMINED BY SUBSTITUTION

Defining product segmentation may appear to be simpler than it is. The European Commission has a Directorate that is focused on merger control. This Directorate has as its assignment to ensure corporate consolidation may not lead to companies upon concentrating getting too large market shares. Too large market shares may give such companies the ability to extract undesirably high prices from consumer/customers. The latter would end up having too limited a choice in buying the products they fancy. As large interests are at stake, in every dossier, the EU Commission has to clearly define and thus ring-fence which product or products constitute a market segment and, most of all, which products do not. This established practice may inspire the strategy professional, if only because market sizing exercises are critical input whenever a company needs to file for merger permission in the EU (or other countries). The EU Commission reports their decisions in their merger control practice in great detail on their website. The cases that relate to your own industry may help to understand how the EU Commission sees market definitions.

In commodity products, a product/market definition is simple, even in the EU Directorate context. Commodities by definition are exchangeable. The metal zinc is traded on the London Metal Exchange. A batch of zinc is defined by it being cast in a particular predefined shape of a particular predefined weight and the metal being of a guaranteed minimum purity. When these conditions are met, it usually does not matter to a buyer which company produced the product; the product is exchangeable. The market for such zinc ingots is as transparent as it is well-defined.

In cars, matters are not so simple. Cars may easily be defined as autonomously driven vehicles aimed to transport passengers and/or freight. Now consider that the EU Commission would receive the request from Ferrari, Maserati, Porsche and McLaren to merge. These car companies could easily show that their common market share in the car market in the EU or any of the countries that make up the EU, even after the concentration, would remain low. Inductively, the companies could argue that the EU should not be concerned that this industry concentration would lead to an increase in market power of the producers or a related future lack of consumer choice. The EU Commission, however, would not likely accept this argument at face value. What is at stake here is not the market for cars as a whole, but the product *segment* for luxury sports cars. The EU Commission could even argue that the market should be segmented as European-made luxury sports cars. The EU Commission may argue that a buyer segment exists that would never buy a US- or Japanese-made luxury sports car, feeling – rightly or wrongly – that these cars lack the European sports car brands' sophistication and/or tradition. The EU Commission may thus restrict or forbid this concentration, even when the common market share in cars of these producers together is rather limited.

For a strategy department doing market sizing work to support a company filing a 'Form CO' to request the EU Commission's approval for a planned acquisition or merger, choosing the right product-mix segmentation definitions and scope is critical. Too narrow a scope may lead to too high market shares and may invite limitations to be enforced by the EU Commission on the requested industry concentration (these are called 'remedies'). Defining segments with too broad a scope may lead to the EU Commission demanding a better product/market definition – with the company possibly losing control over the definitions process.

The EU Commission takes protection of the consumer interest and choice as its leading consideration in defining relevant markets/segments. When, for example, two carbonated soft drink (CSD) companies aim to merge, the EU Commission may not just ask for details on the markets of CSDs, but may also demand data on the markets of dairy drinks, juices and still and carbonated waters. When, due to the concentration, the CSD-company would raise prices, would consumers indeed switch to other drink categories? If so, how would that limit the pricing power of the concentrated CSD company? If the concentrated CSD company's pricing power, due to so-called 'cross-elasticity', would be severely hampered, the EU Commission may be less restrictive in accepting the concentration. If consumer research, however, shows that CSD drinkers will not switch to juice, the Commission may be more restrictive in its judgment.

Product-mix segmentation definitions matter not only in the strategy analysis deliverable phase (e.g., a Form CO), but also in the data sourcing phase. Multiple economic statistics exist on product flows. These may include production statistics and import/export statistics. Zinc metal, as was discussed above, is clearly defined. So is butter. But what about 'dairy drinks'? In practice, most of these statistics, in as far as they do not concern well-defined commodities, are too aggregated to be of major use in market sizing.

As was the case in defining the geo-mix and the channel-mix, in case of the product mix, it is just as critical to a strategy or market intelligence department to define clearly in advance what products are in scope in a market sizing project and why, and which are not and why not. The product-mix scoping definition, once completed, may be so relevant that a strategy department may need to go back to the principal of the market sizing project prior to starting the project to get alignment on and approval of the definitions used.

CATEGORY-MIX: LET CONSUMERS/CUSTOMERS DEFINE THE BOUNDARIES OF THE CATEGORY

Multiple products tend to make up a 'category.' A category is a term that is commonly used in FMCG industries. The category of fresh dairy may, for example, consist of drinking milk, desserts, spoonable and drinkable yogurts, etc., provided all of these products have a shelf life shorter than 45 days. Sizing a category usually requires sizing all the constituent subcategories. Consumer market research exists to reveal the consumer perception of what is or should be included in a category and what should not be. The outcome of this type of research guides both the layout of retail outlets as well as, for instance, the degree in which brands may be stretched across different products. A common research methodology in the FMCG world is simply to put a large number of products on a table and ask consumers to segment these products in categories that to them logically belong together.

In market sizing of categories, it is critical to define in advance what is taken in and out of scope of the category sizing exercise and why.

EXISTING OR NEW PRODUCTS: ANALOGIES MAY HELP TO ESTIMATE NEW PRODUCTS' MARKETS

It makes good sense to distinguish between existing and new products in market sizing (Philips, 1999a). Market sizing is straightforward for existing, properly defined products (or categories) in well-defined geo-territories and channels. Follow the script (that will be discussed later) and a market size estimate with a certain accuracy will be obtained.

It is more challenging to determine a potential market size for a product that does not yet exist or one that is in an early stage of its life cycle. The now classic failure of IBM to properly estimate the market size for PCs and the related impact PCs would have on IBM's mainstream computer business, for example, has been well documented (Gerstner, 2003). When even 'Big Blue', with all the resources at its disposal, could get it so wrong, sizing the market of innovative/new products can, using an authority argument, almost by definition not be easy.

Getting market sizing right for existing products is challenging enough; getting it right for new products is even harder. Philips argues philosophically that correctly assessing the market size for a new product is almost impossible, as consumer response to the new product is not yet known and is virtually unpredictable. This sounds all too negative, but there is some truth in it. What to do?

When a new product replaces a current product, an estimate of the rate of replacement over time (from early adapters to laggard buyers) and of the size of the market for the existing product is a good method to assess the new product's market size. There are simply no easy answers for how to size the market of a new-new thing. Analogies of the market size development over time of other new-new products may be used as a proxy indicator, but uncertainties will remain relatively high.

Prior to executing a market-sizing project, ensure that in the definition phase of the project, it is clearly understood whether existing or new products' markets are to be sized (and what this means for the expected accuracy).

 8.4 # MARKET SIZING AS A THREE-STEP APPROACH

A common methodology to size a market is to follow a process of three consecutive steps, such as practiced at Nokia Siemens Networks (Misund, 2014):

Step 1:   Estimate creation phase
Step 2:   Internal stakeholder validation phase
Step 3:   Dissemination phase

THE ESTIMATE CREATION PHASE CONSISTS OF USING PARALLEL MARKET SIZING APPROACHES

Market sizing is not an exact science, so there is no single best methodology for a particular measurement challenge. Rather, market sizing, like forecasting as discussed before, is best carried out by using as many different approaches as needed to reach a range of estimates. Based on that range, a weighted estimate may emerge as the expected market size. In the next section, five parallel approaches are discussed for coming to a market size. These five approaches by no means form an exhaustive list. Rather than making the approach leading, the problem should be leading in defining the most appropriate market sizing solution. The best approach is the one that solves the problem leading to the most accurate market size estimate at the lowest cost and/or in the shortest time – whatever is more important to the principal. The approaches are thus shared for inspiration. Your own approach is the best! The second step in market sizing is stakeholder validation.

INTERNAL STAKEHOLDER VALIDATION IS AS IMPORTANT AS PROPERLY SIZING A MARKET

Assume that the appropriate methodologies have correctly been used to deliver an estimated market size. This is a good start, but it does not conclude the whole process. Once the market size estimate is available, it is recommended to take the time to go through an internal stakeholder validation phase. This phase may be more political than the more factual first step in market sizing, but the step is equally important. The impact of consultancy work, including strategy work, may be given by the formula:

$$\text{Impact} \quad = \quad \text{Deliverable Quality} \quad * \quad \text{Acceptance}$$

The key is to identify internal stakeholders first. Stakeholders may be colleagues who may in the future find the strategy department's market size suddenly as a budget or personal target guiding their organizational or personal job performance assessment. When, for whatever bad reasons, such stakeholders have not been consulted prior to issuing a market size assessment, resistance and rejection looms just around the corner.

"Who do these Ivory Tower strategy staffers think they are, that they know what *my market* looks like next year?" When these sales staff happen to have built a good track record, management will take their opinions even more seriously and may join them, when applicable, in wondering why strategy or market intelligence is so far off. The next question that may come up is, "Why is strategy charged with doing this work anyway, if they don't know what they really talk about?". The above is, of course, an exaggeration. This is not to say that only salespeople can estimate market sizes based on intuition, tacit knowledge and gut feel. It is to say that involvement and communication with these front-office staff in as early a phase as possible may both facilitate acceptance of the final deliverable, as well as deliver critically valuable input insights on, for example, the most appropriate market segmentation to be used. If your report visibly reflects some of these insights, offer a celebratory moment to the front-office staff that recognizes its earlier contribution. Acceptance is so much easier. What is more, the quality of the output is undoubtedly better.

Amazingly, there is no proportionality between medical doctors in the US being sued by patients for *mistakes* and the percentage of mistakes these doctors make in their treatments of patients (Gladwell, 2005). There is, however, a clear proportionality between the percentage of patients who feel to have been *disrespectfully or arrogantly treated* by an individual doctor and the number of lawsuits an individual doctor faces per thousand treatments. Why would sales staff behave differently from patients?

Once a proper and possibly a more time-consuming, stakeholder management program has been completed, step 3 in market sizing may be started up. The market size estimates may be disseminated to a wider audience.

THE DISSEMINATION PHASE: APPLYING MARKET SIZING OUTPUTS IN STRATEGY DEFINITION

The market share a company holds in a defined market is probably the most elementary business performance indicator. The beauty of having determined a total market size is that it allows a company to calculate its market share by dividing the own sales realized in a particular market by the total size of that market (in value or volume).

When a market is better known (e.g., because retail scanning data is available or because solid estimates have been prepared), the next step is to calculate the market shares for all relevant companies in a market. Dividing the market share by that of either the leading player in a market or by the number two in the market when your position is number one, provides what is known as the *relative* market share.

A relative market share of one means that the number one and number two in a market have equal market shares. A relative market share of two means your own position is not only number one in the market, but also twice the size of the next competitor. Conversely, a relative market share of 0.4 means that your position is a factor 2.5 smaller in share than that of the market leader. Relative market shares tend to be proportional to profit margins in an industry. In many industries, the market leader tends to claim a disproportional share of the industry profit pool. Given the heuristic rule that predicts a likely proportionality between relative market share and profit margin within an (homogenous) industry, the Boston Consulting Group has developed a matrix to assess a company's portfolio of product market combinations. For this, the relative market share is plotted on the horizontal axis of the matrix. The vertical axis typically depicts the total market growth, but it may also depict the Return on Capital Employed (ROC) of a portfolio of businesses. *Diagram 8.1* represents what is now commonly called the 'BCG matrix', using market growth on the vertical axis (in a slightly adapted form).

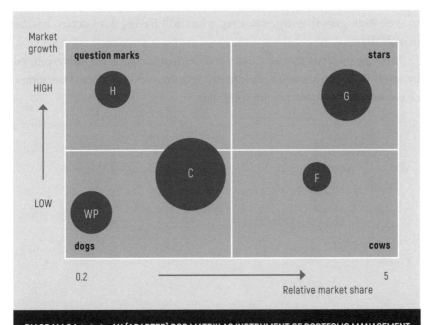

DIAGRAM 8.1 ▶ ▶ ▶ AN (ADAPTED) BCG MATRIX AS INSTRUMENT OF PORTFOLIO MANAGEMENT

In *Diagram 8.1* a fictive example of the portfolio of a dairy ingredient company is given. This company has five business lines. Its G-line is the star of the portfolio, where the company is situated in a high-growth market with a high *relative* market share. Most likely, this business line generates the majority of this company's profits. The WP line, however, is a dog. The market, as such, shows a low growth rate and the company enjoys a weak *relative* market share. Cows are markets that are milked: the *relative* market share of a company is attractive, but the market growth rate is not (or no longer) so. Usually, cows' positions are attractive in a company's portfolio to hold on to as they generate the cash with which star and question mark positions may be funded. Question marks are markets that show a high growth, but where the company does not have an attractive *relative* position.

Provided it has been built on solid market sizing study work, the BCG matrix is a useful tool to assess the current and future strategic position of a company's portfolio of businesses. The tool may well be used for business cash planning purposes of a business portfolio. It assists in determining which businesses generate the cash to fund the growth (cows through their milk, dogs possibly through being divested) and which businesses deserve the cash (stars for their strong overall position and question marks due to their high growth prospects, even when still having a moderate *relative* market share).

It is repeated, perhaps ad nausea, a BCG matrix that is not underpinned by solid market sizing work is more of a risk than an asset. Resist the temptation to use it without having solid data.

8.5 FIVE PARALLEL METHODOLOGIES FOR MARKET SIZING

Five parallel methodologies for market sizing are covered below.

(I) TOP-DOWN MARKET SIZING: STRUCTURED BUT SENSITIVE TO INACCURACIES

The top-down approach is probably the most traditional and frequently used market sizing methodology. A top-down approach starts with using a (reasonably well) known market size of the market of a group of products. This means a market at a high aggregation level. The top-down approach resembles the Fermi Solution approach (see Chapter 1). The example below, using an FMCG-market, elucidates the top-down approach.

Let's look at a fictive example in the Swedish cheese market. The question is what the ex-factory annual value and volume is of the market for *producer-branded light cheese*. It is known for a fact that the total Swedish retail cheese market has a retail value of ~ € 1 bn. The retail value is what is being paid at the cashier, including Value Added Tax (VAT). Retail research has shown that light cheese concepts are sold in 64% of all retail outlets. This percentage is a *weighted* average distribution. In practice, light cheese may only be sold in 40% of all Swedish grocery outlets that sell cheese. That is a *numeric* average distribution. Light cheese, however, is sold in shops that sell relatively high volumes of cheese. As a result, the weighted average distribution is almost by definition higher than the numeric average distribution. This means that the total cheese sales, or in other words, the cheese market, in shops where light cheese is sold equals approximately €640 million.

The same retail research has shown that the shelf space of light cheese is some 15% of the total shelf space dedicated to the cheese category in the stores. Assume retailers to be rational. A rational retailer aims to realize an equal margin per meter of occupied shelf. Assume subsequently retailers' margins on light cheese and other cheese to be equal per unit of sales. Light cheese may rotate a bit slower, but is more expensive per unit (see below) and thus generates a higher margin *per unit of sales* than regular cheese. The latter compensates for the slower rotation. If all assumptions – the rational retailer, the slower rotation, the higher unit price and the similar margin per unit of sales – hold, it means that net sales per meter retail shelf in the cheese category are similar for regular and light cheese. None of the above assumptions are likely to be fully correct, but the error margins may well cancel these assumptions out. That, after all, is the premise we assume to apply when using the Fermi method.

In that case, the retail sales of light cheese in Sweden may be estimated at €640 million * 15% ≈ €100 million. Market research, including shelf studies, has shown that *producer-branded* light cheese has a value market share of about 80% in Sweden. This means that unbranded or retail-branded cheese makes up about 20% in value. Consequently, the retail value for producer-branded light cheese is approximately € 80 million in a year.

Retail gross margins in the fresh/chilled products category in many countries equal between 32 – 42% (VAT included). For Sweden, no independent data is available on retail margins. As business models of retailers across different developed countries tend to be similar, the mid-range of the international benchmark is being used: 37% (VAT included). (For once strategic convergence in a mature industry is an asset to an analyst). As a result, the estimated producer-branded ex-factory **value** of the light cheese retail-channel market in Sweden equals about €60 million/year.

Market research for the total cheese category is available that postulates that the total Swedish retail cheese market has a size of 100 million kg. Given Sweden's population of about 10 million consumers, this figure equals 10 kg/capita. This is a common (retail) cheese consumption per capita figure in Western societies, so the order of magnitude seems at first sight to be correct.

We now know that the ex-factory cheese market equals €640 million in value and 100 million kg in volume. This suggests that the average ex-factory unit value of cheese sold in retail in Sweden is €6.4/kg.

Light cheese tends to be a bit more of a specialty than regular cheese. It tends to be sold in smaller portions, necessitating more packaging cost per kg sold. So an upward correction needs to be made for the unit price of light cheese versus that of average cheese. Retail research confirms that light cheese has an average price premium per unit of 20-25% versus regular cheese. Assume the average ex-factory unit value of light cheese to be €7.5/kg. This unit price allows us to calculate the requested **volume** of the light cheese retail market in Sweden. This volume now equals €60 million/ €7.5/kg = 8,000,000 kg per year.

It is obvious that multiple assumptions had to be made to come to this market size estimate for the volume and value of this market. In this Fermi Solution approach, the inaccuracies of different assumptions tend to be cancelled out, so the quality of the estimate may be better than expected. When, however, a big starting assumption like, for example, the size of the cheese market in Sweden in retail was off by 50%, the resulting sub-market-size estimate will also be way off. Mitigating this risk is best done by executing different sizing methodologies in parallel – and working toward a balanced estimate, obtained through using these multiple methods.

As the example above shows, various research results and figures are needed to come to a market size estimate. Obtaining such research results may both be time-consuming and costly, but working with applicable and accurate in-market research remains the golden standard.

When neither time nor budget permit, comparable market data may be used as proxy. In the above example, proxy data included the double-check of the typical continental European per capita consumption of cheese sold through the retail channel and the retail margin. The use of comparable market analogies as a market sizing method is covered below in more detail. The top-down approach is fastest and cheapest when the research results are either already in place or when they are relatively easy to obtain. For Western (FMCG) markets, a top-down analysis is a common starting point.

(II) BOTTOM-UP MARKET SIZING: POWERFUL INSIGHTS BUT POSSIBLY TIME-CONSUMING

Bottom-up market sizing follows essentially the same Fermi Solution approach as described above in the section on top-down market sizing. The perspective, however, is the opposite. In the case of the Swedish ex-factory, retail-channel, light cheese market in value and volume, the bottom-up perspective could either start at the retail outlet or even with the consumer.

Starting with the consumer perspective, the first step in the market sizing exercise is to do, say, 200 consumer interviews. This type of study borders classic market research. The question to be asked to the consumers could be whether at that moment of time the respondent actually has bought cheese this month and/or has cheese at home. For the positive respondents, the next question could be whether they actually have light cheese at home. Questionnaires like this require specialist (market researcher's) input: asking useful questions is more of a challenge than it may look. Specialist input is also needed to select a representative sample of the population. The sample may be purely randomly chosen. This again sounds easier than it is, because the willingness to actually participate and properly respond to a (telephone) questionnaire may already skew the sample to higher-educated consumers. The latter may buy more light cheese than the average consumer, unintentionally skewing the results of the study. The sample may also be chosen by specifically selecting a town or city that represents both rural and urban Swedish consumers proportionally and accurately.

In 2012, the leading Dutch quality newspaper *NRC Handelsblad* identified a borough within the suburban city of Woerden, the Netherlands, in which the population had voted exactly equal to the average Dutch population at large in the 2012 elections for the Dutch parliament. Subsequently, this specific borough was regularly covered as a proxy for the Dutch population, both in terms of economic developments and public opinions.

The beauty of the bottom-up approach is in the last word of the previous sentence: opinions. When taking the trouble to call a large sample of consumers, it is a great opportunity to also inquire on consumer views on potential and/or current usages of or attitudes toward the product discussed in the interview. In today's connected world, calling people is, of course, too old school to be true. Today, we rather think in methods like online crowdsourcing, for example, as employed by US food giant Kraft (now Kraft:Heinz) to generate a consumer-driven innovation pipeline for its product portfolio (Bodell, 2014).

Let us turn back to the light cheese example. When running well-designed consumer research, the so-called 'penetration' of light cheese is measured. Penetration gives an idea of what percentage of households actually buy a product. Blowing up the output results of a representative sample-based test to a nationwide figure provides an estimate of the volume and value of light cheese bought in the retail channel in Sweden.

A retail-based perspective would consist of retailer interviews. Talking with category specialists and/or simply storeowners on what that they see moving and shaking in a category may just as well deliver building blocks in generating a total market estimate. This type of bottom-up approach works particularly well in emerging markets where syndicate market reports are either not available or quantitatively not sufficiently reliable. As in consumer interview selections, it is all about the representativeness of a sample. In retail-based, bottom-up market sizing, a sample should consist of at least 50-70 stores, preferably geographically distributed over several cities, consisting of different shop formats and distributed over boroughs with clearly different incomes per consumer. As in the (telephone) interviews, the value of this type of bottom-up research is in the insights that may be obtained, next to the quantitative (proxy) data that are obtained (and that needs to be blown up to national level to give a national market size estimate).

The key methodological challenge in the bottom-up approach is handling the dilemma between sample size and cost and/or time. It is essential to choose a sample that is large enough to avoid the inaccuracies of a few more or a few less consumers buying a product significantly affecting the output. It is also essential not to have to call every Swedish citizen individually. Finding that balance, again, requires specialist input. Samples should be as small as possible but not smaller than that.

(III) CONSENSUS-ESTIMATE: ELEGANT, PROVIDED ESTIMATES ARE AVAILABLE

In the world of equity analysts, forward predictions of listed company's share prices are common. These forecasts are often based on the outcome of complex models of company's future earnings multiplied by the companies' anticipated share's price/earnings ratios.

When seven or eight different equity analysts, all working for different boutiques or investment banks, all have released their forecasts, an information provider like Bloomberg provides a consensus estimate. This is a weighted estimate of all estimates.

In market sizing, a strategy or market intelligence analyst can apply the same methodology. It is not uncommon that market sizes (by geo-territory for a product sold through a particular channel in value and volume) are reported by different external sources. For FMCG markets, syndicate information providers like Euromonitor offer such market size estimates for multiple product-market combinations (or PMCs). Similarly, however, Mintel, Datamonitor, Frost & Sullivan and possibly other providers may offer the same or similarly defined market size estimates for the same PMC. Even when none of these providers will have the right figure, a consensus estimate may provide a more balanced view than simply following a single provider's estimate. The disadvantage is obviously that all these providers will charge a fee for delivering their data, so the more balanced the approach, the higher the cost.

(IV) COMPARABLE MARKET ANALOGIES: USEFUL WHEN MARKETS ARE INDEED COMPARABLE

Misund, Räder and Grym refer to the use of analogies as regression analysis (Misund, 2014). The logic of using this term is that data that are available for one market – that is not in the scope of the market sizing study – are correlated in a regression-type analysis to an independent variable. That independent variable should be available for the market that is under study. The (linear) proportionality between the independent variable and the data available for the one market allows us to calculate an estimate of the requested market size.

The example used above may assist to elucidate the concept of regression analysis. It is known that 10 kg/capita/year is a typical continental European retail sales volume for cheese. An independent variable is the population size. Multiplying the known typical figure for continental Europe with the Swedish population size of about 10 million allows an estimate of the volume of the market to be 100 million kg/year.

Independent variables that are easily available for multiple (geo-) markets, nations and increasingly individual cities include the size of the population and of the economy (GDP). Other independent variables may also be used. Consider that, for example, the instant milk powder consumption per capita in three or four African nations with a more or less similar food culture, buying power and agricultural situation is known. Think of states such as the Ivory Coast, Togo and Benin. Knowing these markets' sizes, it is easy to estimate the market in Ghana or Sierra Leone: just multiply the population of the latter two countries with the per capita average annual consumption of the known proxy countries.

This works efficiently and accurately. There is, however, always a catch. Markets must indeed be comparable. Estimating the instant milk powder consumption in Kenya on the basis of that of the mentioned West African countries is useless. In contrast to West African countries, Kenya and neighbouring East African countries have both the climate and the soil situation to provide good conditions for dairy farming. As a result, instant milk powder in Kenya is relatively less important. Fresh (liquid) milk dominates the milk market. Even when the spending power per consumer may be similar to that of West African consumers, overall dairy consumption in kg per capita per year in Kenya may well be tenfold of that in most West African countries.

The above example elucidates that an independent variable like per capita consumption of instant milk powder only works in countries with a comparable food culture. Kenya, where dairy is a staple, cannot be compared with Togo, where dairy is an imported luxury.

The tricky thing is that market size estimates based on market analogies are sensitive to a degree of comparability that may not be immediately obvious. For assessing consumer market sizes in Africa, GDP/capita seems a great independent variable. For many products, the market size/capita will likely increase with an increase in GDP/capita. This is a good default assumption. It doesn't work for dairy, though. In dairy, countries with a domestic dairy tradition like Kenya are a completely different class compared to countries without a dairy tradition like Togo. Along the same lines, the per capita consumption of dairy in volume in India is double (!) that of Singapore, even when the average spending power of Singapore's consumers is a multitude of that of average Indian consumers. In India, dairy is a staple; in Singapore it never was. The value of the *formal, measurable* dairy market in Singapore per capita, however, is much higher than that in India. In India, 80-90% of the dairy market is informal. It consists either of on-the-farm consumption or of barter trade. Singapore is among the world's most premium consumer dairy markets per kg, where only A-brands are being sold.

In summary: comparable market analogies may be an efficient and powerful tool to estimate an unknown market size, provided the market dynamics are comparable. When using a comparable market analogy approach, ensure there is evidence at hand that proves that consumer/customer usage and attitudes regarding the product are close enough to be truly comparable. If such evidence is not available, consider whether the speed (and low-cost) of this approach justifies the risk of overlooking fundamental but invisible differences between less than perfectly comparable markets.

(V) INTERNAL/EXTERNAL INTERVIEWS: AN INEVITABLE MIX OF KNOWLEDGE AND BIAS

There are two slightly different approaches to a multiple interview method in market sizing. The first approach is to extract the wisdom of (a group of) experts; the second is to capture the wisdom of the crowd. We will start with the expert approach.

Misund, Räder and Grym encourage the use of multiple expert interviews to estimate market sizes (Misund, 2014). These authors refer to a particular script called the 'Delphi Method'. The script consists of a few consecutive steps and may include several iteration loops:

- The strategy department selects an anonymous group (5–20 people) of experts.
- Each expert independently receives a questionnaire, asking for a market size estimate.
- The input estimates from all experts are collected and mean/median results are determined.
- All experts receive the mean/median estimate results they together, but without knowing who is in the group, have compiled and are asked for feedback on their earlier estimate.
- All experts are invited to revisit their earlier provided estimate and send their revised estimate. There is no pressure to revisit the estimate. A confident expert may stick to his opinion.
- The potentially revisited input estimates from all experts are again collected and, where applicable, adapted mean/median results are distributed.
- This loop may be repeated until a stable mean/medium group estimate has been obtained.
- The final figure weighs the final estimates from the individual experts equally.

The Delphi Method is a more advanced form of obtaining a consensus estimate than the one described above. A consensus estimate does not have an iteration loop that allows for learning and that may lead to an expert reconsidering their earlier estimate.

To execute a Delphi Method, securing the participation of the different experts is one of the challenges. Getting the experts to willingly provide their time may require cost and time. A second challenge is to get an expert group of sufficient diversity.

When ten experts have a similar background and thus look at the same limited set of indicators to predict a future market size, the Delphi Method is only a costly and time-consuming way to magnify a common and subsequently confirmatory bias.

Surowiecki, in his book *The Wisdom of the Crowd*, has substantiated the value of the second approach to interviewing: capturing the wisdom of the crowd. The methodology traditionally was simply to ask the same question (e.g., How many coins are in this glass container?) to a large sample of random people who were physically present (Surowiecki, 2005). With today's internet connectivity, global polls with thousands of respondents can be held in a matter of minutes on high-traffic websites. Across multiple areas of prediction, it can be shown that the larger and more diverse the sample, the more accurate the outcome. The average estimate of the crowd almost by definition is more accurate than the estimate of any single participant in the crowd.

Based on these results, it has been shown that under some conditions the crowd outperforms the expert, any expert, in predictions. Four conditions define a wise crowd (Surowiecki, 2005):

- Diversity of opinion: each crowd member has some particular private information – it does not need to be correct as long as it is unique.
- Independence: crowd members do not have a chance to mutually influence each other.
- De-central: crowd members may have different specializations and thus draw on diversely built sets of experiences.
- Aggregation: there is a mechanism to bring all opinions together in a balanced way.

In the case of organizing a poll (e.g., in a shopping mall, asking how many coins are placed in a glass container), the latter condition is easily met. The poll forms the aggregation mechanism. Assuming the shoppers in the mall form a diverse and independent lot and through ensuring discretion of each estimate cannot influence each other, the *average* actual prediction may come remarkably close to the actual figure.

Applying the remarkable accuracy that the 'wisdom of crowds' predictions can give to market sizing predictions is a methodological field that is still in its infancy, but that merits much, much more attention. Strategy departments that may capitalize on this methodology in a smart way will almost certainly offer their firms a strong competitive advantage.

WHEN MARKET SIZES ARE HARD TO DETERMINE, DO PROVIDE DISCLAIMERS

In rare cases, where due to lack of data neither of the above methodologies delivers useful market size estimates, modelling may have to be applied. Modelling takes the comparable market analogies method a step further. Even when it cannot be certified that markets are comparable, they are modelled as comparable anyway.

Modelling has its potential dark sides. When a market size estimate heavily relies on modelling, ensure that in the internal stakeholder validation and management phase, this fact is communicated well. Ensure also the principal of the project understands the challenges the strategy department encountered when attempting to size this particularly elusive market. Additionally, ensure the principal's commitment to issuing the output figures, even when the underlying facts may be felt to have a disproportionally large uncertainty. The bad thing about figures is that they are remembered well – while the disclaimers that come with the presented figures are instantly forgotten.

 # 8.6

CONCLUSION

Market sizing of most business markets is valuable and feasible with the aforementioned range of methods. To be successful, it is essential both to manage stakeholders of the market sizing output and to keep market sizing methodologies' limitations and risks clearly in view. *Table 8.2* summarizes market sizing as a tool in strategic analysis.

DIMENSIONS	DESCRIPTION
What use does this tool have?	Market sizing is among the most common activities in strategy and market intelligence. Market sizes are broadly used to underpin strategic, marketing and other business plans. A typical output of a market sizing study helps use strategic portfolio analysis tools like the BCG matrix.
When to apply this tool?	Market sizes determine the 'size of the price'. The current and future market size is a leading indicator needed to justify efforts in a business to capture or maintain business positions. In M&A decision-making market sizes, market shares and market growth rates are among the most important strategy-derived parameters in a target company's valuation.
Who to involve when applying this tool?	For determining market sizes, multiple sources in a business may be needed. Choosing unbiased sources and especially sources that do not have a vested interest in the decisions based on the outcome of the market sizing exercise is critical.

TABLE 8.2 ▶ ▶ ▶ APPLICATION OF MARKET SIZING AS A TOOL

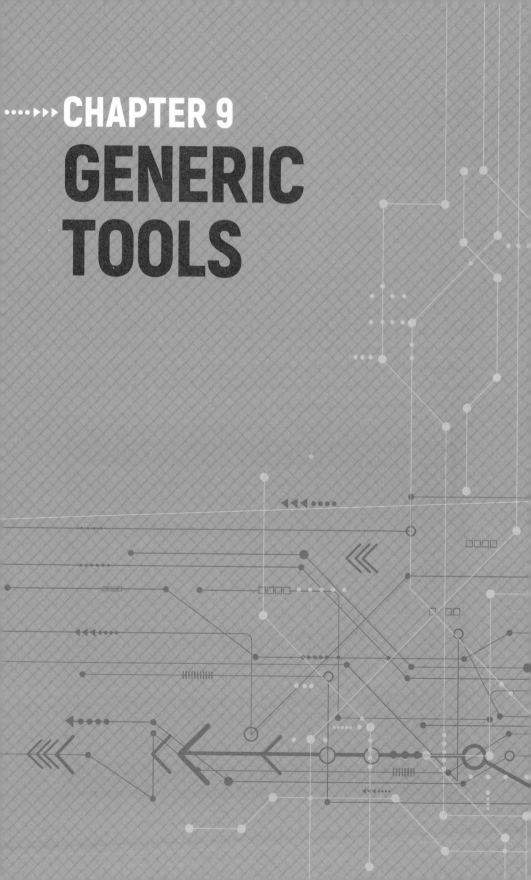

CHAPTER 9

GENERIC TOOLS

9.1 INTRODUCTION

In strategic analysis, there are a number of multiple-purpose tools. The three tools that I present in this chapter all focus on group dynamics, harvesting the best strategic insights from a group of business executives. First we discuss brainstorming. This tool looks easier than it is. Coming toward truly new ideas may require more preparation than one may think. Secondly, I cover *structured challenge*. This tool assists in imagining particular future situations, capitalizing on the full power of the question 'what if?' Finally we discuss a tool called 'pre-mortem analysis'. Consider a business. Assume that a year from now it has become insolvent. What pathways could have led the company to that bankruptcy? With what probability could it have occurred? What events could trigger such a situation? The pre-mortem analysis tool is useful in, for example, risk analysis. Applying each of these tools may require some preparation, but when their timing is properly chosen, each tool generates relevant and often unexpected strategic insights.

BRAINSTORM

Brainstorming is an analysis tool commonly used in strategy design. It facilitates individuals or groups to generate new ideas or solutions to solve problems or harvest opportunities. Brainstorming is so common that discussing it seems superfluous.

It looks so simple. Put people in a nice conference room or connect them through a nice web tool and let them generate original ideas. We have all done that.

For a twist, below there is a summary of learnings of how not to do brainstorming, inspired by Coyne and Coyne (Coyne, 2011). The manual how-to most effectively waste time in brainstorming prescribes to (in my words):

- Invite an outside facilitator who knows nothing of your business.
- Ask the facilitator to urge participants to 'think outside the box' but forget to ask them not to use too much airtime in showing what creativity should look like.
- Have loud participants promote their well-known pet ideas again.
- Invite most participants for political stakeholder management reasons rather than for their specific competences, knowledge or creativity.
- Avoid managing the scope of the brainstorm by asking the questions within the brainstorm focus area, ensuring you end up with many ideas that are sufficiently far outside the box to be useless.
- Ensure having the session as much as possible in a large plenary group setting. In small groups everybody contributes, instead of only the loudest participants in a plenary environment.
- Limit contributions of knowledgeable staff by inviting their intimidating bosses' bosses as well.

- Ensure enough experts are around whose main contribution is to shake their sad, wise heads, mumbling that executing these new ideas requires violating fundamental laws of physics (or economics or whatever other discipline).
- Avoid sharing at the end of the session what next steps will be taken after the session and what criteria will be used to select the best ideas.

This cheerful list is not provided to suggest brainstorming cannot be done. It is provided as a checklist to properly prepare a brainstorm session, rather than just schedule it. Invite some colleagues and run a session. Similar to a wargame, the trick in brainstorming is also solid preparation.

One step to improve brainstorming is to carefully distinguish the idea-generation step from the idea-evaluation step. Really new ideas by definition are unconventional. To avoid such ideas being suppressed for the sake of group conformance, secure a safe and protected, trusted environment to the participants where judgment is deferred (Heuer, 1999b). Brainstorming really is a two-step approach. Do not start judging or filtering ideas prior to making sure all fresh ideas have been generated.

One attractive way to unleash creativity is to host an 'impossible-to-possible' session (Bodell, 2014). In such a brainstorm, syndicate groups are challenged to answer questions like:
- "Our customers would never say X about our industry."
- "We would never sell our product/service in X way."
- "You will never see us change X."
- "Customers would never pay for X."
- "Our customers would never do X."

The aim of an 'impossible-to-possible' session is to reverse beliefs. Maybe there are ways to redefine our products, creating a differentiating angle that indeed *never* had been chosen before.

The strategy department may easily take the full responsibility for defining, planning, organizing and following up on a brainstorm, provided the brainstorm is exclusively focused on a strategy-design topic. Avoid, as a strategy department, becoming known for your competency in organizing and running brainstorms as such: not every useful task in a company is worth pursuing for a strategy department. *Table 9.1* summarizes aspects of the tools of brainstorming, focused on its application in strategy design.

DIMENSIONS	DESCRIPTION
What use does this tool have?	Xenocentrically imagining the competences and intent of other companies in the business environment as a basis for predicting their future actions is a core activity in strategy design. Paradoxically, brainstorming is a tool to *structure* imagination.
When to apply this tool?	The output of brainstorming typically feeds several strategy processes and/or other tools, including but not limited to: competitor executive profiling, pre-mortem analysis, scenario analysis, trend analysis and market sizing. When business stakes are high and uncertainty about the future business environment is significant using methods to, in a structured way, 'imagine' possible futures and their implication on the firm is usually worth the time spent.
Who to involve when applying this tool?	Brainstorming requires free thinkers. Assuming the brainstorm output should offer an imagined future business environment, or xenocentrically imagined future steps of a competitor or customer, do invite staff who are not too conditioned by corporate, often implicit, mental barriers. What 'we will never do' may not be 'what they will never do'. R&D staff may qualify as unorthodox thinkers. Trusted outsiders may also add value, e.g., selected staff of an advertisement agency who are specialized in creative thinking, or innovation-focused consultants. In principle, any creative mind that is not a naysayer qualifies as a potentially valuable contributor.

TABLE 9.1 ▶ ▶ ▶ APPLICATION OF BRAINSTORMING

9.3   STRUCTURED CHALLENGE

Like brainstorming, a 'structured challenge' is a tool that is commonly applied. A structured challenge is both useful in strategy design and in the strategy execution phase; it also looks to be among the easiest tools to apply. After all, it seems the only thing to ask is, "what if?". First looks, however, may be deceiving, so I think this tool deserves more attention than just providing the tool's key question.

Similar to brainstorming, a company's strategy department is well-suited to taking the responsibility for the execution of a structured challenge and for the approach to be chosen. Although asking "what if?" sounds easy, in a structured challenge good preparation pays off. To organize a structured challenge some choices are to be made, for example:

- How to do it?   – parallel individual challenge (as in the Delphi method in market sizing, see *Chapter 8*) or a concurrent group challenge
- Who to ask?   – what participants to invite and why
- When to do it?   – as so often, timing is everything
- What questions to ask?   – choice of a business problem that may be solved through structured challenge

To make matters a bit more tangible, I would like to use an example of when a structured challenge tool may well be applied strategically.

A STRUCTURED CHALLENGE SERVES TO DISCOVER FUTURE STRATEGIC REALITIES

To illustrate the use of structured challenge, let me first provide a business problem and a bit of context. In July 2014, flight MH17 was shot down over the Ukraine, with the loss of 298 lives. In response, several boycott measures were taken against

Russia by the EU. As a result, Russia became economically isolated from Western Europe. As a counter measure, Russia closed its borders for several categories of Western food imports, among them fruits, vegetables and cheese. At the time of the Russian boycott hitting Western produce, the Russian ruble/euro exchange rate was about 40. In the spring of 2016, however, rumours started spreading that Russia would be prepared to reconsider its boycott of Western produce, provided the EU would also lift some of its trade bans. Due to the global over-supply of crude oil in a slow-growth economy, oil prices in 2015 and early 2016 had crashed. With it, the Russian ruble/euro exchange rate had dropped to levels of around 70–80. A typical structured challenge tool application could now be:

"What if Russia re-opened its borders for Western-made cheese?"

The answer to this strategic question could be substantiated by asking and answering auxiliary questions like (list not exhaustive):

- "What could trigger Russia to lift the ban?"
- "What would the Western cheese import volume become six months after the ban has been lifted?"
- "What price level would cheese retail for (per kg)?"
- "What producers/sellers would benefit most from a lift of the ban and why?"

A strategy department could choose to send out these questions independently and concurrently to a number of selected in-house/external sources or to gather the same sources together in a room and try through a group discussion to reach a common view.

Even more elegant is to first send out the questions, preferably with a short deadline for the answers to be given. The email recipients should get the explicit request not to align their answers with each other. Subsequently, after all the answers have been received at the strategy department, the strategy department may organize a meeting to present the various answers. The meeting serves to discuss the meaning of the answers and subsequently allows one to define the possible next steps for the company. This two-step method ensures – provided all respondents indeed act independently – the harvesting of multiple different opinions and insights prior to the meeting. In a one-step process, some answers and opinions may have been lost in the typical turbulence of meetings where big boys interact.

A *STRUCTURED CHALLENGE* REQUIRES A SIMILAR ORGANIZATIONAL APPROACH TO A WARGAME

Like a wargame, structured challenges should have a principal, that is, a line manager for whom the outcome of the structured challenge acts as an input to their decision-making. As with the application of many tools, executing a structured challenge only has a merit when this principal is indeed prepared to act upon the outcome of the challenge and has the authority to do so.

For the strategy department, the preparations thus focus on this principal. Together with the line manager, the setup and the process choices must have been agreed upon before starting.

The strategy department should make sure that management feels comfortable with all the individual participants to a possible structured challenge initiative. A structured challenge loses most of its values in a low-trust, political environment. In the absence of a suitable 'political' environment, neither propose nor run a structured challenge.

A SUB-TOOL LIKE DEVIL'S ADVOCACY IS PREFERABLY USED BILATERALLY

Within a structured challenge, three sub-tools may be distinguished (Bruce, 2008):

- What if?
- Devil's advocacy.
- High-impact/low-probability analysis.

The latter sub-tool relates to improbable events with a high impact that in practice are less improbable than they intuitively feel to be. These have been popularized as the Black Swans of Extremistan (Taleb, 2007). Dreaming up high-impact/low-probability events could benefit from a tool like brainstorming. Once some high-impact/low-probability events have been listed, risk mitigating strategies may be defined using the structured challenge of the "What If?" type.

Devil's advocacy in strategy design is also a form of structured challenge, but it is politically often difficult to use. As a strategy department, taking the role of devil's advocate toward an internal 'in-company' line manager is not easy. This is especially true when the discussion centres around the company's own management decisions.

A devil's advocate may ask a question like: "So you really think that, with the resources you've asked for, you can achieve a 5% increase in market share?" Even when this may rationally be a fair and relevant challenge, it may not be conducive to the strategist's popularity, impact or credibility. The latter especially matters when the strategist does not have a line management track record of success – as they have mainly or only worked in staff and/or consultancy roles.

Like it or not, but the response from an angered line manager may all too often be defensive, with them thinking, if not saying,: "Who exactly do you think you are to ask this?"

Prior to devil's advocacy being applied successfully, a relation of deep trust between the 'devil's advocate' strategist and the line manager needs to have been developed. Even then, this role is probably best played in bilateral and discrete setting.

Table 9.2 describes how to apply structure challenge generically in a strategy setting.

DIMENSIONS	DESCRIPTION
What use does this tool have?	Structured challenge is a way to operationalise xenocentrism. The word 'structured' in structured challenge refers to the fact that, by using the questioning approach, the strategic question is reviewed from all imaginable perspectives. Structured challenge, like a wargame, aims to make a strategy department and the related business executives team sweat in mental training rather than to have both bleed in business battle.
When to apply this tool? & Who to involve when applying this tool?	Structured challenge assists by preparing for all sorts of relevant external environment eventualities prior to executing a strategic move, e.g., an acquisition. A structured challenge exercise usually requires a correct and complete (new) business environment data set. The exercise helps turning data into actionable market intelligence. Structured challenge only has value when the output of the thinking process is translated into actions. Even when structured challenge requires management commitment to act upon the outcome to ensure it is time well spent, that does not mean that it may only proceed on a demand-driven basis, i.e., with a reactive attitude from the strategy department. A strategy department may of course proactively and internally do a "what if?" analysis to think through potential changes in the firm's business environment. In such cases, prior to starting, it is recommended to consider how the results of such analyses will be made actionable. It is essential to avoid not-invented-here reflexes from those who are authorized to *do* something with the outputs. Internal proactive "what if?" analysis may, for example, be great input to corporate risk (and opportunity!) assessments.

TABLE 9.2 ▶ ▶ ▶ **APPLICATION OF STRUCTURED CHALLENGE**

PRE-MORTEM ANALYSIS

Pre-mortem analysis may have a role both in strategy design and in strategy execution. The elegance of pre-mortem analysis is that, when properly applied, it generates possible logical *pathways* to future situations that are otherwise hard to imagine (Heuer, 1999c). It changes the focus from *whether* something might happen – which may become a yes/no discussion – to *how* it might happen. The latter discussion has much more potential to generate new insights.

PREDICTING PATHWAYS TO BANKRUPTCY OF A CUSTOMER – AND WHAT TO DO ABOUT IT

The idea in a pre-mortem analysis is to first imagine a possible future state e.g., two years from now. For example, company XYZ has gone bankrupt even when its financial health today looks fine. Assume company XYZ to be one of our company's major customers today. For a pre-mortem analysis to be effective and worthwhile, the future state should preferably have a low probability and a high impact.

The future state now is a given: XYZ does not pay its invoices to anyone anymore. The question now in a pre-mortem analysis is: "How could this have happened?" If XYZ is in the food business, a path to bankruptcy may have been that XYZ suddenly lost all the consumer trust in its brand due to a food poisoning scandal, leading to some consumers dying in the aftermath. If XYZ is a passenger airline, a plane crash related to blatant negligence in maintenance or safety may have been a cause.

The question sequence that subsequently develops for company XYZ could look like this:

- How could this food scandal at food company XYZ happen? It happened because a single disgruntled employee intentionally left essential nutrients out of the recipe of a key product.
- Why was this employee disgruntled?
- How could quality control measures have been so sloppy that a single employee could have so much impact?
- What does this tell about the vulnerabilities of company XYZ?

The next phase may then be to identify probabilities to the pre-mortem chain of events and/or to gather insights for your own company that may invite to be acted upon. In the latter case, a question like the following may become relevant:

Could our company think of ways to mitigate the risks for company XYZ by, for example, offering an essential nutrient pre-mix that makes company XYZ's operating procedures less vulnerable?

Unlikely events, such as the bankruptcy of a financially healthy company like XYZ, are suddenly less implausible than they seem: there are more black swans than one can see at night (Taleb, 2007).

Especially prior to committing to a major investment or a major acquisition, management may benefit from a pre-mortem analysis. For a cheerful note, assume in the pre-mortem the investment has gone up in smoke.

Use the analysis to see how solid the assumptions and their probabilities in the business case really are. Most of all, the exercise may assist in spotting a few black swans that otherwise would have remained in hiding. Knowing where these swans are and how they look assists management in taking better-informed decisions.

A brainstorming session may identify a list of, for example., five high-impact/low-probability risks to a long-term strategy or a major investment to be executed.

Also, for this tool, it is critical that the decision-makers have to buy into acting upon the outcome of a pre-mortem analysis, before the analysis should be made. For the strategy department, it is critical to define responsibilities upfront. The strategy department may take the responsibility for defining the five high-impact/low-probability risks, for facilitating the process of the analysis and for reporting the output. The decision-makers take the responsibility to consider acting upon the outputs.

Table 9.3 summarizes the application of the pre-mortem analysis tool.

DIMENSIONS	DESCRIPTION
What use does this tool have?	Pre-mortem analysis is a tool to identify pathways to self-defined high-impact, low-probability events. In identifying such pathways, the analysis may also offer early warning indicators of pathways to misery that may unravel.
When to apply this tool?	Preferably the tool is used prior to deciding to commit to major investments, to spot black swans in hiding.
Who to involve when applying this tool?	The most important people to involve are the decision-makers who are considering the investment. For this tool to be useful, solid commitment to the tool and its outputs is required of the decision-makers to ensure they act upon the outputs. In the absence thereof, the tool's application may lead to nice-to-know results. Such results are even more frustrating when the investment has not delivered the anticipated returns – and the pathway to why this happened had correctly been identified but ignored.

TABLE 9.3 ▶ ▶ **APPLICATION OF PRE-MORTEM ANALYSIS AS A TOOL**

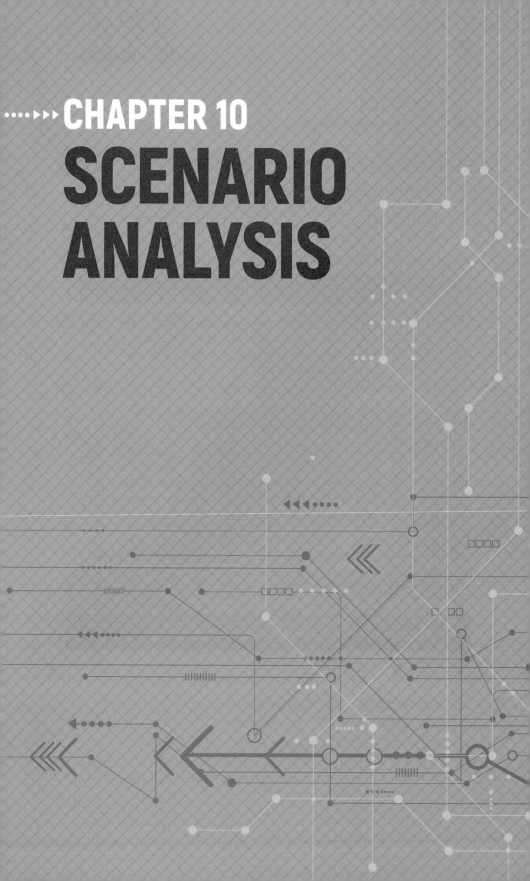

······▶▶▶ **CHAPTER 10**
SCENARIO ANALYSIS

>>>> 10.1 INTRODUCTION

Scenario analysis (also referred to as 'scenario planning') is a complex strategy and/or planning tool. Scenario analysis involves so many steps and may become so complex that dedicated volumes have been written about applying it in a business context. A good introduction to scenarios is Van der Heijden's book *Scenarios – The Art of Strategic Conversation* (Heijden, 1997a). Van der Heijden's work has inspired this section. The reason for briefly covering scenario analysis is that this tool is commonly used in strategy design, even when it is not too often a full scenario analysis. More often, rather modest exercises in terms of time and effort take place in strategy work, where only bits and pieces of real full-blown scenario analysis methodologies are being used.

Strategy departments sometimes are tasked to contribute to or even manage scenario analysis exercises. This section will introduce scenario analysis in sufficient depth to allow the reader to determine when, why and how to use the tool. When deciding, however, to embark on a detailed scenario analysis for a business, more specific handbooks such as Van der Heijden's work may well be helpful to complement this introduction.

ROYAL DUTCH SHELL HAS PIONEERED THE USE OF SCENARIOS IN BUSINESS

Scenario analysis exercises find their origin in wargames (see *Chapter 5*) (Heijden, 1997b). In the early 1970s, Royal Dutch Shell introduced scenario-based planning into the oil industry. Shell's choice to develop scenario analysis capabilities resulted from anxiety in its planning department. In Shell's planning, it had already in the late 1960s been observed that the accuracy of its forecasts in most cases gradually improved, but in some cases had deteriorated alarmingly (Wack, 1985).

Shell decided that, rather than hire even more forecasters who would have to develop even more sophisticated single forecasts, it would explore a new methodology: scenario analysis. With scenario analysis, Shell no longer worked with a single most likely forecast, but with multiple possible futures. Shell's planners aimed to prepare the behemoth oil company for each of these possible futures. The oil industry faces long lead times between investment decision and cash flow from capital allocated to such investment. The industry's high capital intensity contributed to the planner's anxiety. When forecasts were wrong in the oil industry, the implications were grave. Scenario analysis indeed worked out well for Shell (a bit tongue in cheek, but otherwise we would probably never have heard about it).

As a result, Shell developed superior foresight after having properly prepared for possible futures based on scenario analysis. This allowed Shell in the 1970s and early 1980s to significantly outperform its industry. This proven track record of success and the successful marketing thereof in business literature has strongly contributed to the interest in and application of scenario analysis in business (Wack, 1985).

Like wargaming, scenario analysis is a tool, not an aim in itself. Scenario analysis is a form of cognitive augmentation, not cognitive replacement. In an elegant way, it is framed as the 'art of strategic conversation' (Heijden, 1997a). Prior to embarking on the tool as such, we need to discuss the language of that conversation.

'SCENARIO' IS A TERM THAT IS OFTEN INCORRECTLY AND CONFUSINGLY USED

In business, the word 'scenario' is so loosely used that it has a merit to define what in this chapter is meant by a scenario and by scenario analysis. Business literature is not helpful here, as the word scenario is not very well defined (Heijden, 1997c). A scenario is defined here as:

A range of possible future developments and outcomes in the business environment that are beyond the firm's control.

Scenario analysis is the methodology to deliver a set of different individual scenarios that allow for the analysis of their implications of these possible futures on our firm. Scenarios are to guide your firm's decision-making today in anticipation for a fundamentally unknowable future.

10.2 THE MECHANICS OF SCENARIO ANALYSIS

How scenario analysis works is shown in *Diagram 10.1*. The process starts at the left side of the diagram. First agreement is needed on generic inputs to the analysis that will be constant in any scenario. Demographics form a category of data that tends to develop almost independently of any other factor in an economy or society. This allows demographics to be taken as a constant, no matter what external future (or scenario) will emerge. Demographics thus become a fixed, external input.

Subsequently, scenarios or possible external futures are defined by defining a set of external independent input parameters. These parameters are preferably orthogonal. They vary for each scenario. Typical orthogonal input parameters include global economic growth (high/low), trade liberalization (high/low import duties), political stability (high/low), interest rates (high/low), etc. The interaction of these external inputs together leads to the possible distinctly different external futures in the end year of the scenario analysis, e.g., 10 or 15 years from now. By choosing four distinct sets of input parameters, four possible futures, called scenarios, emerge.

As a third step, internal company choices have to be defined. Those are the inputs into the scenarios. The generic and the specific external inputs determine how the world looks 10 or 15 years from now. The choices made for the company now determine how – in the defined scenario world 10 or 15 years later – the company will fare. Inputs now may be investments that are made or not made, acquisitions that are made or not made, etc. Outputs, one for each distinct scenario, may be cash flows, balance sheets, market shares or profits, to name just a few typical output parameters.

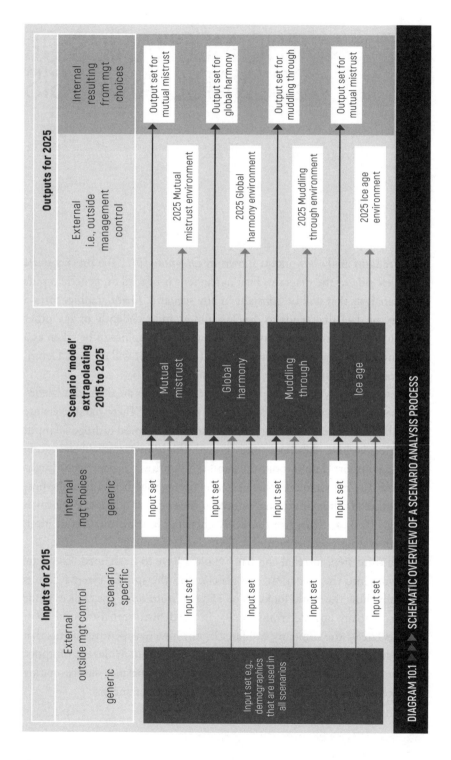

DIAGRAM 10.1 ▶ ▶ ▶ SCHEMATIC OVERVIEW OF A SCENARIO ANALYSIS PROCESS

One of the valuable outputs of scenario analysis is that upon 'stress testing' the various business choices for various possible futures (called scenarios), some choices will prove to come out as positive for the company at stake, no matter which future emerges. These are 'no regret' moves: executing those choices will most likely benefit the company, no matter what the future will look like. Some other choices may only be beneficial to the company when a particular future indeed emerges. The possibility to assess which of today's choice will lead to what outcome in what future indeed is a great input to a strategic conversation of a senior management team.

 10.3

WHEN AND WHY TO PLAN A SCENARIO ANALYSIS

SCENARIO ANALYSIS IS CARRIED OUT IN FUNDAMENTALLY UNPREDICTABLE ENVIRONMENTS

Multiple occasions are mentioned when a scenario analysis may be the most appropriate tool to help a business design or execute its strategies. Two occasions seem to stand out:

- In challenging, uncertain market conditions, such as Shell faced in the late 1960s and early 1970s. In such fundamentally unpredictable, volatile business environments, scenario analysis is a tool to prepare for the unpredictable that, in a scenario, may be imaginable. In such environments, linear planning with a single point prediction is and has proven to be irresponsible.
- Scenario analysis may also be appropriate when trends affecting an industry exceed an industry's typical planning/time horizon, with the impact of the trends as yet being impossible to predict.

Scenario analysis may well be positioned in a concurrent process with a company updating its strategy. As I indicated above, a scenario analysis feeds multiple possible futures into the strategic dialogue, sketching imaginable futures that may allow stress testing various strategic choices.

SCENARIO ANALYSIS AIMS TO DELIVER ROBUST DECISIONS PRE-EMPTING MULTIPLE FUTURES

The fundamental reason to apply scenario analysis lies in acknowledging that business volatility is unpredictable and by implication that any single-point forecasting is to be wrong (Heijden, 1997d). In response, smart business leaders prepare their companies for multiple, independent, different yet equally plausible futures. Imagining these different futures allows coming up with decisions that are stress tested against what may happen within our imagination.

Upon reviewing the outcome of decisions, it will become clear that some decisions may not deliver value when one scenario materializes, but they strongly build a firm's competitive advantage when another scenario materializes. Thus, when comparing the outcome of decisions in different scenarios, implicitly the sensitivity of the outcome of decisions to the resulting firm-specific scenario output parameters emerge (Heijden, 1997e).

Cash flow generation could be such a firm-specific scenario output parameter. This output parameter may, for a firm taking certain decisions, for example, show to depend mainly on the growth rate of a particular product market combination within a firm's portfolio. This informs management going forward to monitor that growth rate with great care. When that growth rate disappoints, an unfavorable scenario may emerge. In such an unfavorable scenario, contemplated or even committed investments will yield unsatisfactory returns. In contrast, when that growth rate exceeds values even the most positive scenario, the firm is likely to be on the right track for a great performance.

Based on such sensitivity insights, management can usefully hold strategic conversations, weighing choices and their upsides and risks. In addition, it allows management to set up an early warning system – involving either a market intelligence or strategy function – defining cues that may point at certain scenarios ready to emerge. Based on market intelligence reporting the observation of particular cues, management may in advance define decisions, which will conditionally be taken, depending on cues being observed. In a military metaphor, this could be framed as 'rules of engagement'. When the cue is positively identified, however, the gun is ready to fire. Scenario analysis thus contributes to shorter management response times to business environment change (Heijden, 1997f).

Scenario analysis may serve other purposes than the one discussed above. In the intermezzo, I discuss some other possible purposes of scenario analysis.

INTERMEZZO: BUSINESS CONTEXTS WHERE SCENARIO ANALYSIS MAY ADD VALUE

The fundamental reason to apply scenario analysis lies in acknowledging that business volatility is unpredictable and by implication that any single-point forecasting will be wrong. Scenario analysis may, however, also serve other business purposes, some of which are described below.

Challenging conventional wisdom

The market intelligence and/or a strategy or planning department may at times believe a business faces a paradigm shift in its 'rules of the game' (Roxburgh, 2009). An example of such a shift may be the change of buying behaviour of customers from high-street retail to e-shops. So far, however, management does neither seem to see nor to act on the first whispers of this change. Introducing a scenario analysis allows changing the existing mental models of decision-makers by, in this example, introducing a scenario where a limited number of years from now, 90% of global shopping in this category is predicted to flow via e-shops (Heijden, 1997g). In doing so, a company's business environment is reframed, which may lead to management vividly experiencing the change in the scenario exercise, turn the corner and adapt their choices to pre-empt the possible future and be successful in it. Scenario analysis in this approach is an elegant tool in stimulating organizational learning (Heijden, 1997h).

Identifying inevitable futures before somebody else does

In a volatile market, management may overreact by thinking that nothing can be predicted, so only short-term focused decisions make sense. This may not be fully true. Scenario analysis is a tool that allows discovery of what could be defined as 'inevitable futures' (Roxburgh, 2009). Inevitable futures may both emerge in the market conditions a company faces in any scenario at the end of the planning horizon, as well as in some company-specific outputs (like free cash flow generation). The more creative and imaginative the different scenarios that have been used, the more convincing when in all scenarios certain outputs are predicted. As a result of a scenario analysis, management will not only be confirmed in their knowledge that some volatility-related outputs are fundamentally unpredictable, but also that some other things do appear to be predictable. The latter insight, which is uniquely derived from scenario analysis, may be remarkably powerful in guiding management decisions.

Reducing complexity

Markets may not only be perceived as too volatile to predict, but also as too complex. The rigidity of scenario analysis may support managers identifying non-fashionable and weak signals in the business environment timely and yet without overwhelming the managers with complexity (Geus, 2002).

Combatting groupthink

In cohesive management teams, the outside voice and opinion may over time have become muted, leading to a tunnel vision on a firm's own position and its environment. Scenario analysis as tool may bring in the outside voice – provided management approves of imagining the unpredictable (Heijden, 1997h). Management in groupthink must first see a call for change, prior to their starting to act upon change. Scenario analysis as a tool may help as a change agent, but its value should not be overestimated versus a stuck-in-the-mud opinioned team.

Leading the world's view on potential multiple futures of your industry

The output of a scenario analysis – especially one with a renowned third-party expert input – may be successfully used to communicate to external stakeholders. In doing so, a firm may gently and profitably shape a business world by making their desired future a bit more inevitable. An example of this use of scenario analysis is what Finnish ship engine builder Wärtsilä did in 2014 (Wärtsilä, 2014). As Shell faced volatile oil markets and yet approached these markets using scenario analysis, ship engine builders also face volatile markets. The similarities between shipping and oil are remarkable. In both cases, capital investments are large and once done are committed for decades. Also, in both cases, the return on investment depends on the global economic growth and, in the case of shipping, in particular on trade across the globe. Wärtsilä in response developed four scenarios on the world of shipping toward 2030, utilizing inputs from multiple external stakeholders. The market condition outcomes at the end of the scenario time horizon were made available to a broad audience. In a sort of crowdsourcing way, the scenarios were enriched further. The outcome of this process almost unintentionally developed in the world's view on the possible futures of shipping. In instigating and gently leading this process, Wärtsilä opened multiple doors to itself and established itself as thought leader in shipping; not a bad position for a ship engine builder to be in!

10.4 ANTECEDENT SUCCESS FACTORS

Scenario analysis is a great tool, but it only works under certain favourable organizational conditions. For scenario analysis to deliver value to a firm, these conditions need to be met. In this section, we frame these conditions as antecedent success factors. When not meeting most of these factors, scenario analysis may not lead to desired results or worse, will prove to have been a waste of resources.

The first factor is **starting** with a **minimum organizational capability level** of the firm where the tool is to be applied (Heijden, 1997i). Embedding a scenario analysis in a firm is not a plug-and-play activity. A minimum sophistication level of management is required to grasp the concept of scenario analysis. A management that lacks this level and also lacks the eagerness to lift itself to this level is unlikely to provide the right context for a successful application of scenario analysis.

An additional factor is that management should **have time to spare** to think beyond tomorrow's cash flow. A management team that faces a crisis is not in the right mood. No matter whether such a crisis is seemingly permanent – as some teams sometimes seem to radiate – or whether it is temporary, timing is everything.

Management should also **feel the need to change** from single-point planning to considering multiple futures. When management does not see the flaws in its current poor forecasting capabilities, scenario analysis is an answer to a question that is not being asked. A bit of management anxiety is a must have, prior to starting scenario analysis. In short: uncertainty, but not panic, is a good breeding ground for rationality. Genuine management uncertainty favors rational analyses like scenario analysis to be fruitfully applied.

Another factor that matters is management's **positive attitude to learning**. Scenario analysis often works out to be scenario learning. Sometimes management teams are so dysfunctional that, in the team, shared learning is impossible. Power-related dynamics may, for example, prohibit the team members to implicitly admit that there is a need to learn. For scenario analysis to be successful, an implicit presupposition is that a team wants to learn. Through learning, the team must have a desire to be enlightened with insights that none of them already has. When the team doesn't show the ownership for the learning, a good facilitator (e.g., the strategy department) cannot compensate for this. Schoemaker puts it nicely when he says that the top management has to do the 'heavy lifting' of challenging an industry's or firm's current paradigms (Schoemaker, 2009). In the absence of a genuinely felt management need to revisit their industry paradigms through scenario analysis, chances are modest that management will indeed act upon a scenario analysis' outputs.

Without pretending to present an exhaustive overview of antecedent success factors, a final factor that matters is, of course, the **professionalism of the facilitator** of the scenario analysis. The first choice to make is whether the facilitator is an in-house team member or an outside party. In Royal Dutch Shell, an in-house team was used. Given the size and resources of Shell, the capability to facilitate scenario analysis in-house could well be developed. At a privileged company like Shell, several intellectual and highly competent staff could each gradually clock more than 10,000 hours of working experience, developing themselves into world-class experts (Gladwell, 2009d). Only truly large companies will both have the size, the internal need and the luxury of the resources to develop such capabilities in-house. When outsourcing scenario analysis, the one-off, out-of-pocket cost will increase versus running an analysis in-house. This may raise the barrier for a management choosing to apply this tool. In addition, what is worse, the learnings that, in particular, the facilitation team accumulates are not or at least not fully retained within the organization when outsiders do the analysis.

Another dimension of professionalism of a facilitator is their ability to be original and bright in their thinking (Heijden, 1997j). Futures may not be predictable, but when they are not even imaginable, even a business operating a scenario analysis may still be caught off-guard by an unimagined future.

Scenarios **need** to be built on as **solid** and **undisputed** a **fact-base** as it gets. Meeting this antecedent success factor often but not only requires having a good market intelligence department involvement. Given that scenarios often look one or two decades ahead, having facts that also go back a long time may add both to credibility and to new insights. Statistics such as interest rates for some countries go back more than 300 years (Roxburgh, 2009); some other statistics go back more than 800 years (Reinhart, 2009). Viewing such truly long-term movements of scenario inputs may assist in not limiting the imagination to too narrow an actuality range. After five days of sunshine, imagining a sixth day of sunshine is all too human. Thinking back at the rains that flooded the nation a month earlier is not.

For scenario analysis to become successful, **resources** need to be sufficiently available. Shell refers to scenario analyses having taken two full years to complete – not to mention the total resources spent in those two years. Deciding to embark as a business on a scenario analysis exercise implicitly requires a commitment of serious resources.

DESIGN PRINCIPLES FOR A SCENARIO ANALYSIS EXERCISE

Scenario analysis works best when a number of design principles are incorporated in the analysis. Without pretending that this list is exhaustive, the following principles seem to apply to any scenario analysis exercise.

Developing **four scenarios** is recommended. When using one scenario, we essentially make a single-point prediction, which scenario analysis was set up to prevent. When using two scenarios, we most likely underestimate how varied the future may look. In the case of three or even five scenarios. the disadvantage is that management tends to 'take the middle one', again essentially falling back on the trusted comfort-zone habit of working with a single-point prediction. Having more than four scenarios tends to complicate the strategic conversation the management participants are to have on the basis of the scenarios' outputs. When having, for example, six scenarios, the inputs to the different scenarios may more easily be mixed up and the resulting confusion may impede clarity. In conclusion: having four scenarios is usually best.

All scenarios should be **equally plausible** (Heijden, 1997k). A basic tenet of scenario analysis is that each scenario is perceived by the management team that bases its strategic conversation on it to be equally plausible. When management sees one scenario as rosy and likely, it is more apt to ignore a 'doomsday' scenario, which although technically equally likely, is so much less fun to experience when that future materializes. Scenario design requires preventing scenarios seeming like 'bad' versus 'good'. Scenarios are possible futures, exclusively determined by factors that are outside management's control. In preparing a company for these possible futures, it is utterly irrelevant whether management 'likes' one possible future more than another – and in response therefore prepares better for the more likable possible future. A scenario analysis facilitator should challenge management when, during an analysis, that management is skewed to only prepare for a scenario they all like, but of which the liklihood of occurrence is only 25% (assuming four different scenarios are reviewed).

Management should **recognize** themselves in the outcomes of the scenarios. When none of the scenarios occur, no matter how well crafted, it's perceived to be likely that management may start to doubt the usefulness of applying the tool altogether. One way to prevent this is to have one base-case scenario. This scenario is essentially a forward projection of trends and developments management recognizes. Recognizing that uncertainty is fundamental, a management team's effectiveness improves when there is at least one scenario for which they already today feel well equipped to handle. As was said above: rational analysis thrives in uncertainty, but not in panic. Allow a management team enough comfort zone areas to ensure their collective thinking remains rational.

ATTRIBUTES OF A GOOD INDIVIDUAL SCENARIO

Individual scenarios within a scenario analysis need to have several attributes to make them useful. A good scenario is:

- Imaginative
- Relevant
- Actionable
- Original
- Internally consistent
- Smartly named
- Narrating

Below the individual attributes are discussed in a bit more detail.

IMAGINATIVE

The future in volatile industries may be unpredictable. That fact, however, does not justify management – or the scenario preparation team they assign – to fail to *imagine* relevant and plausible futures. Scenarios should be chosen that delicately balance between too much of an unimaginative forward projection and too outlandish as to be implausible (Heijden, 1997f). The former and the latter are both useless. The former, because it fails to identify discontinuities that single-point forward projection will not plan for and the latter, because they implicitly or explicitly will be rejected by management as too bizarre to plan for. Finding the right balance is the specialist's work. Scenario writing may well be more complex than it may look.

RELEVANT

Scenario analysis is only useful when it addresses real and actual top management concerns. In the absence of perceived uncertainty, scenario analysis is an answer to a question that either was not perceived to be relevant or that never featured in the minds of management (Geus, 2002) (Heijden, 1997j) (Heijden, 1997k). To ensure the relevancy of scenarios, management should be able to identify themselves both with the possible overall futures, but also with the implications thereof for the business they are responsible for. Too abstract or disconnected futures portrayed in glossy but vague general scenarios may be perceived as at best nice-to-know, but may not trigger action to prepare the firm for those futures.

A potential approach to accomplish management identification with both the general market conditions and the specific implications for their own industry is to split the narrative of the scenario in two parts. The first part narrates about society/the world/the market in general terms. The second part of the narrative should concern with the business line the company is active in. A 'bridging sentence' may connect the two:

> In the scenario, 'mutual mistrust' global trade flows may decline. Globalization will falter, protectionism will return. Import barriers that had evaporated over decades will be lifted again. *In this global business environment,* cross-trade-block trade in our industry will also decline. Exports across continents will in 2025 be half when taking 2015 as base year.

ACTIONABLE

The language of scenarios is the future. Scenarios describe possible futures for the relevant business environment of a firm. Scenarios in business, however, should be so concrete and tangible that they invite management to take actions now to pre-empt being surprised in those possible futures (Heijden, 1997f).

ORIGINAL

Scenarios must be sufficiently imaginative to provide a new perspective on the issues of management (Heijden, 1997f).

INTERNALLY CONSISTENT

Even when not mentioned as first attribute, this attribute may well be the most relevant. Summarized, the requirement of internal consistency means (Heijden, 1997k):

Events within a scenario must be related through cause/effect lines of argument, which cannot be flawed.

SMARTLY NAMED

Scenarios should have telling and memorable names. The name should efficiently and aptly trigger the right image of the future the scenario is describing in its narrative (Heijden, 1997i). The names used in *Diagram 10.1* such as Ice Age and Muddling Through meet the requirement that they summarize the narrative a scenario could tell.

NARRATING

Storytelling is among the most persuasive and memorable forms of communication. Human brains are simply well equipped to think in stories. A good scenario banks on the human ability to work with and remember stories.

Stories allow multiple data to be communicated in a correlated form that allows their logic of connection to be remembered. The use of stories is no luxury. Scenario analysis often is an instrument of change management. Change in scenario analysis requires management to be prepared to review and possibly leave their current comfort zone of accepted wisdom. You'd better have a good story to get them to do so (Schoemaker, 2009).

In the case of the scenario Mutual Mistrust, the narrative presented above under the attribute 'relevant' could be made more vivid by adding a character with whom people can identify, turning an abstract into a personal story. Journalists love to pick a peculiar and particular *personal* case to illustrate a larger phenomenon through a story. Wherever casuistic, personal stories are being told, persuasiveness and impact goes up.

 10.7

THE FLOW OF A SCENARIO ANALYSIS EXERCISE

In spite of the air of sophistication that may sometimes surround scenario analysis as a tool, applying the tool in an organizational context is straightforward. A common project flow is described below. By using the word 'project', we already implicitly acknowledge that a scenario analysis has a beginning, a deliverable and thus an end. Scenario analysis is and should not be a process that lingers on and on, without delivering tangible deliverables that a management acts upon.

The first step in a scenario analysis is to define the **key questions to be resolved** for management. Examples of such questions may be: Should we develop a market position in Latin America? Or should we invest in a world-class e-commerce capability? Or should we set up production plants for our company's most profitable product range in every major global customs union?

The question determines whether scenario analysis is the right tool, not the other way around. Getting the answer is way more important than, out of love for a tool, looking for a fitting question.

Of the above three questions on geo-expansion, capability building and supply chain set-up, the third question seems so strongly dependent on independent socio-economic-political external factors that it at first looks more suitable to be tackled with scenario analysis than the second question, where the only externally relevant factor at first sight seems to be the possible change of consumer and/or customer/channel buying behaviour. When Michael Dell revolutionized the computer industry by introducing a fundamentally new e-ordering business model, it is doubtful whether that was the outcome of a scenario analysis.

Once a management team or its staff has neutrally checked and confirmed that scenario analysis is indeed the most suitable tool to answer the question that a management team wants to get answered, a formal management decision is needed to start a scenario analysis project.

As in any project, a scenario analysis project requires a **project team** to be established, a budget, a well-defined brief and scope, well-defined deliverables, a time schedule and a risk assessment.

The first step of the scenario analysis itself is the **definition of the possible futures** or scenarios themselves. Scenarios emerge as the output of sets of input data and of the assumptions on the correlation between these data.

An example of a causal set of events that could make up a scenario is described here as an illustration. The example aims to show how scenarios may be developed. The example may be worked out qualitatively, recognizing correlations between factors, but without quantifying these relations. Scenarios may also be worked out quantitatively.

The latter is way more time-intensive, but may for some decisions be needed. When choosing a quantitative approach, ensure well-experienced staff are involved to ensure the complexity remains manageable.

Consider the narrative below as a possible line of thinking in a scenario:

In emerging markets, increasing inflation, especially of food products, may easily trigger social unrest. Social unrest may trigger violence. Violence may trigger political instability. Political instability is threatening and thus unwelcome to any government. So in response to rising world market bulk food prices (e.g., whole milk powder or rice), the government of a particular emerging market nation-state announces formal price ceilings for food products. Doing so artificially pushes down inflation. This example may be followed by other emerging market nations. This whole set of events is external and virtually outside an individual company's control. When a scenario – as a possible future – predicts a future of high inflation in emerging markets, the impact thereof on the profit pool of a food industry operating in such markets may be massive, as the food companies cannot compensate the rising global raw material cost by lifting their in-market prices, due to the government price ceiling.

To the above scenario, key input data would, for example, be (list not exhaustive):

- World population growth, granular by country
- World food production growth

- Economic growth, granular by relevant country
- Trade balance, granular by individual relevant country

Interim outputs, granular by individual country, could be currency exchange rates and inflation rates. The inflation rates thus correlate with political stability, government anti-inflation policies – which could also include import duties on goods or other measures – and possibly with the government pushing agricultural development projects to drive food self-sufficiency. The long-term market attractiveness for an international consumer food producer of different countries *assuming ceteris paribus business choices* could thus be mapped for any scenario, e.g., high economic growth, low economic growth, high inflation, low inflation and any imaginable useful combination of other external input parameters.

The trick in scenario design is to **identify original thinkers** inside and, where needed, outside a firm to dream up the possible futures which, on the one hand, must be sufficiently original, and on the other be sufficiently feasible to remain credible.

Brainstorming and workshops may be good tools to define the individual scenarios. Moreover, using such co-creation work forms may, in a later stage, help in building stakeholder and decision-maker commitment to using the output of the scenario analysis.

Once the possible futures have crystallized out as scenarios, the next step is to **define what (combinations of) business choices to evaluate** in the analysis. This is a task where the decision-makers need to sign off in advance, even when the scenario analysis project team prepares the menu of choices. The only way to get management to use the output of a scenario analysis is to ensure they see the scenarios themselves and the business choices as credible and relevant.

The output of a scenario analysis is the input to the **management's strategic conversation**. The result of such conversation should be a (renewed) corporate or business strategy that is value-creating and resilient in two, maximum three of the four scenarios. In parallel, a contingency plan should be developed should scenario four emerge, where the business strategy likely is not going to create value.

The *real* future as it will over time unfold will most likely be a mix of all the *possible* futures, or, as we now know them, scenarios. When, as management, having used sufficiently imaginative scenarios, the real future may differ in intensity from the possible futures in the scenarios, but the real future should not have too many surprises when it unfolds. Scenario analysis also in this respect resembles wargaming. It forces a management to sweat in training, to be well-prepared for the real battle in the real future. Moreover, scenario analysis enables management to identify no-regret moves that should be executed right away.

So, as output of a scenario analysis, a management team selects actions to execute after having conversed about possible futures. In parallel, this management team should also set up or fine-tune its **early warning system** to define, measure, report and act upon cues that point to some scenario being more likely to emerge than another as *the real future*. Even when usually a market intelligence department will not be leading a scenario analysis project, the set-up of the early warning system obviously is and should be an exclusive market intelligence department's responsibility.

≫≫ 10.8 COMMON PITFALLS IN SCENARIO ANALYSIS

A scenario analysis is a complex exercise, which does not automatically yield useful results. Below three common pitfalls in scenario analysis are described as examples (Roxburgh, 2009). This list is, unfortunately, not exhaustive.

Analysis paralysis is one pitfall. Scenarios as possible futures may describe a lot of uncertainties that a business may face. A management team facing too many uncertainties may, instead of moving into an action-oriented mode, as a result now themselves feel uncertain what to do next. Moreover, discussing the possible futures in a strategic conversation may not lead to a consensus-view by the team on what next steps to take. Both in the case of overwhelming uncertainty and in the case of differences of opinion, what is easier than to ask for more research and analysis? In doing so, the team postpones the hour of truth of having to make choices about *what* but, most of all, about *what not* to do. The subsequently executed meticulous analysis rarely solves the root cause of the management's problem. It does have merit though. It at least forces the management team to face the truth that either they are having different opinions, which seem hard to resolve or that they just don't dare (yet) to take the measures that the situation requires. For a strategy or market intelligence department, doing the extra analysis work is inevitable, but not always rewarding. So be it. The world, even in the world's best companies to work for, cannot always be fair.

Foggy communication is another pitfall. Scenarios are possible futures against which to test today's management choices. Once choices have been made, these need to be communicated firmly and persuasively. The latter also requires communicating what will *not* be done. A politician, as a rule, may wish to keep all their options open, but a leader has to make choices.

When a company's leadership has more than its fair share of politicians, communication of the choices may become foggy, if only because the leadership may not wish to be pinned down on having or not having made choices all too clearly. Unclear communication may obviously reduce the effectiveness of a strategy's execution and by implication the value of a scenario analysis that underpinned it. In other words, when a management team doesn't want to make firm choices, consider carefully whether this management team should spend time and effort on a scenario analysis in the first place.

Unimaginative scenarios form another pitfall. When a scenario analysis team has not been able to locate enough original thinkers, the real future a company will be facing will still look different from any scenario that has been imagined. In this case, having gone through a scenario analysis gives a management team a false sense of certainty.

This sense of certainty, even when false, may make them more decisive than they otherwise may have been. This is generally a good thing. The question remains whether the team took the right decisions in the light of how the *real* future will unfold.

Overlooking tactical challenges is the final pitfall discussed here. A scenario analysis, with an as-per-the-book long-time horizon, will not likely reveal a competitor planning a price war the next quarter. Neither will it discover a competitor planning a heavy promotion campaign later this year or predict an intensification of a competitor's innovation activity planned for next year (Alvarez, 2007). Scenarios focus on long-term uncertainties and rarely serve in solving tactical problems. A management team that is too busy with handling tactical issues should not embark on a scenario analysis.

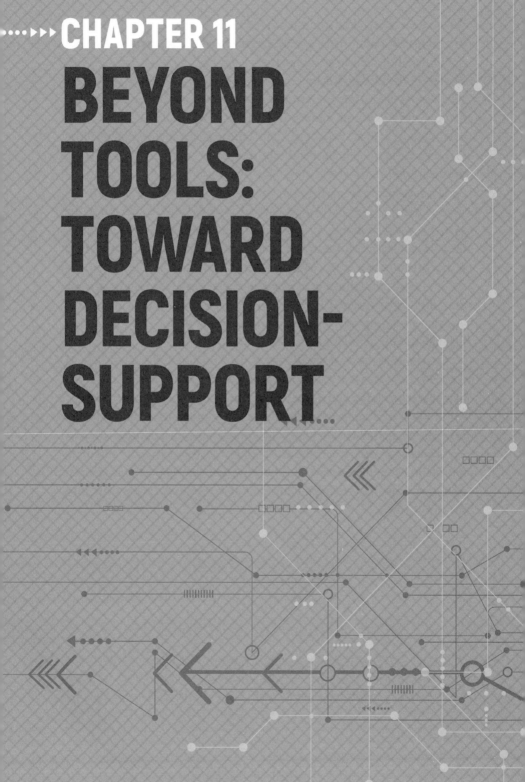

CHAPTER 11

BEYOND TOOLS: TOWARD DECISION-SUPPORT...

11.1 INTRODUCTION

In the introduction of *Chapter 1*, I emphasized that tools are the means to an end. Now that we have discussed the various strategic analysis tools, I would like to return to where we started: by recognizing that tools are instruments of decision-support.

In business strategy-making, it is common to distinguish three different activities during each of which decisions are made and by implication decision-support may be needed:

- Design
- Execution
- Monitoring

These activities link back to the common plan-do-check-act loop. First we plan a strategy in the design phase, next we execute the plans we made and subsequently we monitor whether our actions proceed as per the plan. This allows us to identify whether adaptions of the strategic design and/or execution may be needed.

Common outputs of the strategy **design** phase in business are either:

- An overall strategic plan for a business, including all business disciplines.
- A functional plan, e.g., a supply chain strategy or a marketing strategy.
- A business development plan, e.g., expanding a company's geo- or product-mix.

Outputs of the **execution** phase are usually investment approval requests for capital expenditures, market entry plans and M&A (funnel) related plans and documents. All relate strategy (the making of choices for allocating a company's resources) with execution (the actual spending of resources).

Finally, outputs of the **monitoring** phase include the annual business budget book and the typically monthly or quarterly business review related documents.

In the section below, I have, for the design, execution and monitoring of strategy, based on my experience, summarized what particular tools suit what particular management decision (document) best. These tables should not be treated dogmatically. Some analysts may use tools in cases where I have not mentioned them to be commonly applicable. Similarly, some analysts may not have found the application of a particular tool useful for a particular decision in strategy making. The tables reflect my practitioner's experience. Strategy design is an art; the tools described in this book I often grab from my toolbox – and I do so to support the decisions mentioned in the tables below. Any reader should make their own choice – the only purpose of providing the tables below is to share some insight – for better or perhaps for worse!

11.2   TOOLS IN RELATION
TO DECISION-SUPPORT
DOCUMENTS

In *Table 11.1* below, I have followed along the vertical axis of the table the tools presented in the various chapters of this book. Horizontally I have listed four typical strategy design documents: a long-term holistic and multifunctional business strategy, an R&D strategy, a supply chain strategy and a marketing and/or sales strategy. For each such strategy, I am typically used to writing documents/slide shows. To substantiate the choices in such documents, you need either group process-based or desk research-based analyses or a combination of both. The tools mentioned below can either contribute to the group process or be part of the desk research.

CHAPTER	SECTION	LONG-TERM BUSINESS PLAN	R&D PLAN	SUPPLY CHAIN PLAN	MARKETING OR SALES PLAN
Competitor capability profiling	Competitor profile	✓	✓	✓	✓
Competitor capability analysis	Benchmarking	✓	✓	✓	✓
	Cash flow analysis	✓			✓
	Product portfolio analysis		✓		
	Patent analysis		✓		
Competitor management analysis	Executive profiling				
Competitor future moves analysis	Wargaming	✓			✓
Market environment analysis	Country analysis				✓
	Technology analysis	✓	✓	✓	
	Volatility analysis	✓			✓
	Trend analysis	✓	✓		✓
Market segment analysis	Industry cost curve	✓	✓	✓	✓
	Profit pool analysis	✓			✓
Market sizing		✓	✓	✓	✓
Generic tools	Brainstorm	✓	✓	✓	✓
	Structured challenge	✓			✓
	Pre-mortem analysis	✓			✓
Scenario analysis		✓			

TABLE 11.1 ▶ ▶ ▶ CONNECTING ANALYSIS TOOLS WITH STRATEGY DESIGN DELIVERABLES

The take-out of *Table 11.1* is that many tools suit multiple strategy design purposes. Some, like market sizing, benchmarking, and competitor profiling or brainstorming, are relevant to almost any business (strategy design) plan.

Table 11.2 provides the same overview for strategy execution related documents.

CHAPTER	SECTION	MARKET ENTRY PLAN (GEO/PRODUCT)	CAPITAL EXPENDITURE	M&A FUNNEL OR TARGET APPROACH
Competitor capability profiling	Competitor profile	✓	✓	✓
Competitor capability analysis	Benchmarking	✓		
	Cash flow analysis			
	Product portfolio analysis	✓		✓
	Patent analysis			✓
Competitor management analysis	Executive profiling	✓		✓
Competitor future moves analysis	Wargaming	✓	✓	✓
Market environment analysis	Country analysis	✓	✓	✓
	Technology analysis	✓	✓	
	Volatility analysis			
	Trend analysis			
Market segment analysis	Industry cost curve		✓	✓
	Profit pool analysis	✓	✓	✓
Market sizing		✓	✓	✓
Generic tools	Brainstorm	✓		
	Structured challenge	✓	✓	✓
	Pre-mortem analysis	✓	✓	✓
Scenario analysis				

TABLE 11.2 ▶ ▶ ▶ CONNECTING ANALYSIS TOOLS WITH STRATEGY EXECUTION DOCUMENTS

Also in the phase of strategy execution, some tools seem to apply broadly. Wargaming is typically a tool that suits a strategy execution phase. In *Table 11.3*, the final table of this chapter, I look at tools and their suitability to strategy monitoring.

CHAPTER	SECTION	ANNUAL BUDGET PROCESS BOOK	QUARTERLY BUSINESS PERFORMANCE REVIEW BOOK
Competitor capability profiling	Competitor profile	✓	✓
Competitor capability analysis	Benchmarking		✓
	Cash flow analysis		✓
	Product portfolio analysis		
	Patent analysis		
Competitor management analysis	Executive profiling		
Competitor future moves analysis	Wargaming		
Market environment analysis	Country analysis	✓	
	Technology analysis		
	Volatility analysis	✓	✓
	Trend analysis		
Market segment analysis	Industry cost curve		
	Profit pool analysis		
Market sizing		✓	✓
Generic tools	Brainstorm		
	Structured challenge		✓
	Pre-mortem analysis		
Scenario analysis			

TABLE 11.3 ▶ ▶ ▶ **CONNECTING ANALYSIS TOOLS WITH STRATEGY MONITORING DOCUMENTS**

What is most striking when looking at *Table 11.3* is that in the monitoring phase, most tools do not really contribute to the quality of a management team's decision-making.

Strategic analysis predominantly contributes in a business strategy design and execution phase. I enjoy repeating, as a final word, a message I gave earlier; the best tools are those that are tailor-made for the problem at hand. No analyst should ever feel restricted by the fact that for a problem there is no off-the-shelf tool. Hopefully, the off-the-shelf tools discussed in this book stimulate analysts even more to create their own tools to crack whatever strategic analytic challenge fruitfully and efficiently.

····▶▶▶ ACKNOWLEDGEMENTS

This book has mainly been based on office experience in Akzo Nobel and Royal FrieslandCampina. Multiple colleagues deserve my gratitude, but there are a few who deserve special attention. At AkzoNobel, Huub Cuijpers was among those who decided in favour of me being recruited. Later it was Huub who encouraged me to develop actionable strategic analysis as functional discipline for the Base Chemicals business; thanks for that, Huub.

Tjerk Gorter persuaded me to join him in professionalizing innovation, strategy and analysis in a predecessor to Royal FrieslandCampina, because he believed in me. His larger-than-life commitment to pulling strategic analysis through the unavoidable dip in any experience-based learning curve has resulted in our five-year common journey toward developing world-class strategic analysis in FrieslandCampina. Tjerk, you were great!

FrieslandCampina has been and is a great environment to work on strategic analysis, not the least due to the stimulating context in which individuals are challenged to make the most of themselves and their work. Within Business Group Cheese, Butter and Milk Powder, a special word of thanks goes to Bas van den Berg, John Habets and Yves van Coillie. In addition, Thom Albers, as former Corporate Director of Strategy, Fabian Dooijeweerd and Tom Booijink as peers in Corporate Strategy, Konstantine Maggioros in the Business Development Unit in Kuala Lumpur, Malaysia, Heidi van der Kooij and Damianos Vainas at Corporate Legal Affairs, and Jan-Willem ter Avest as thought leader at Corporate Communication deserve my gratitude.

Many friends have proofread parts of this book at various stages of its development. My gratitude goes to Irma Kluifhooft, Jasper Lambregts, Dr

Peter Perla, Shirley Lau, Hella Schmidt, Godfried Wessels, Martin Wijsman, Wim de Koning, professor Bob de Graaff and Egbert Philips for the encouraging messages and most helpful suggestions you provided me with.

One more individual deserves special thanks. Hans Steensma as co-founder of Military Formats In Business and long-term wargaming-in-business partner deserves special gratitude. Hans, knowing my strategy work experience, convinced me that I should write this book. About five years after his strong urge to do so, the writing has been finished. Without your encouragement, Hans, the book may never have been written.

This book also would never have been written if the team at LID Publishing Ltd had not believed in the idea. I am especially indebted to Martin Liu, Sara Taheri and Liz Cooley for their support.

Last, but not least, two people deserve the largest gratitude of all: my patient wife Marieke, who had to make do with my solitary writing, and my daughter Louise, to whom I have dedicated this book – as a way to compensate for the many games of chess we could have played had this book not been written.

⋯▶▶ APPENDIX

CHECKLISTS FOR PROFILING COMPETITOR CAPABILITIES

In the appendix below, checklists with questions are provided by traditional functional discipline. The sharp reader will notice that the segmentation of the functional disciplines is slightly different from that presented in *Diagram 2.1*. *Diagram 2.1* is focused on representing the output of an analysis. In contrast, the segmentation below is focused on the collection phase of the analysis. The latter follows the more traditional organizational lines that (probably) also will be relevant in the case of the competitor to be analysed. When there is evidence the competitor has a different split of functional roles, the analyst needs to consider whether to follow the competitor's split (and risk confusing their people sources during the collection work) or to stick to the traditional split of functions to facilitate talking to human sources during collection and to adapt the segmentation during the analysis. In the end, the analysis output should depict the competitor's real structure.

The checklists may assist in defining what data and analysis may need to be collected and worked out for compiling a particular competitor profile. As always in strategic analysis, the decision to be substantiated drives the analysis that is to be prepared. The analysis drives what data are needed. It is clearly not recommended to prepare, based on these questions, encyclopedic competitor reviews that serve no other purpose than to offer facts and answers to questions that had not been and most likely will never be asked by the ultimate end-user of the analysis. As a result of the above, the checklists below can, by definition, never be complete. A tailored strategy need will lead to a tailored analysis that is translated into tailored market intelligence questions to be collected from specific sources.

The questions below may seem to be a bit skewed to FMCG marketing but are *mutatis mutandis*, also believed to be useful in B2B. The checklists, after all, are aimed to inspire the process of defining the tailored analysis for the problem to be solved.

CONSUMER MARKETING

Competitor product portfolio analysis

- *What constitutes the overall product range?*
- *What marketing synergies exist within the range that add to the competitor's competitiveness (e.g., Mercedes A-type benefitting from quality image of Mercedes S)?*

Qualitative marketing and brand analysis (to be worked out for brands in-scope of the analysis or for the entire brand portfolio where applicable)

Who are they?

- *What is the brand promise? What is the brand's image? What are the brand values?*
- *What is the brand's identity? Why is this identity credible or on-trend?*
- *How has the identity developed over time? What is the vitality of the identity to adapt to changing consumer/customer interests? How has the identity been leading trend change?*
- *What does the identity change over time (where applicable) tell us?*
- *Where will the identity positioning move next? Why?*
- *What identity will the brand – given the identity it is perceived to be having today – never be able to have in the future (e.g., Julie Andrews will never be a rock star, Madonna will never be a virgin)? What does this tell us about the competitor's weak spots: positions the competitor will never be able to own in the consumer/customer's mind to which the competitor itself may be blind (think of IBM the mega-computer company arrogantly ignoring simple PCs that could never live up to the 1980's IBM brand values)?*

- *What is the apparent policy on working with talents/celebrities in brand communications? What has this delivered to the brand image/identity over time? What, if anything, went wrong?*

Who talks and to whom?
- *What target group(s) does the brand focus on?*
- *What advertising agency do they use? What is the nature of the contract with the advertising agency (national, international, multi-year)? What does this tell us about current and future creative/unexpected moves of the brand's communication? When is the contract up for renewal? What agencies would your firm want to lock in prior to the competitor being able to do so?*

Where do we see them?
- *What is the international scope (where applicable) of the brand? How consistent is the communication of the brand internationally, or the recipes/pack types/identity/functional benefits/emotional benefits/reasons to believe? What does this implicitly tell us about the competitor's organization/structure and flexibility (or not) to act in individual markets?*
- *What communication channel(s) have been and are being used? Think of: events marketing, product placements in media, online, TV (what TV?), outdoor (for what audience to see?), magazine (what magazine?), radio (with what programmes?)? What does this tell us about the focus (or lack thereof) in the competitor's media policy? How consistent is the use of the various channels over time? What does this tell us about apparent learnings the competitor has gone through and acted upon?*
- *What is the mix of the communication spent by channel? What channels does the competitor want to own 'exclusively' for this brand? Why? How do they lock in the channel?*

What is the news?
- *What apparent innovation roadmap do we see? How (where applicable) are international roll-outs of innovations managed: simultaneous in multiple markets, or one-by-one? If the latter is true, which market tends to be first to roll-out an innovation? Why? What does this tell us about how much time we have in our market to pre-empt a future competitor innovation roll-out?*
- *What speed of innovation do we observe? What apparent autonomy do local country organizations have in tailoring innovations to local market needs? What does this tell us about the potential/authority of local country organizations to respond to our firm's proactive innovations?*
- *What are the reasons to believe that the brand communicates to underpin the products' functional benefits? What policy does the brand team apparently have regarding the product features that relate to the functional benefits (i.e., 100% IP-protected, exclusively sourced at locked-in suppliers, 'branded benefits' that are trademark protected or free to use or copy)?*
- *What if any licenses does the brand give or take (e.g., on branded benefits)?*
- *What quality/sustainability programmes does the brand relate to (e.g., UTZ in cocoa sourcing)? What stakeholders endorsements do they have (e.g., recommended by WWF for meeting minimum animal welfare standards)?*
- *What formal claims does the brand make? With what substantiation? What entry barrier does that imply for other brands/companies?*
- *What is the brand's price positioning versus competing products by channel, by occasion, by pack type, by concept, by country and why?*
- *What campaign strategies do we see? What are the thematic campaigns about?*

Quantitative marketing and brand analysis (to be worked out for brands in-scope of the analysis or for the entire brand portfolio where applicable)
  What is their market position?
- *What is the sales size of the brand by channel, by country, by product, etc.? What are the overall sales we*

calculate per competitor brand in their portfolio? What if we add up all relevant brand sales and compare the calculated combined sum with the company's reported sales? What differences do we see? How to understand these?

- *What sales growth do we see by channel, by country, by product, etc.?*
- *What profit do we believe this brand generates? (Profit sanctuaries often are specific channels that are overlooked by other companies – this means that a particular company has a disproportional market share and often profit pool in a particular channel.)*
- *What gross profit do we think is being generated by this brand?*
- *What is the market share (volume/value) by channel, by country, by product?*
- *How is the market being measured? What coverage of the various channels do these measurements have? What channels may be overlooked in market share analysis? How big could these channels be? What does this mean for the total size and market share of this competitor's brand? How large do we believe their consumer base/customer base to be? How does that base change over time? Who are the heavy users and why?*
- *What is the growth potential of the markets this brand is sold in? How does this market momentum (by brand) compare with the competitor's overall growth rate and growth ambitions? What does this tell us about the probably priority this brand will have in the competitor's portfolio when it comes to resource allocation?*

What is the support they give?

- *What advertising and promotion (A&P) spend do we measure (by media, by channel)? What part is used Above the Line, what part Below the Line? Why? What Share of Voice, Share of Spent in the category does this A&P spent represent? How do SoV and SoS relate to the market share the competitor has with this brand?*
- *What percentage of net sales does the A&P amount constitute? How does this percentage compare to industry benchmarks or your own firm's choices?*
- *How does this amount relate to the amount required to get 'above the clutter'?*
- *What part of the competitor's R&D budget do we think is available for supporting this brand with new functional benefits?*

What is their position in the consumer's/customer's mind?

- *What brand awareness (aided/unaided, top-of-mind percentage) does this spend result in or has historical spend resulted in?*
- *What percentage of brand loyal customer/consumers do they have? Why? Why are these customers loyal? What functional or emotional benefits that the brand delivers drives this loyalty?*
- *What is the brand's penetration (in households, where applicable) by country?*
- *What is the frequency of use/purchasing (by occasion, by channel)?*

TRADE MARKETING, SALES AND DISTRIBUTION

Qualitative trade marketing, sales and distribution analysis (to be worked out for business in-scope of the analysis or for the entire competitor where applicable)

What pricing do we see?

- *What pricing strategies do we see (by channel, by customer type)? Value based or cost plus? How does pricing vary by brand, by channel, by market? What seems to be the apparent pricing logic? What triggers price changes?*
- *What policy is used when raw material prices change? When is the competitor changing its prices? As an early adapter or as a laggard? What does this implicitly tell us about the competitor's strategic intent?*
- *Where does the competitor have a price leadership position? How does it show?*
- *What is the basis for the competitor's promotional mix?*

What physical distribution do they operate?

- *What physical distribution policies do we see by channel? What is insourced, what is outsourced? What (logistics) partners are involved? What other companies' products may these partners also ship simultaneously?*

What customers do they sell to and how?

- *What cross-selling or up-selling strategies do they employ toward their customers?*
- *What sales sophistication does the competitor use: e.g., sales staff with handhelds?*
- *How efficient is the sales ordering process from a customer perspective? How much time does it take from order to delivery? What is the differentiator (if any) in this? How does this meet specific customer needs best? What is the customer value of this differentiator?*
- *What sales methods do they employ: direct, indirect, online, via bricks-and-mortar?*
- *What does the competitor's customer mix look like (by channel, by country, by segment or market)? What is the characterization of the competitor's customers (value-buyers, premium-buyers, volume-buyers, etc.)? Why do exactly these customers buy at the competitor (choice of suppliers, winners-picking-winners, long-term relation, physical proximity of customer and supplier, etc.)?*
- *What customers do we know? What special customers do they have: e.g., government?*

What channel strategies do we see?

- *What channels (where applicable) always get the innovations first? What pricing policies are used by each channel?*
- *What trade terms and credit policies are used by channels? What does this tell us about channel priorities in the competitor's strategy?*
- *What point-of-sale strategies does the competitor employ? What in-store/out-of-store activation materials do we see? How effective do we rate these to be? Why?*
- *What sales process advantages does the competitor offer to its customers (think of: e-ordering, electronic stock monitoring and replenishment, allocation of contingency stock)?*
- *What exclusivity agreements do they have with customers/re-sellers (where legally possible)?*
- *What products do they offer by channel, by outlet? What (where applicable) category management and shelf-planning initiatives and capabilities do they have? What customers do they employ these initiatives with?*

What non-monetary features does the sales policy have?

- *What product returns and service policies does the competitor use?*
- *What e-commerce connections exist between distributors, customers and the competitor?*
- *What in-store equipment does the competitor provide (e.g., fridges in the case of a yogurt producer)?*
- *How well does the stock replenishment planning work? How often do we see out-of-stock or 'out-of-shelf-life' products?*
- *Who 'owns' the customer: the distributor or the competitor?*

Quantitative trade marketing, sales and distribution analysis (to be worked out for business in-scope of the analysis or for the entire competitor where applicable)

What customer and consumer prices do we see?

- *What prices and price lists do we see? How often do the price lists change?*
- *What promotional budgets does this competitor operate with?*
- *What customer incentive schemes do we see? Quantity-based? Exclusivity-based?*
- *What distributor margins are offered? Why? How do these change in time, if at all?*

What sales operations do we see?

- *What is the size of the sales force (by channel, by country, etc.)?*
- *What is the typical amount of sales realized per sales representative?*
- *How many sales offices does the competitor operate? How many sales reps operate per office? What seems to determine the set-up and size of a (new) sales office?*
- *What are the sales and distribution cost as a percentage of sales?*
- *What incentives schemes are used for the competitor's sales staff? What is the bonus, what is the fixed salary? How many sales calls are the competitor's staff making per week?*

What sales results do we see?

- *What sales does the competitor report (by channel, by customer, by country, by product, etc.)?*
- *What is the sales volume in relevant units? How do volume sales relate to value sales? What changes in unit prices do we see? In how far do these changes cover inflation?*
- *What is the direct and indirect coverage of the market?*
- *How many customers does the competitor have that pay invoices directly?*
- *What is weighted distribution in percentage for the competitor's product (by geo, by product)? What is the numeric distribution? How do these change in time? What does this tell us?*
- *What is the customer base? What percentage of sales is generated by the top-five customers?*
- *What customer service levels do we see (by product, by channel)? Why? What seems to work well for the competitor, what doesn't seem to work too well yet? Why? How can we turn the competitor's mishaps into our competitive advantage?*

SUPPLY CHAIN AND PROCUREMENT

Qualitative supply chain and procurement analysis (to be worked out for business in-scope of the analysis or for the entire competitor where applicable)

What is the supply chain strategy?

- *How does the supply chain strategy link to and realize the competitor's overall strategy?*
- *What is the supply chain strategy of the competitor? What elements in the supply chain does the competitor see as so critical that the competitor always owns and operates them, and which elements does the competitor preferably outsource? Why?*
- *How are the supply chain assets linked to the sales and distribution organization (e.g., all plants produce for the global sales organization or every country has its own optimized production and sales process)?*
- *What, if any, are the major suppliers the competitor outsources (semi-) finished goods production to? What selection criteria has the competitor apparently used?*
- *What is the competitor's policy on (off-balance) leasing versus owning equipment? Why?*
- *What is the process/production technology philosophy of the competitor (only proven technology, innovative first-mover, own in-house new technology development, etc.)?*
- *What is the competitor's focus in its supply chain operations: cost control, standardization, bulk and conversion cost focus, flexibility, and small batches/high prices, etc.? How does this differ by plant/by country/by product range? How much is the supply chain organization attuned to delivering the strategic imperatives for today's and tomorrow's markets?*
- *What does the competitor do with fixed assets it no longer needs? To whom do they sell assets (if at all)? Why?*
- *What drives the production planning: production-for-stock or production-for-order?*
- *What is the importance of raw materials, respectively conversion cost for the competitor's total profitability?*

What fixed asset base do they operate?

- *Where are the competitor's plants located? How are the plants positioned for supplying today's and tomorrow's markets? How are the plants divided geographically over the world's major customs' unions? How many contingency options does the competitor have when one plant suddenly has to stop operations? What bottlenecks do we see for capacity expansion?*

- *What problems would be caused by sudden reductions of demand? What implications would this have on numbers of permanent staff that are employed? How dependent is the asset base (or the individual plant on a single customer or market)?*
- *What are the possibilities for the various production locations to expand (i.e., availability of neighbouring plots, permit situations, political/societal view on this type of industry)?*
- *What restructuring options does the competitor have, given its own manufacturing asset base? What merger or acquisition with another industry player would greatly enhance both parties' asset optimization programmes, and result in significant cost synergies?*
- *What is the competitor's track record of expansion and/or restructuring?*
- *What inevitable links exist between product ranges (think: salt leads to chlorine and caustic, milk leads to cheese and whey)? If such links exist, what product drives the business in terms of sales and/or profits? What does this mean for supply chain operations?*
- *What investments have recently been finalized? What was the purpose of these investments: quality, health, safety, environment, replacement, efficiency, expansion, etc.? What is the state of maintenance and the age of the equipment used?*
- *How are raw material and finished goods inventories managed (off-site, on-site, FIFO)? What is the size of the finished goods storage on-site (expressed in days of production)?*
- *What natural advantages do the plant location(s) of the competitor have (e.g., close to hydropower unit, close to river, major harbor, railway, major roads, major customer distribution centres, etc.)?*

What technology do they employ?

- *What (production) technologies does the competitor apply? Which of these technologies are proprietary? How does technology contribute to the competitor's competitive edge, if at all? What technologies that are applied are so well protected to create an entry barrier for competitors?*

What is the network we see?

- *What (technology or production in/out-sourcing) partners does the competitor work with? Why?*
- *What physically close connections do competitor plants have (e.g., share power/steam unit with neighbouring plant from another company; have an on-site oxygen unit of an industrial gas producer; have an on-site bottle plant owned and operated by a packaging material supplier)?*
- *What major suppliers does the competitor work with? Why? What is the nature of the contracts with these suppliers? How much technological cooperation or operational integration exists between the competitor's major suppliers and the competitor's own operations? What does this say, for example, about the competitor's flexibility to innovate production processes or products (rapidly)?*

What else differentiates the competitor?

- *What seasonality affects the competitor operations e.g., in raw material supply (e.g., sugar industry) or in demand (e.g., ice cream in Northern Europe)?*
- *What are the quality, health, safety, environment standards at the competitor? What is the competitor's reputation? What does the competitor do to strengthen that reputation (if anything)? What was the largest serious mishap (e.g., factory fire, product recall, etc.)? What was the competitor's response? How effective did the competitor act? What did this say about the competitor's organizational professionalism in its supply chain operations?*

Quantitative supply chain and procurement analysis (to be worked out for business in-scope of the analysis or for the entire competitor where applicable)

What equipment and outputs do we see?

- *What production lines are operated per plant? How many of each? How versatile are the lines in terms of producing different recipes/pack sizes, etc.?*
- *What product ranges are produced in which plants?*
- *What is the production capacity per plant/per product?*
- *How many plants are being operated?*
- *What is the design capacity (ensure a clear definition of capacity is consistently used: a capacity/day may not equal 24 times a maximum hourly capacity, etc.)?*
- *What are the reported outputs by plant? By implication: what is the effective utilization rate of the plants (by product line)?*
- *How many different distribution centres/depots are used?*
- *How many shifts are operating at the plant (by plant, by product line where relevant)?*
- *How large is a production worker shift?*
- *How many route-to-market related assets does the competitor have?*

How effective is the supply chain organization?
- *What is the typical lead time for producing a truly innovative product?*
- *What CapEx/Depreciation ratio does the competitor use (use a long-term average)? What CapEx/Sales ratio does the competitor have (use a long-term average)? What Capital Employed/unit output does the competitor require? What are characteristic output ratios (e.g., kg product/man-hour or sales/employee/ year)? What does the output ratio tell about the competitor's operations? How do the above ratios compare to industry benchmarks?*
- *What cost position does the competitor have in its operations (consider preparing an industry cost curve and/or an competitor profit and loss account)?*
- *What numbers of staff does the competitor employ in its operations? What does this say about competitor efficiency measures and competitor capabilities?*

RESEARCH AND DEVELOPMENT

Qualitative research and development analysis (to be worked out for business in-scope of the analysis or for the entire competitor where applicable)

What is the R&D programme and what is the position?
- *What are the focus areas of technology/research? What do we know about the current ongoing R&D portfolio of projects? What businesses likely will benefit most from these projects' outputs?*
- *In what areas (if any) does the competitor lead in R&D?*
- *How does R&D now and in the future contribute to the firm's competitiveness?*
- *What publications, participations to conferences, etc. do we see? What do these publications and presentations tell us about the apparent focus areas of the competitor's R&D?*
- *What is the biggest achievement in the competitor's R&D of the past decade? Why? What (unique) capabilities have supported this achievement? What business success has this R&D achievement resulted in? How could the competitor benefit further from capitalizing on the capability?*

What intellectual property and which intangible assets do we see?
- *What patent policy does the competitor pursue (blanket of patents to cover an entire field, incidental patents in separate technology fields, etc.)?*
- *What is the value of the competitor's patent portfolio?*

What network does the competitor have in science and technology?
- *Who are the competitor's open innovation partners? What science cluster(s) does the competitor work with?*
- *What key suppliers transfer technology to the competitor? What does this say about the competitor's real technological clout?*

- *What technology or technologies have been licensed in? From whom? Why?*
- *What large technology institutes cooperate with the competitor?*
- *What technology-linked acquisitions or ventures has the competitor closed in the last five years?*
- *What participations to multi-party sponsored R&D programmes do we see? With whom does the competitor partner? Why? Who are the competitor's programmes most common sponsors?*

What organization do we see?
- *How has R&D been organized (central, divisional, by country, by product range, etc.)?*
- *How many R&D facilities does the competitor have? Where are these facilities based?*

Quantitative research and development analysis (to be worked out for business in-scope of the analysis or for the entire competitor where applicable)
What resources do we see?
- *What is the competitor's R&D budget? How does this budget compare to the absolute amount spent by the competitor's competitors? What does this say about the competitor's current or future likely technological edge?*
- *What is the competitor's R&D budget as a percentage of sales? How does this ratio compare to the industry benchmark?*
- *How many people are employed by the competitor in R&D (globally, by R&D centre, by country, by product or business line, etc.)?*

STAFF, ORGANIZATION AND OWNERSHIP
Staff, organization and ownership analysis (to be worked out for business in-scope of the analysis or for the entire competitor where applicable)
What HR policies do we see?
- *What is the compensation and benefits policy at the competitor? How does the competitor pay compared to peer companies?*
- *How does the bonus system work? Who at the competitor is eligible for variable payments? What is the basis for such variable payments?*
- *What training programmes does the competitor offer? What institutes/universities/business schools often train the competitor's staff? What does this tell us about the capabilities and professionalism the competitor aims to build?*
- *Which staff are eligible for training? On what basis?*
- *What do we know the competitor spends on training?*
- *What diversity policies do we see? How diverse is the competitor's management and staff (gender, nationality, culture, etc.)?*
- *How do expatriate contracts work (when applicable)? How many expatriates does the competitor employ? What assignments are characteristically taken up by expats?*

What workforce do we see?
- *What employee morale do we see? How does employee morale change over time? Why?*
- *What labour unrest have we seen in the last five years? What triggered this unrest? How have the issues (if any) been resolved?*
- *What staff retention rates do we see? What triggered retention rates to go up or down?*
- *What is the size of the workforce (in total, by country, etc.)?*
- *What relations does the competitor have with trade unions?*
- *What companies often recruit the competitor's staff?*

What management do we see?
- *How can the competitor's management style be characterized?*

- *What capabilities does the competitor's leadership team have?*
- *Who are the competitor's leaders (by functional discipline, by country, by culture, etc.)? What competitor executive profiles are available (if any)?*
- *Which of the competitor's top team leaders are particularly close? Why?*
- *What is the internal succession rate of (top) management?*
- *What characterizes senior executives at the competitor?*
- *Which individuals would be hard to replace at the competitor? Why? How would their leaving affect the competitor's performance?*
- *What companies are the typical hunting ground for competitor recruitment efforts targeting mid- to senior-level staff?*
- *What relations/connections does senior management at the competitor have with other stakeholders (e.g., board memberships in other companies)?*
- *How is the competitor's supervisory board connected with other companies?*

Where is the competitor's point of gravity?
- *What is the country of origin of the competitor (culturally)?*
- *Where is the global head office based?*
- *What is the relation of the competitor with its home country's government?*

What structure do we see?
- *What is the current structure of the competitor (central or decentral, divisional, segmented by country, category, matrix, etc.)?*
- *When has the current structure been implemented? By whom? What triggered the change? To what issues/questions was the current structure the answer? Why? How far have these issues meanwhile indeed been resolved?*

What owners do we see?
- *Who owns the company? What role does the competitor serve in the owners' portfolio of businesses (where applicable)?*
- *What is the owners' expectation from the company (e.g., top-line growth, bottom line growth, stable dividends, share price growth, etc.)?*
- *How stable is the ownership? What changes have we seen over time?*
- *What changes have we seen in ownership structure? What changes can we predict or expect to happen in the future? What could trigger such changes (e.g., passing away of retired founding father)?*
- *What does the formal governance look like?*
- *How, if at all, are the owners involved in running the day-to-day business?*
- *Where is the company formally registered?*
- *When the competitor is listed: how is the liquidity of the share? What percentage is freely traded? On what stock exchange(s)? What different classes of shareholders exist, if any? What different rights do different classes of shareholders have? How, if at all, is the company protected against hostile takeovers? Who are the current major shareholders? What is the (informal) link between the major shareholders and the competitor? What, if any, emotional ties exist?*

FINANCE

Qualitative finance analysis (to be worked out for business in-scope of the analysis or for the entire competitor where applicable)

What choices do we see being made?
- *What financial strategies and policies does the competitor pursue (e.g., aggressive leverage or conservative debt-free growth)?*

- *What is the quality of the competitor's equity? What if any hybrid equity does the company have on its balance sheet? Who holds the hybrids?*
- *Who is the competitor's house bank? Who is the accountant? Who used an M&A advisor most often? Why?*
- *Which banks underwrite the competitor's syndicate loans (where applicable)? Who holds the competitor's debt? What are the loan doc conditions?*
- *What financial capabilities does the competitor have in its own team? How does this show?*
- *What (financial) IT-systems does the competitor operate? How well are these integrated with other systems (e.g., ERP)?*
- *How fast does the company publish its accounts after the closing of its financial year? How often does it release figures? How detailed are the statements (e.g., sales segmentation by product line, geo-area, capital allocation and profitability by business line, etc.)?*
- *What is the procedure for allocating capital (i.e., what are the minimum investment amounts that require approval by what governing body)?*

What financial targets do we believe the competitor aims for?
- *What financial targets does the competitor aim for (think: sales, sales growth, free cash flow, ROCE, ROS, solvency, etc.)?*
- *How do these targets compare to historic performances by the competitor?*
- *How ambitious/realistic are these targets?*
- *How do the competitor's results compare to that of peer companies? Why? What drives the competitor's outperformance or underperformance?*

Quantitative finance analysis (to be worked out for business, product, geo-mix etc., in-scope of the analysis or for the entire competitor where applicable. More than for any other analysis, for this analysis, the data to be collected, analysed and reported truly depends on the strategy assignment that has been given. Often, financial parameters that are tailor-made for the assignment show the competitor's performance best. Think of a financial indicator like the ten-year compound annual growth rate of net sales/unit product during a period (corrected for consumer price inflation). This single indicator may tell the whole story of a competitor's performance over time. Defining that indicator is the challenge for the analyst; plainly reporting known facts is not).

What figures do we see?
- *What financial results does the competitor deliver: think of (list not exhaustive; actuals, historic comparables, like-for-like or reported, projections; absolute and also as percentage of net sales):*

- *Profit and loss statement*
  - *net sales (including currency mix of net sales)*
  - *cost of goods sold*
  - *gross profit*
  - *EBITDA*
  - *EBIT*
  - *net interest*
  - *tax (also as a percentage of taxable profit)*
  - *net profit*
  - *dividend (also as a percentage of net profit)*

- *Cash flow statement*
  - *depreciation and amortization*
  - *cash flow from operations*

- *investments*
- *free cash flow*

- *Balance sheet*
  - *goodwill*
  - *total assets*
  - *equity*
  - *long-term debt*
  - *net debt*
  - *solvency (total equity/total assets)*
  - *adjusted solvency ((total equity – goodwill)/total assets)*

- *Other ratios and parameters (where applicable)*
  - *net debt / EBITDA*
  - *interest coverage (i.e., net interest payment/EBITDA)*
  - *market capitalization*
  - *share price (and development over time + projection)*
  - *earnings per share (and development over time + projection)*
  - *p/e-ratio for the current share price (and comparison with peer companies)*
  - *valuation (i.e., market capitalization + net debt)*

···▸▸▸ NOTES

CHAPTER 1

1. The approach was referred to by Joyner in his amusing book *Simpleology: The Simple Science of Getting What You Want* (Joyner, 2007). The author acknowledges Surasak Jintananarumit for alerting him to this highly readable book.

CHAPTER 3

1. H.I. Ansoff starts his classic 1957 HBR-article on "Strategies for Diversification" with a quote from L.J. Carroll's *Through the Looking-Glass* (New York, The Heritage Press, 1941) (Ansoff, 1957):

   "The Red Queen said, "Now, here, it takes all the running you can do to keep in the same place. If you want to get somewhere else, you must run at least twice as fast as that.""

   Ansoff proceeds with, *"So it is in the American economy. Just to retain its relative position, a business firm must go through continuous growth and change."*

   Ansoff's advice has stood the test of time. To monitor the absolute position of a business' internal data will do. To monitor the relative position, benchmarking is critical.

CHAPTER 5

1. Zook emphasizes the difficulty for senior management to reach out to frontline staff in larger organizations. A Commander's Intent may be crystal clear in the ivory tower of corporate strategy in the head office of a global company, but getting the Commander's Intent embedded in the actions of all frontline staff is a different thing. Even when the top really aims to put customers first, it is the staff at some remote foreign call centre that needs to live such values in their day-to-day operations and be encouraged by the right incentives and enabled by the right authorities to do so.

CHAPTER 6

1. Other options include hedging commodity price fluctuation risks. These are outside the scope of this book.

2. Credits are due to Steven van de Ridder for his innovative unpublished work in this field.

·····▶▶ LITERATURE

AchieveGlobal (2010), "Winning Account Strategies Training Program"; see www.achieveglobal.com visited February 2012.

Alvarez, A. (2007) "Situational Early Warning", *Competitive Intelligence Magazine*, Vol. 10, No. 1, January-February Issue, pp. 14–18.

Ansoff, H.I. (1957), "Strategies for Diversification", *Harvard Business Review*, Vol. 35, Issue 5 (Sep-Oct) pp. 113–24.

Axelrod, A. (1999), *Patton on Leadership – Strategic Lessons for Corporate Warfare*, Prentice Hall Press, Paramus, NJ, pp. 205–6.

Bales, C.F. et al. (2009), "The Business System: A New Tool for Strategy Formulation and Cost Analysis", *McKinsey Quarterly*, April Issue.

Bodell, L. (2014), "Beyond The Brainstorm", *Strategy & Business*, September 2015.

Bosomworth, C. (1993), "The Executive Benchmarking Guidebook", *Management Roundtable*, Boston, MA.

Bradley, C., Dawson, A, Montard, A. (2013), "Mastering the Building Blocks of Strategy", *McKinsey Quarterly*, October 2013.

Bruce, J.B., Bennett, M. (2008), "Foreign Denial and Dception: Analytical Imperatives", In: R.Z. George, J.B. Bruce (Editors), Analyzing Intelligence – Origins, Obstacles, and Innovations, *Georgetown University Press*, Washington DC, pp. 126-135.

Büchler, J.P. (2013), "Zukunftsorientierte Steuerung – Mit Business Wargaming Entscheidungen optimieren", Paper presented at Wargaming Symposium TU Hamburg-Harburg, 1 March.

Chan Kim, W., Mauborgne, R. (2005), "Blue Ocean Strategy", *Harvard Business School Press*, Boston, MA

Clark, C. (2013), *The Sleepwalkers – How Europe Went to War in 1914*, Penguin, London, p. 183.

Clark, R.M. (2007a), "Intelligence Analysis – a Target-centric Approach", *CQ Press*, Washington DC, pp. 72–4.

Clark, R.M. (2007b), ibid, p. 111.

Courtney, H., Horn, J.T., Kar, J. (2009), "Getting Into Your Competitor's Head", *McKinsey Quarterly*, no. 1, pp. 128–37.

Coyne, K.P., Coyne, S.T. (2011), "Seven Steps to Better Brainstorming", *McKinsey Quarterly*, March issue.

Drucker, P. (2004), "What Makes an Effective Executive?", *Harvard Business Review*, June Issue, pp. 59–63.

Friedman, G. (2014), "Taking the Strategic Intelligence Model to Moscow", *www.stratfor.com*, analysis column, 2 December 2014.

Gadiesh, O., Gilbert, J.L. (1998), "How to Map Your Industry's Profit Pool", *Harvard Business Review*, May-June Issue.

Gerstner, L.V. Jr. (2003), *Who Says Elephants Can't Dance? Inside IBM's Historic Turnaround*, HarperCollins Publishers, London, pp. 119–20.

Geus, A. de (2002), *The Living Company – Habits For Survival in a Turbulent Business Environment*, Harvard Business Review Press, Boston, MA, pp. 44-54.

Gilad, B. (2006), "Neither a War, Nor a Game", *Competitive Intelligence Magazine*, Vol. 9, No. 6, Nov-Dec. pp. 6–11.

Gladwell, M. (2005), *Blink – The Power of Thinking Without Thinking*, Little Brown and Company, New York pp. 21–38.

Gladwell, M. (2009b), *Outliers – The Story of Success*, Penguin, London, pp. 206–61.

Heijden, K. van der (1997a), *Scenarios - The Art of Strategic Conversation*, J. Wiley & Sons, Chichester.

Heijden, K. van der (1997b), ibid, p 15.

Heijden, K. van der (1997c), ibid, p. 5.

Heijden, K. van der (1997d), ibid p. 7.

Heijden, K. van der (1997e), ibid, p. 17.

Heijden, K. van der (1997f), ibid, pp. 118–19.

Heijden, K. van der (1997g), ibid, p. x.

Heijden, K. van der (1997h), ibid, p. 51.

Heijden, K. van der (1997i), ibid, pp. 273–6.

Heijden, K. van der (1997j), ibid, p. 43.

Heijden, K. van der (1997k), ibid, pp. 53, 187 and 198.

Heilmann, U. (2013), Command & Control Leadership Competence Improvement – An Education and Training Project, paper presented at UK Connections Conference, 3–4 September, London, King's College, Department of War Studies.

Heuer Jr., R.J., (1999a), *The Psychology of Intelligence Analysis*, Centre for the Study of Intelligence, CIA, p. 140.

Heuer Jr., R.J., (1999b), ibid, p. 77.

Heuer Jr., R.J., (1999c), ibid, pp. 70–1.

Hoffman, D.E. (2011), *The Dead Hand*, Icon Books, London, p. 190.

Horn, J. (2011), "Playing War Games to Win", *McKinsey Quarterly*, March Issue.

Hoyer, M. (2013), Strategic Wargaming, Paper presented at Wargaming Symposium TU Hamburg-Harburg, 1 March.

Joyner, M. (2007), *Simpleology – The Simple Science of Getting What You Want*, J. Wiley & Sons, Hoboken, NJ, pp. 184–6.

Keutmann, K. (2013), Competitive Intelligence zur Strategie-Entwicklung bei Henkel, paper presented at Wargaming Symposium TU Hamburg-Harburg, 1 March.

Kodalle, T. (2013), Wargaming, Interaktive Ausbildungsverfahren zum Wargaming in den Streitkräften, Paper presented at Wargaming Symposium TU Hamburg-Harburg, 1 March.

Lauder, M. (2009), "Red Dawn: The Emergence of a Red Teaming Capability in the Canadian Forces", *Canadian Forces' Canadian Army Journal*, Vol. 12, Issue 2 (summer), pp. 25–36.

Lemarre, E., Pergler, M., (2009), "Risks: Seeing Around the Corner", *McKinsey Quarterly*, October Issue.

Long, A (2007), "Competitor Cost Profiles Drive Predictive Price Modeling", *Competitive Intelligence Magazine*, Vol. 10, no. 1, January Issue, pp. 58–9.

Manchester, W. (1978), *American Caesar*, Bantam Doubleday, New York, p. 68.

Misund, K, Räder, A., Grym, A. (2014), Acquire Market Sizing and Forecasting Best Practices, workshop manual at GIA Conference June 2-4, 2014, Helsinki, Finland.

Perla, P. (1990), *The Art of Wargaming*, The Naval Institute Press, Annapolis, MD.

Philips, E., Vriens, D. (1999a), "Business Intelligence", *Kluwer Bedrijfsinformatie*, Deventer, Netherlands, p. 155 (in Dutch).

Philips, E., Vriens, D. (1999b), ibid, pp. 166–8.

Philips, E., Damhuis, C. (2009), Executive Profiling Training Course – Tailored Training to FrieslandCampina, www.bcintelligence.com.

Polya, G. (1957), *How To Solve It*, 2nd Edition, Princeton University Press, Princeton, NJ.

Porter, M.E. (2004a), *Competitive Strategy: Techniques For Analyzing Industries and Competitors*. The Free Press, New York pp. 47-74; in particular pp. 48–9 (reprint from 1980 edition).

Porter, M.E. (2004b), ibid, p. xviii.

Reinhart, C.M., Rogoff, K.S. (2009), *This Time Is Different – Eight Centuries of Financial Folly*, Princeton University Press, Princeton, NJ.

Ries, A., Trout, J. (2006), *Marketing Warfare*, 20th Anniversary Edition, McGrawHill, New York.

Rothberg, H.N. (1997), "Fortifying Competitive Intelligence with Shadow Teams", *Competitive Intelligence Review*, Vol. 8, No. 2, pp. 3–11.

Roxburgh, C. (2009), "The Use and Abuse of Scenarios", *McKinsey Quarterly*, November Issue.

Sabin, P. (2013), The Stigma of Wargames, paper presented at UK Connections Conference, 3–4 September, London, King's College, Department of War Studies.

Salinas, G. (2009), *The International Brand Valuation Manual*, J. Wiley & Sons Ltd, Chichester.

Sandman, M., Fuld, L. (2003), "War Games in an Era of Collaboration", *Critical Eye*, September-November, Issue, pp. 8–11.

Schoemaker, P.J.H. (2009), Eyes wide open: embracing uncertainty through scenario planning, *HBR-blog*, http://knowledge.wharton.upenn.edu/article/eyes-wide-open-embracing-uncertainty-through-scenario-planning, visited 8 November 2014.

Schwarz, J.O. (2013), Testing Strategies in a Business Wargame, Paper presented at Wargaming Symposium TU Hamburg-Harburg, 1 March.

Shalev, A. (2014a), *Israel's Intelligence Assessment Before the Yom Kippur War*, Sussex Academic Press, Eastbourne, p. 78.

Shalev, A. (2014b), ibid, p. 164.

Strother, R. (2006), "Post-Saddam Iraq: The War Game", *National Security Archive Electronic Briefing Book* No. 207.

Sunstein, C.R., Hastie, R. (2015a), *Wiser – Getting Beyond Group Think to Make Groups Smarter*, Harvard Business Review Press, Boston, MA, p. 89.

Sunstein, C.R., Hastie, R. (2015b), ibid, p. 92.

Surowiecki, J. (2005), *The Wisdom of Crowds*, Anchor Books, Random House, New York, p. 10.

Taleb, N.N. (2007), *The Black Swan – The Impact of the Highly Improbable*, Penguin Books, London.

Thom, N., Rohrbeck, R., Dunaj, M. (2010), Innovation Instruments for Translating Future Insights into Managerial Actions, ISPIM Conference 2010, Bilbao, Spain.

Underwood, J. (1998), "Perspectives on War Gaming", *Competitive Intelligence Review*, Vol. 9 (2) pp. 46–52.

Vella, C.M., McGonagle, J.J. (2000), "Profiling in Competitive Analysis", *Competitive Intelligence Review*, Vol. 11 (2) pp. 20–30.

Von Baeyer, H.C. (1993), *The Fermi Solution; Essays on Science*, Chapter 1, Random House, Portland, OR, pp. 3-12.

Wack, P. (1985), "Scenarios: Uncharted Waters Ahead", *Harvard Business Review*, September-October, pp. 73–89.

Wärtsilä (2014), www.shippingscenarios.wartsila.com, visited 11 April 2015.

Watters, D.C. (1981), "The Industry Cost Curve as a Strategic Tool", *McKinsey Foundations*, pp. 26–8, Issued 2009.

Weber, M.S. (2004), "Profiling for Leadership Analysis", *Competitive Intelligence Magazine*, Vol. 7, No. 4, July/August, pp. 6–13.

Zook, C., Allen, J. (2012), *Repeatability – Build Enduring Businesses for a World of Constant Change*, Harvard Business Review Press, Boston, MA, pp. 88–91.

AN INTRODUCTION TO
ERIK ELGERSMA

ERIK ELGERSMA is Director of Strategic Analysis at FrieslandCampina, one of the world's largest dairy companies. He speaks and lectures frequently at universities and at business seminars on the topics of strategic analysis, competitive strategy and related data analysis and management. He holds a PhD from Delft University of Technology, the Netherlands and is an alumnus of the International Institute for Applied Systems Analysis in Vienna, Austria. He lives with his wife and daughter in the Netherlands.